ORAL NARRATIVE RESEARCH
WITH BLACK WOMEN

ORAL NARRATIVE RESEARCH WITH BLACK WOMEN

KIM MARIE VAZ
EDITOR

SAGE Publications
International Educational and Professional Publisher
Thousand Oaks London New Delhi

Copyright © 1997 by Sage Publications, Inc.

All rights reserved. No part of this book may be reproduced or utilized in any form or by any means, electronic or mechanical, including photocopying, recording, or by any information storage and retrieval system, without permission in writing from the publisher.

For information address:

SAGE Publications, Inc.
2455 Teller Road
Thousand Oaks, California 91320
E-mail: order@sagepub.com

SAGE Publications Ltd.
6 Bonhill Street
London EC2A 4PU
United Kingdom

SAGE Publications India Pvt. Ltd.
M-32 Market
Greater Kailash I
New Delhi 110 048 India

Printed in the United States of America

Library of Congress Cataloging-in-Publication Data

Main entry under title:

Oral narrative research with Black women: collecting treasures / edited by Kim Marie Vaz.
    p. cm.
  Includes bibliographical references (p.).
  ISBN 0-8039-7428-0 (cloth: acid-free paper). — ISBN 0-8039-7429-9 (pbk.: acid-free paper)
    1. Women's studies—Biographical methods. 2. Women, Black—Research—Methodology. 3. Afro-American women—Research—Methodology. 4. Oral history—Methodology. 5. Oral tradition—Methodology. I. Vaz, Kim Marie.
HQ1185.O73 1997
305.48'896'0730072—dc21   97-4842

97 98 99 00 01 02 03   10 9 8 7 6 5 4 3 2 1

Acquiring Editor:	Marquita Flemming
Editorial Assistant:	Frances Borghi
Production Editor:	Diana E. Axelsen
Production Assistant:	Karen Wiley
Typesetter/Designer:	Janelle LeMaster
Cover Designer:	Ravi Balasuriya
Cover Photographer:	Deborah Plant

Contents

Preface	vii
Acknowledgments	ix
1. Introduction: Oral Narrative Research With Black Women KIM MARIE VAZ	1

PART I Ancestor Mothers

2. Ophelia and Me: Tribute to an Early Narrative Researcher MARTIA GRAHAM GOODSON	7
3. Professions of Faith: A Teacher Reflects on Women, Race, Church, and Spirit JOYCELYN MOODY	24

PART II Research Processes: Giving Voice

4. What Do Women Know? . . . As I Was Saying! CHRISTINE OBBO	41
5. You Haven't Seen Anything Until You Make a Black Woman Mad ARLENE HAMBRICK	64
6. Oral History: Louisiana Black Women's Memoirs GEORGIA W. BROWN	83

PART III Research Processes: Health and Well-Being

7. Talking About Sex and HIV: Conceptualizing a
   New Sociology of Experience   99
   RENÉE T. WHITE

8. Methodological Issues in Triangulation: Measuring
   Weight Control Behavior of African American Women   119
   JACQUELINE A. WALCOTT-McQUIGG

9. Where Have All the Nice Old Ladies Gone? Researching
   the Health Information-Seeking Behavior of Older
   African American Women   143
   CLAUDIA J. GOLLOP

10. African American Women and the Emergence of
    Self-Will: The Use of Phenomenological Research   156
    ELIZABETH A. PETERSON

PART IV Research Processes: Negotiating Institutions

11. Reconstructing the History of Musicians' Protective
    Union Local 274 Through Oral Narrative Method   177
    DIANE D. TURNER

12. Methodological Considerations in Field Research: Six
    Case Studies   197
    PATRICIA GREEN-POWELL

13. Social Conformity and Social Resistance: Women's
    Perspectives on "Women's Place"   223
    KIM MARIE VAZ

14. European American and African American Men and
    Women's Valuations of Feminist and Natural Science
    Research Methods in Psychology   250
    LESLIE ANN KINGMAN

    About the Authors   260

Preface

*ollecting Treasures* answers the question "Why conduct oral narrative research with African and African American women?" This research method allows the unique knowledge domains of black women to come into full view. The anthology consists of personal portraits by oral narrative researchers on the strategies they have found useful in unearthing the experiences of African and African American women. While reading these articles, I was struck by the enormous time and financial commitments required to successfully complete their respective research projects. The researchers invested themselves wholly—their own money and their time over and above official work hours, often putting their own lives "on hold" to fulfill the numerous obligations that are incurred in carrying out fieldwork. The gains to be had, they report, are not only professional development and contribution to their fields of study; uniformly, the contributors conclude that their investigations have led to increased personal affirmations and feelings of validation about being black and being a woman. These contributors focus on research areas not covered by androcentrically and Eurocentrically inclined researchers. In doing so, these contributors

must also confront the prejudice of colleagues who assume that because one is black and engaging in research with a black populace, the research is not "real." Importantly, the contributors discuss how presenting more diverse portraits of black women is sometimes challenged by white researchers who, because they accept certain stereotypes about black women as true, again conclude that such research is "biased." Contrary to popular images of black women as either "strong" or "overburdened and overwhelmed," some black women are strong and some are not, and others are both at varying times; but most women of African descent throughout the world are overcoming the odds. The contributors to this anthology discuss fully how this is so.

Kim Marie Vaz

Acknowledgments

When I was a graduate student at Indiana University pursuing a doctoral minor in African studies, I had the good fortune of having met and studied with C. Halisi, a political theorist whose area of concentration was South Africa. Once, while attending a conference about the discipline during an early phase of my graduate studies, Halisi gathered about a half dozen African American women academics in the lobby of the conference site. All of these women had conducted research in South Africa. He did this for my benefit to demonstrate to me, in a way that I could never dismiss, the absolute possibility of my following in their footsteps. These bespectacled, natural-hair-wearing sisters had all conducted their research while apartheid sought to strangle black South Africans and at a time when African Americans were not necessarily welcomed in the region. They indeed were impressive as they surrounded us. Needless to say, that image has stayed with me, and never after did I doubt that I, too, could accomplish my dream of going to Africa and carrying out research. Although not in my field of study directly, Sheila Walker, a developmental psychologist, agreed to become my dissertation committee advisor and opened her home and her heart to me. She shared her experiences living and working in Nigeria and provided me with a contact who would greatly facilitate my academic growth while carrying out research in Ile-Ife, Nigeria, Tola Olu Pearce. Dr. Pearce is a medical sociologist whose research interests include women's studies. She spent many hours discussing my research speculations on women's roles in Nigeria and introduced me to the methods of qualitative research. I have been conducting qualitative research in Africa and about black women ever since and am indebted to the support of these people. This volume is dedicated to them.

1

INTRODUCTION

Oral Narrative Research With Black Women

KIM MARIE VAZ

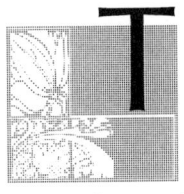This book consists of chapters on methodological issues by Africana (African and African American) women scholars who have successfully employed oral narrative methods in their research. Methodological chapters on conducting oral narratives from an Afrafeminist/ womanist standpoint are rare, and book-length works are almost nonexistent. This volume participates in the growing movement of Afrafeminist/womanist scholarship whose intention is to fill this void. The contributors to this book represent diverse disciplines: psychology, education, history, literature, nursing, and anthropology. They have much to offer students and scholars who want not only to include black women in their research but also to learn the fundamentals of the research process. These chapters explore in detail how new information about Africana women is being created and how it is currently being used. The interdisciplinary nature of this book renders it useful throughout academia. What makes this book a valuable teaching tool are the pedagogical suggestions and research artifacts contained within. Contributors have described one or two activities that may assist instructors' efforts to teach oral narrative methodologies. Most contributors have a book or several articles in print that can be used to expand the lessons contained in the chapters. Some contributors have

included photographs of themselves in their interview settings and other photographs as they see fit; abridged versions of interviews; and other artifacts from their field/interview experiences.

The contributors were given chapter guides and were asked to develop their chapters around the following themes: (a) the strengths of oral narrative research for expanding and transforming knowledge about black women; (b) how these scholars learned to conduct oral narrative research and descriptions of the types of narratives they are gathering; the difficulties they have encountered and how these were overcome; and the ethical dilemmas faced; (c) a discussion of the different "moments" in oral narrative research; what role, if any, participant observation plays in their work; their methods of record keeping; and how they go about "analyzing" their interviews, observations, field notes, intuition, insights, and hunches; (d) to what extent they involve the people they interview beyond the actual interview itself, and the comments, observations, emotions, and attitudes expressed by those interviewed in relationship to the research/er; (e) what they think is important for people new to oral narrative research to know about the methodology; (f) how being a black woman affects their research and how their "social class" and other personal factors influence their interviews and interactions in the field; (g) how they have presented their research to a diverse audience (or how might they present it) and the ways their research has been applied in various settings (or how might it be applied); and (h) how carrying out oral history research has affected their professional lives (e.g., opportunities created/lost); how their department or unit perceives their oral narrative research; how conducting oral narrative research has affected their personal growth and development; and how they manage the enormous time demands involved in conducting oral narrative research.

The title of the book, *Oral Narrative Research With Black Women: Collecting Treasures,* was selected in honor of the late South African writer Bessie Head. Ms. Head wrote a book of short stories entitled *The Collector of Treasures.* The stories were informed, in part, by her life in a village in Botswana. In this village (where she settled after leaving South Africa), Ms. Head "forcefully created for [her]self, under extremely hostile conditions, [her] ideal life." Here she walked slowly through the village, observing the "flow of everyday life." She felt that nothing in the village would interest a historian—for far too much necessity living was going on. Historians, she believed, did not record "how strange and beautiful [people] are—just living." So Ms. Head recorded the history of the village from its elders; took down the life histories of "ordinary" villagers; and counted "with love" the chairs and tables used in development projects. This work is recounted in *Serowe: Village of the Rain Wind*. Before settling in this village, she was a refugee in Northern Botswana. There, Ms. Head recorded the dialogue she had with a young freedom fighter from Zimbabwe. These dialogues are recounted and reshaped in her first novel, *When Rain Clouds Gather*. This novel contains her vision of young people rejecting the "wild rush for power," opting instead to absorb themselves in activities that would benefit people. Throughout her writings, Ms. Head formed new worlds where literate and semiliterate people worked together to battle tough problems—"everyone had a place in [her] world."

Given the totality of her works, Ms. Head herself became a "collector of treasures" and stands as an avatar in oral narrative research. The black women scholars who contributed to this book share many values and life experiences with Ms. Head: a broken sense of history and rootlessness that she regained through an exploration of ancient African ways; "a reverence for ordinary people"; and a philosophical examination of the nature of evil that underlies her grasp of the patterns of racism and sexism and their consequences. Moreover, Ms. Head valued African Americans and saw the Goddess in one woman who came to live in her village. Ms. Head was impressed by this woman's compassion for the underdogs of the world and believed that this compassion could come only from African Americans, given their history. Ms. Head, who identified herself as an underdog, absorbed from her Goddess the capacity to identify with people the world over who live under oppressive conditions. Learning and absorbing from other black women is part of the process of oral narrative research as carried out by black women. Ms. Head's statement "I have recorded whatever hopeful trend was presented to me in an attempt to shape the future, which I hope will be one of dignity and compassion" rings true of the research process engaged in by the contributors to this anthology.

PART I

ANCESTOR MOTHERS

EDITOR'S NOTE: Joy James uses the term *ancestor mothers* in referring to black women who demonstrated through a lifetime of writing and activism a commitment to the economic, political, educational, and moral uplift of the race. See Joy James's article "Searching for a Tradition: African American Women Writers and Activists and Interracial Rape Cases" in K. Vaz (Ed.), *Black Women in America: Confronting Gender, Race, and Class* (Thousand Oaks, CA: Sage, 1995).

2

OPHELIA AND ME

Tribute to an Early Narrative Researcher

MARTIA GRAHAM GOODSON

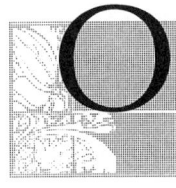Ophelia Settle Egypt (1903-1984) was a native Texan who spent most of her life—from 1939 until her death—in the District of Columbia. She graduated from Howard University there in 1925 with a degree in sociology; by the time she returned to serve on Howard's faculty 14 years later, she had already

Taught school in North Carolina (1926-1928)
Received a master's degree from the University of Pennsylvania (1928)
Conducted fieldwork at Fisk University in Tennessee (1928-1933)
Practiced social work in Missouri (1933-1934)
Directed the Social Service Department in a Louisiana hospital (1934-1939)

The focus of this chapter is the 5-year period in Egypt's early life—she was still in her 20s—when she collected ex-slave reminiscences in Tennessee, Alabama, and Kentucky for Fisk University. Egypt began listening to and collecting ex-slaves' stories, and those recollections were published in typescript form (typed) in 1945 as *Unwritten History of Slavery* (Egypt, Masuoka, & Johnson, 1945). Although they constitute

---

AUTHOR'S NOTE: Quotations from *Unwritten History of Slavery*, by O. Egypt, J. Masuoka, and C. S. Johnson, © Fisk University, Nashville, Tennessee, are used with permission.

some of the first and best of 20th-century oral narrative research on slavery, Egypt's name is not widely known.

In addition to what we can learn from the content of the slave stories that Egypt collected, her narrative research is instructive because of what we can learn about collecting treasures by studying her methodological techniques. Equally informative are the glimpses of Egypt's philosophy and of how she lived her life.

I had the opportunity to meet Ophelia Settle Egypt. Doing so greatly enriched my life both personally and professionally.

MEETING OPHELIA

My dissertation was finished. My degree was in hand. In arranging to meet Ophelia, I was, in a leisurely way, following up on a lead that I had been given during my doctoral research but that I had not been able to pursue.

She could, I was told, provide a start in my current hunt for living interviewers of ex-slaves. My doctoral research had focused on WPA-sponsored ex-slave narrative collection projects. Those projects usually excluded black workers from the ranks of their interviewers. I had grown tired of hearing the oft-repeated criticisms of these ex-slave narratives: They were invalid because they had been easily faked, the interviewers were unskilled, the ex-slaves got paid to tell their stories, many bad aspects of slavery had been left out; mostly Uncle Toms and/or Aunt Thomasinas had been interviewed and they were unrepresentative, and so on. I believed, and still believe, that narratives are a rich source of information on American slavery. But these weaknesses do not, in my opinion, invalidate them as a source of information on slavery.

I was now searching for people who I thought might have been the most skilled interviewers of ex-slaves—black people, the same black people to whom, I assumed, ex-slaves would most *want* to transmit their slavery-time stories. I wanted to talk with people who had worked in the 1920s and 1930s and 1940s on the several ex-slave interviewing projects I had identified as having black interviewers. Ophelia Egypt was the most accessible of them. She responded to my letter and invited me to visit her and talk about her now-distant Fisk days. Her recollections of interviewing slaves represent only a part of what she shared with me. Her life itself was a great lesson. But first, her oral narrative collecting days.

GOING TO FISK

Ophelia Egypt's opportunity to interview ex-slaves came through her work at the Social Science Institute at Fisk University in Nashville. Under President Thomas Elsa Jones, the late 1920s was a time for attracting people who were to become well known in 20th-century African American history. Sociologists Charles S. Johnson and E. Franklin Frazier, who were trained at the University of Chicago, joined the Fisk faculty as head of the Social Science Institute (1928) and as Research Professor of Sociology (1929), respectively. Interracial worker Juliette Derricotte, who would die tragically only 2 years later, came to Fisk as its first black dean of women (1929) after distinguishing herself in YWCA work (Lerner, 1973b, p. 384). In retirement, Arthur Schomburg (1874-1938) had been named curator of Fisk's Negro Collection (1929-1932). James Weldon Johnson was soon to be appointed professor of creative literature and writing (1933). Other people of distinction were already on the faculty, including physicist Elmer S. Imes, pianist C. Warner Lawson, chemist St. Elmo Brady, linguist Lorenzo Dow Turner, and philosopher Alain Locke (Richardson, 1980, p. 114). Among the students beginning at Fisk around this time was John Hope Franklin, a Phi Beta Kappa and magna cum laude graduate in 1935 (see Logan & Winston, 1982, pp. 356, 241, 348; and Salley, 1993, pp. 201-202, 266).

In recruiting for the Social Science Institute, Charles S. Johnson wrote to various graduate schools, searching out black sociology graduates who might join him, a recent Ph.D., in research at Fisk. Ophelia Egypt, having just received her master's degree in sociology from the University of Pennsylvania, accepted Johnson's invitation to become a Fisk instructor and research assistant at the institute. The institute's fieldwork was concentrated on the conditions in the Black Belt, including Tennessee, Kentucky, and Alabama, particularly in Macon County, home of Tuskegee Institute (Johnson, 1934). Egypt's initial fieldwork had brought her across older people. When they were asked to provide family background for the researchers, they began to tell stories of slavery. Egypt considered these stories to be so fascinating that she found herself devoting more time to these older people than she thought wise. She found the stories fascinating especially because they reminded her of similar stories she had heard from her grandparents. After consulting with Johnson, Egypt plunged into the work of collecting these ex-slave reminiscences in a systematic way.

THE FIELDWORK

The university furnished Ophelia Egypt with a stenographer, who traveled with her as she searched for interview subjects, and a typist. Together these three black women comprised the team that collected and transcribed 100 ex-slave stories, of which 37 were published a dozen years later.

First, Egypt found the subjects by going back to people she had met earlier. They, in turn, directed her to others. She created the interview questions, scheduled the fieldwork, conducted the interviews, and supervised the transcription. She wanted to tell the ex-slave stories with the care she had learned both as a descendant of slaves and as a sociologist. At Penn, she had studied with James H. S. Bufford, whose emphasis was similar to that of Charles S. Johnson's mentor at the University of Chicago, Robert E. Park. They both stressed letting the informant tell his or her own story, recording carefully to make the person's testimony come alive.

Lacking audio-recording devises, Egypt worked with a "crackerjack stenographer" who sat in the background at all interviews and took notes in shorthand. After they returned to the Fisk campus, they got together with the typist and tried to reproduce the interviews as they were given.

In addition to Egypt's formal training in data collection, she was a member of that special generation born after slavery that had the opportunity to hear of the slave's experience from family members who had direct experience. She recalled her grandfather's stories of slaves "turning down pots" at their secret gatherings, of runaways and songs, and of cowhide beatings. Egypt knew what these stories meant when she heard them in her work.

When Egypt and her staff approached the task of reproducing the "interviewees' words" for their preservation, they operated from the vantage point of being descendants of ex-slaves. Ophelia told me that each of the three women was from the South and that she worked to try to make the dialect they were reproducing real. Some interviewees used perfect English at times, and at other times in the same interview, they would switch to dialect. Egypt tried to follow the interviewee's pattern, rather than to keep the responses consistent.

The trio of Egypt and her two assistants on the project collected and recorded 100 interviews with ex-slaves. These transcriptions never, apparently, received much posttranscription editing. Soon after the interviews were completed, the staff and faculty at the university were hit with reductions. Egypt left Fisk and Tennessee, her sociology career interrupted by the Depression and the narratives unpublished.[1]

Fisk was hard-pressed for funds, and after one round of reductions, Egypt was provided with alternative employment. Because most people didn't distinguish between sociology and social work, she was thought suitable to take on an assignment in Missouri.

Egypt reported to the Provident Association in St. Louis, where her assignment was to help in the establishment of public relief programs. Private agencies, like Provident, had to show public agencies how to run such programs. Egypt was interested in the assignment and worked in the In-Take Department. Provident, a family agency, operated the relief program, distributing relief funds. After the public program had been established, Provident workers went back to private work.

PUBLICATION OF *UNWRITTEN HISTORY OF SLAVERY*

In going to the Missouri job, Egypt left sociological fieldwork and, in fact, the whole field of sociology. The Depression, her subsequent employment, and her continuing academic training all led her in the direction of social work, the career to which she devoted her years from 1933 until her death.

She gave little further thought to her narrative collecting as she moved to the job in Missouri, and later to work in Louisiana, immersing herself in her newly found career in social work. Fourteen years after she had completed her undergraduate work there, Egypt returned to her alma mater, Howard University, where she joined the faculty as assistant professor in the gestating School of Social Work, a position she held from 1939 to 1949. While at Howard, she married Ivory Lester Egypt and subsequently gave birth to Ivory Lester Egypt Jr. In 1953, Egypt Sr. died.

According to Egypt, in 1945 she received news that Charles S. Johnson, who by then had become president of Fisk, was planning to publish the ex-slave narratives that Egypt had collected earlier. She was asked to review a manuscript, entitled *Unwritten History of Slavery, Autobiographical Account of Negro Ex-Slaves*. It was "Social Science Source Documents, No. 1 Social Science Institute" and contained about three dozen ex-slaves' recollections and an introductory essay signed by Ophelia Settle Egypt, Jitsuichi Masuoka, and Charles S. Johnson. Masuoka was an instructor in sociology and a researcher in the field of race relations and became a longtime Fisk faculty member in sociology. Evidently, Masuoka drafted the introduction to the published interviews and supervised the preparation of the interviews for publication of *Unwritten History of Slavery*.

And so the narratives that Egypt had collected saw the light of day as they were made available to the public for the first time. Charles S. Johnson's name added much stature to the publication. As a well-known sociologist, spokesperson, advocate for black people, and by this time, president of Fisk, Johnson was well known nationally in his fields. The introduction to *Unwritten History of Slavery* bears his imprint and his thinking, according to Egypt.[2]

To understand the significance of the publication of *Unwritten History of Slavery*, a brief review of slave narrative collecting may be helpful. Prior to the Civil War, fugitive slave narratives were common and familiar. The popularity of collecting slave stories faded as the coming of the Civil War necessitated new and more powerful propaganda weapons for abolitionists. As a consequence, new heroic figures—for example, the black soldier—emerged to replace the fugitive slave as the central figure in the literature on slavery (Goodson, 1977).

By the second decade of the 20th century, the collecting of slave narratives was actively resumed, this time at the instigation of African American teachers and students in the segregated colleges of the South. At least three systematic collections were conducted.

First, John B. Cade conducted interviews with ex-slaves in Louisiana in 1929-1930. He reportedly collected interviews from ex-slaves from 13 states while he worked at Prairie View College in Prairie View, Texas (Cade, 1935).

Chronologically, Ophelia Settle Egypt's work at Fisk came second. Also during the 1930s, the Federal Emergency Relief Administration (FERA), while providing jobs for the unemployed, assigned workers to collect interviews from ex-slaves in five states bordering the Ohio River. Before this project ended in 1936, more than 400 narratives had been collected under the supervision of Lawrence D. Reddick, a professor at Kentucky State College.

These efforts were followed by a third, large project to interview ex-slaves, sponsored by the federal Works Progress Administration (WPA). The umbrella organization for collecting the slavery reminiscences was the Federal Writers Project (FWP). The FWP solicited stories in 17 states; the result was 2,000 interviews that have come to be known as the Slave Narrative Collection. This collection, now on deposit at the

Library of Congress, was obtained by staffs of mostly white nonprofessional interviewers.[3] The Slave Narrative Collection is the largest group of ex-slave stories collected after the Civil War.[4] However, they were not published until 1972 (Rawick, 1972). Prior to this time, it appears that only Egypt's ex-slave interviews had been published as a collection in the 20th century.

Thus, the Egypt interviews—begun in the 1920s, elicited by a black interviewer, taken down in shorthand, and transcribed by people who were sensitive to the content—represent some of the earliest and best postwar slave reminiscences that we have. The systematic organization of the project and the social environment of the interview sessions themselves also help make the resulting testimony significant.

THE PUBLISHED INTERVIEWS

The narratives of *Unwritten History of Slavery* contain material that is both familiar and distinctive. On the one hand, they provide the familiar descriptions of slave masters (Old Master, Massa, Marster), masters' wives (Ole Miss, Big Missy, Missus), and their children (Young Marster, Young Missy). We also find descriptions of the work the slave had to perform and his or her reaction to the news of Emancipation. We find familiar stories of slaves bought and sold, of the debts and deaths of masters, which often precipitated such sales. In *Unwritten History of Slavery*, we find recollections of prayer meetings, punishment, broom jumping, ashcake, and slaves' gardens.

On the other hand, *Unwritten History of Slavery* also has some distinctive qualities. First, some testimony gives new insight into familiar phenomena: running away, hiring out, and the support networks that existed among bondspeople. Second, in interesting and amusing anecdotes, these interviews give us glimpses of slaves' forthright opinions about the slavery system. And third, in a related vein, these collected memoirs offer stories of the type not thought to be appropriate for sharing with whites—stories of the type that went untold to white collectors of ex-slave stories. A few examples must suffice:

"Some of Them Just Wouldn't Take a Whipping for Nothing"

Egypt interviewed many ex-slave informants who described slaves who reportedly "wouldn't be whipped." What happened when a person (slave) decided that she or he would not be whipped? What things made the person reach that consequential decision? How did the decision affect others around him or her? Egypt's collected slavery recollections paint a picture of a complex web of relations that flowed from and to that truly fateful decision to resist.

Which came first, the whipping or the refusal to be whipped? Sometimes the slaves reporting here made the decision not to be whipped after *already* having been whipped; they vowed there would not be another. Others ran away, refusing a whipping that was being threatened. Still others—often black women—forced their masters to hire them out, rather than sell them because they wouldn't be whipped.

In contrast with the slave stories of fugitives trekking by night and resting by day, heading toward freedom in the North, a different kind of "running away" is described here. When slaves ran away, they often did not run far. A reluctance to leave family and become a fugitive on the move, a sense that one's awaiting punishment was negotiable, or a group of friends who would supply food and information—these are some of the factors that induced slaves to hide out in the vicinity of their plantation, rather than try to leave for a distant point unknown.

Some of the most interesting testimony found here concerns women who wouldn't be whipped and who, as a consequence, were sent to work for someone else—hired out while her family (usually her children) remained with the master. Thus, these interviews provide contradiction to the notion that, in slavery, the slave had to submit to the master and that the master determined where the slave would work. Here, in these recollections, the slave makes the decision not to be whipped and presents the master with the problem of what to do with her. Because the slave women were willing to be "hired out," a neat solution was found, even if only temporarily.

Those not able to negotiate hiring out could simply remain away from the plantation. When talking with Egypt, ex-slaves told of their taking food to those "hiders" who were hiding out in the woods. Egypt recorded stories of entrepreneurial whites who bought and sold slaves who were hiding out in the woods. The captured slaves were purchased by traders, who knew that the particular slave was willing to go to a new master and called this "buying him in."[5] Other slaves returned from hiding after they got some concession from the master concerning more considerate treatment in the future (Egypt et al., 1945, pp. 97-98). This testimony reveals the extent to which negotiations were involved in the slave's experience. Being able to get a slave owner not to whip you suggests powerful negotiating skills and something important about which to negotiate.

Terms of Address

The stories that Egypt collected also provide interesting glimpses into the mind of the slave and nuances that imply feeling. In contrast with revealing feelings about broad subjects like slavery, freedom, Emancipation, or the master, *Unwritten History of Slavery* gives us a chance to glimpse subtler nuances in the slaves' cerebral lives.

How, for example, did adult slaves and slave children feel about addressing white children as "Master" and "Missus"? Their feelings are suggested in testimony that was offered years after slavery had ended but that reflected resentment toward the slave-society convention regarding this "social amenity."

> When your marster had a baby born in his family they would call all the niggers and tell them to come in and "see your new marster." We had to call them babies "Mr." and "Miss," too. (p. 150)

> When we got to the house, my mistress came out with a baby in her arms and said, "Well, here's my little nigger. Shake hands with me." Then [the master] come up and said, "Speak to your young mistress," and I said, "Where she at?" He said, "Right there," and pointed to the baby in my mistress' arms. I said, "No, I don't see no young mistress, that's a baby." (p. 133)

Stories for Black Ears

This collection contains stories that, I contend, ex-slaves would have been reluctant to tell to white interviewers, stories their interviewers would probably have been reluctant to hear. Given that some of the interviewers were descendants of former owners of the interviewees, it is hard to imagine whites in 1929 receiving either of the following stories.

> One time when [the slaves] were singing, "Ride on King Jesus, No Man Can Hinder Thee," the padderollers told them to stop or they would show them whether they could be hindered or not. Sometimes the white folks

would come in when the colored people would have prayer meeting and whip every one of them. Most of them thought that when colored people were praying it was against them. For they would catch them praying for God to lift things out of their way, and the white folks would *lift them*. (p. 60)

One time a white man came over to my hack and asked me whose hack it was, and I told him that it was Mr. Farley's, and he said, "Well, how much for a trip?" and I told him 50 cents. After I made the trip he said, "Here is 50¢ for your boss and $1.00 for you." He was supposed to be a wealthy man, and I was glad to get that $1.50. Mr. Farley was myself, but he didn't know it, so I didn't tell him nothing but the truth and got $1.50. (p. 61)

These sensitive stories are meant for sensitive ears. In the Jim Crow era in which these ex-slaves and their interviewers lived, it could not be surprising that there are things the ex-slaves would not tell to just anyone. And, for seasoned storytellers, multiple versions of a story can be told, depending on the audience. (For discussion of white interviewers and black interviewees offering ex-slave testimony, see Goodson, 1985.)

WHAT I LEARNED FROM OPHELIA

I would describe the Ophelia Egypt that I knew as an active, resourceful, self-directed person and an excellent typist of breezy, responsive personal letters. For most of her years, she worked in the same Washington, D.C., southeast neighborhood in which she lived. The granddaughter of slaves, she raised her son after her husband died. She was an unassuming person with a quick and warm smile. I willingly and respectfully learned quite a few things from her. Three of them come to mind.

First, don't let anyone abuse you. When I interviewed Ophelia Egypt, I wanted to know the most memorable thing that she heard during her interviewing project. What message had the voice of the slave left to be heard by succeeding generations? What did they want us to know? She replied, recalling the admonition of a slave mother to her daughter in one of the most often quoted of Egypt's Fisk narratives, known as "My Mother Was the Smartest Black Woman in Eden":[6]

Don't let nobody run over you, don't let them mistreat you. *If you can't hit, kick. If you can't kick, bite, do something but don't let them abuse you,* was her word. *Don't let 'em 'buse you, Puss.*[7] (p. 143)

Although she did not say so, I believe that this mother's admonition was a part of Egypt's credo as well. Fifty years after she first heard it, she still remembered it. That, I felt, was reason enough for me to consider the advice seriously myself.

Don't let nobody 'buse you.

I have repeated it often in the years since I heard it from Ophelia. And I quote it often to my children. That caveat is part of a legacy that I can, personally, through Ophelia, trace back to slavery and, perhaps, earlier. I understand it as a message of self-defense and self-affirmation for which I—not others—am responsible.

Don't let nobody 'buse you. Evidently, it worked for Fannie and Cornelia and Ophelia; it works for me.

A second thing that I, as an oral historian, learned from Ophelia Egypt is to believe in my informants. On the one hand, slavish acceptance of everything one hears would be inappropriate for a student of the black oral tradition. But on the other hand, one must believe that one's informant has something of worth to say. And because researchers don't always know what interviewees are going to say, we must accept that they will, at times, say things we will not be prepared for or not understand when we hear them. That does not mean, however, that things unclear to us have no validity. To the contrary, we are there to learn. Therefore, we must be prepared to encounter things we don't know about and must conduct research following our interviewing in order to understand what we have heard.

In my conversations and correspondence with Ophelia, I learned that she and I shared an interest in some of the particular things the former slaves talked about. She believed in the stories the former slaves told her, even when she didn't quite understand the testimony herself and even when others might be either reluctant to believe or quick to dismiss that testimony when it was new or different.

For example, she took the ex-slaves seriously when they frequently reported they "turned down [iron] pots" during their nighttime prayer meetings in order to suppress the sounds of their exuberant worship. But could placing a pot in a brush arbor or on a dirt cabin floor, near the door, actually absorb or muffle sound? Could it keep the slaves' worship from being detected by their masters or by patrollers? Egypt thought it might. She remembered that her grandfather had talked about this same practice. She believed that the use of the pot was more than "symbolic."

Some researchers, however, disagree. George Rawick, who edited the publication of the WPA/FWP project in the 1970s, also commented on the widely reported practice of turning down pots during religious worship. He concluded that the use of the pot has nothing to do with keeping sound down, but was purely symbolic. Rawick (1973) said,

> It is clear that the iron pot could not have in fact been very effective in actually deadening the sound of the slaves' religious sings, particularly when we know that they were not quiet affairs. . . . Clearly the iron pot or kettle is a symbolic element, the original associations of which have been lost. . . . [Among the Yoruba] the pots are special symbols of the gods who afford protection to men and women. . . . With such protection men and women in Africa and in related ways, under slavery in the New World, had the courage to gather at night for prayer meetings to assert and develop their community even though such meetings were prohibited. (pp. 41-43)

If we say that the use of the pot is symbolic, how do we understand an informant who, when asked about "turning down pots" on her plantation, responds as follows:

> No, we didn't *have to* [italics added] turn the pot down on our place, but an old man lived up in the country named Mr. Compton and his folks would have prayer meeting and the people would slip there, and they would have the pot down to drown the sound. They would be scared to death that the white folks would hear them. We had wooden shutters and they would just pull those shutters to and do the door some way, and pray and sing in the room together. (Egypt et al., 1945, p. 5)

Does "we didn't have to" mean that when masters disallowed the meetings, the pots were used to conceal a covert meeting? And if meetings were allowed, they didn't "have to" use the pots to keep their gathering secret? Or perhaps they didn't "have to" use the pot because their cabins were sealed enough to contain the sound?

This detail, of the pot "helping" keep the sound down, clarifies an ex-slave's recollection that Rawick (1972, Vol. 6, p. 40) cites:

> Some of de niggers get happy and get to shoutin' all over de meadow where dey built a bresh arbor. Massa John quick put a stop to dat. He say, "if you gwine to preach and sing you must turn de wash pot bottom up"; meaning 'no shoutin'.

Perhaps, as Egypt's informants suggested, the upturned pot did, indeed, help keep the sound down, a "fact" that even Massa John knew and accepted. But why did the use of the pot disappear? When the end of slavery ended the need for secrecy in religious worship, when the invisible institution of slavery became visible, why did the use of the pot disappear? Didn't it disappear?

Also, why do so many slaves describe a phenomenon that was *ineffective* in drowning out sound? In other words, if turning down pots didn't work, why did they keep doing it? The questions to which I am seeking answers remind me of earlier ones I have asked regarding the slave women's use of botanical medicine.

Ophelia and I spoke briefly about the slaves' use of medicinal plants. In this regard, she thought it was important to use the knowledge she already possessed to help interpret this slave testimony. She told me she paid attention to what the slaves said about medicines and cures because she had known of plant medicine when she was growing up. Further, when her brother was studying pharmacy and she would help him prepare for exams, she told me she ran across "things that my grandmother used" that were in the medications being made up into pharmaceutical prescriptions.

Our discussions encouraged me to continue with research on the Slave Narrative Collection interviews. My research suggests some of the many medical botanical contributions of African women to the American medical community and to American medicine. The demonstrated effectiveness of the botanical cures and treatments employed by slave women compelled the young Southern (and later national) medical community to accept and imitate—without sentiment or traditions—the slave women's plant medical practice.

The American medical community learned about medicine from slave women, and Egypt was one of those who believed that medical botany was a part of the efficacious and enduring legacy of Africa that the slaves preserved for us (Goodson, 1987).

A third thing that I learned from Ophelia was about life and how to live it. Ophelia Settle Egypt remained tied to her black people throughout her life. She became someone whom I wanted to imitate, someone whose life on which I wanted, in some manner, to pattern mine.

Clearly, she was independent—traipsing around the South in the early 1930s with an Ivy League master's degree, collecting slave stories. Throughout her life, she worked at those things to which she was committed. And she was committed to her people. A brief look at a few periods of her life will illustrate:

One of her Howard classmates, Helen Brown, recalled that in her undergraduate days, Ophelia Settle was "always engaged in Christian work." She was very involved with the Phillis Wheatley YWCA activities; and although she lived off-campus, she often led the before-breakfast Devotionals ("a song and a prayer and a song and prayer") on campus with her female Howard classmates (H. Brown, personal communication, July 14, 1995).

While at Fisk University, she was an active member of the research staff but was not too busy to be involved in student life. Regularly, she had Sunday morning breakfasts with at least one 1st-year student, Ramona Lowe, advising her about college and about life (R. Lowe, personal communication, July 17, 1995).

Following her time at Fisk, Egypt had two jobs that molded the remainder of her career. After 2 years of social work in St. Louis at Provident Association, Egypt moved to the new field of medical social work as director of the social services at Flint Goodridge Hospital in New Orleans.

Then, Egypt returned to Howard University—13 years after she had graduated. This time, however, she had her mind on social work, rather than sociological research; and now she was ready to teach social work, not just practice it.

At Howard, she worked with E. Franklin Frazier again. Since the time they had both been at Fisk, Frazier had directed the Social Work School at Atlanta University. Now, Egypt would work with him and their colleague Inabel Burns Lindsay to develop Howard University's School of Social Work.[8]

Ophelia taught in Howard's School of Social Work for a decade (1939-1949). While there, she earned a second master's degree, this one in social work from New York School of Social Work, now Columbia University School of Social Work. She took more courses in social work at the University of Pennsylvania School of Social Work as well.

The bulk of Ophelia Egypt's working life was undertaken when she moved out of academia and waded into the very real waters of providing social work services. One of her first efforts when she left Fisk was to reestablish the recently closed Ionia R. Whipper Rehabilitation Home, which serviced unmarried black women. Later, she directed the Parklands Neighborhood Clinic, Planned Parenthood of Metropolitan Washington, D.C., which she established in 1957 and led until she retired in 1968. Through this clinic, Egypt taught community residents about "planning for parenting" in her contacts with them in churches, in beauty parlors, in their homes, in grocery stores, and at soda fountains (Planned Parenthood Federation of America, 1957).

At the time she worked at the Whipper Home, her job was made difficult, in part, by attitudes toward unmarried pregnant women. Her

Planned Parenthood job gave her an opportunity to make an impact in an area that mattered to her. At first, she had some difficulty getting women interested in Planned Parenthood. Gradually, however, she found that the problem was not getting into, but getting out of, women's homes when they discovered how her birth control knowledge satisfied their hunger for information.

In her retirement, this dynamic woman continued her activities and found new ones. She authored a children's biography of James Weldon Johnson (Egypt, 1974). She spent a considerable amount of time speaking to various groups (Scouts, libraries, churches, schools), for which she received recognition and awards. Finally, she had the time to return to the slave narratives with which she began her career.

Egypt worked on *Raggedy Thorns,* the title she had selected for her own compilation of the slave reminiscences that she had collected nearly 50 years earlier. Of this book it was said,

> The final chapters of "Raggedy Thorns" will give her personal opinion of how racism is a heritage of slavery and how it affects the lives of 20th century Americans, black and white. She hasn't written it yet but it will conclude that "it is terribly hard to change attitudes of racism which are deep in the subconscious." (Trescott, 1971, p. H-4)

Ophelia Settle Egypt died on May 25, 1984, before this work was completed, yet she inspired me and, I hope, other narrative researchers, social workers, historians, anthropologists, and sociologists, as well as other black women and humanity in general, by her example.

> Her [narrative collecting] studies provided a solid basis for new scholarship. But her work in the area of social service met an important need in the black community. It enabled her to provide social and emotional relief to black youth, unmarried mothers, and needy blacks throughout the several communities in which she unstintingly gave her expertise and time. (Smith, 1992, p. 305)

Ophelia. We need more Ophelias. I think we have them.

NOTES

1. Evidently, Egypt was able to provide some immediate description of her slave narrative collecting project. She published "Social Attitudes During the Slave Regime: Household Servants Versus Field Hands" in 1933, in publications of the American Sociological Society. For reasons that are unclear to me, the author is listed as "E. Ophelia Settle." Settle is Ophelia's family name (see Meier & Rudwick, 1969).

2. This introduction states that the narratives "help us understand the manner in which personality enters into social change." It goes on to describe the institution of slavery as

> first and foremost an adjustment of divergent and dissimilar individuals to an impersonal competitive process ... an exploitative system, in which ... individuals, equipped with superior technology and capital, directed and controlled the energies of a numerically superior, but culturally inferior, population.

The result of this system, according to the introduction, was the development of a "form of racial symbiosis within a single society."

3. Only the Virginia Writers Project had an all-Negro unit to collect ex-slave stories. Roscoe Lewis of Hampton Institute was "Supervisor of Negro Workers" in the statewide project, which produced *The Negro in Virginia* (1940). The frontmatter states, "Compiled by the Workers of the Writers' Project of the Works Progress Administration in the State of Virginia." The Foreword of *The Negro in Virginia* explains:

> Late in 1936, a Negro section was added to the Federal Writers' Project in Virginia. Its purpose was two-fold: to provide work for educated negroes on relief and to contribute to Negro literature.... In the months that have followed approximately one-fifth of the personnel of the Virginia Writers' Project has been made up of Negroes.

4. The first descriptive article on the Slave Narrative Collection was written by Benjamin Botkin, folklore editor of the Federal Writers Project in 1944, in *Library of Congress Quarterly Journal of Current Acquisitions*. Perhaps this publication prompted Charles S. Johnson to redirect his attention to the narrative collection that was lying dormant at Fisk. Botkin's article was followed 2 years later by his *Lay My Burden Down* (1945), a book of short excerpts from the Slave Narrative Collection.

5. "Some time they would be in the woods two years, and be sold to the highest bidder" (Egypt, Masuoka, & Johnson, 1945, p. 14).

6. This narrative was, I believe, one of Egypt's favorites. It was probably one on which she spent time, refining it from an interview transcript into a narrative story for popular audiences. It is quoted in Lerner (1973a, p. 34) and Wallace (1978, pp. 128-129).

7. The theme reoccurs in various forms throughout the ex-slave story. "The one doctrine of my mother's teaching which was branded upon my senses was that I should never let anyone abuse me. 'I'll kill you, gal, if you don't stand up for yourself,' she would say. 'Fight, and if you can't fight, kick; if you can't kick, then bite.' "

As the slave child's mother is to be sent away for refusing to be whipped, she advises her child, "She called me and told me that she and pa were going to leave me the next day, that they were going to Memphis. She didn't know for how long. 'But don't be abused, Puss.' She always called me Puss. My right name is Cornelia."

Later, separated from her mother, Puss reflects on an earlier time when she "was thinking all the time that slavery did not seem so cruel. Master and Mistress Jennings were not mean to my mother. It was she who was mean to them." Now, with her mother and father gone, the slave child's view changed, "Yes, Ma had been right. Slavery was chuck full of cruelty and abuse. During this time I decided to follow my mother's example. I intended to fight, and if I couldn't fight, I'd kick; and if I couldn't kick, I'd bite.... Everyone began to say, 'Cornelia is the spit of her mother. She is going to be just like Fannie.' And I delighted in hearing this. I wanted to be like [Ma] now" (p. 145).

8. Lindsay, like Egypt and Frazier, was a Howard graduate (1920). And like Charles S. Johnson and E. Franklin Frazier, she had done graduate work at the University of Chicago, where she received a master's degree in social work administration (1937). She was invited to return to Howard to help set up a School of Social Work there. After the new school was fully established, Lindsay was named its first dean, in 1945 (see Hill & King, 1990; Logan, 1968; Smith, 1992).

REFERENCES

Botkin, B. (1945). *Lay my burden down.* Chicago: University of Chicago Press.
Cade, J. B. (1935, July). Out of the mouths of ex-slaves. *Journal of Negro History, 20*(3), 294-337.
Egypt, O. (1933, December). Social attitudes during the slave regime: Household servants versus field hands. *Racial Contacts and Social Research, 27,* 95-98.
Egypt, O. (1974). *James Weldon Johnson.* New York: Thomas Y. Crowell.
Egypt, O., Masuoka, J., & Johnson, C. S. (1945). *Unwritten history of slavery* (Social Science Resource Document #1). Nashville, TN: Fisk University. (Also published by NCR Microcard, Washington, 1971)
Goodson, M. (1985). The significance of race-of-interviewer in the collection and analysis of ex-slave narratives: Considering the sources. *Western Journal of Black Studies, 9*(3), 126-134.
Goodson, M. (1987). Medical-botanical contributions of African slave women to American medicine. *Western Journal of Black Studies, 11*(4), 198-203.
Goodson, M. G. (1977). *An introductory essay and subject index to selected interviews from the Slave Narrative Collection.* Unpublished doctoral dissertation, Union Graduate School.
Hill, R. E., & King, P. M. (Eds.). (1990). *Guide to the transcripts of the Black Women Oral History Project.* Westport, CT: Meckler.
Johnson, C. S. (1934). *Shadow of the plantation.* Chicago: University of Chicago Press.
Lerner, G. (1973a). Fight, and if you can't fight, kick. In *Black women in white America.* New York: Vintage.
Lerner, G. (1973b). The life and death of Juliette Derricotte. In *Black women in white America.* New York: Vintage.
Logan, R. (1968). *Howard University: The first hundred years.* New York: New York University Press.
Logan, R., & Winston, M. (1982). *Dictionary of American Negro biography.* New York: Norton.
Meier, A., & Rudwick, E. (1969). *The making of black America: Essays in Negro life and history* (Vol. 1). New York: Athenaeum.
Planned Parenthood Federation of America. (1957, Winter). Mission in Washington. *Planned Parenthood News, 17.*
Rawick, G. (Ed.). (1972). *The American slave: A composite autobiography.* Westport, CT: Greenwood.
Rawick, G. (1973). *From sunset to sunrise: The making of the slave community.* Westport, CT: Greenwood.
Richardson, J. (1980). *A history of Fisk University, 1865-1946.* Tuscaloosa: University of Alabama Press.
Salley, C. (1993). *Black 100.* New York: Citadel.
Smith, J. C. (1992). *Notable black American women.* Detroit: Gale Research.
Trescott, J. (1971, March 7) "Raggedy Thorns": Slave narratives. *Sunday Star* (Washington), p. H-4.
Virginia Writers Project. (1940). *The Negro in Virginia.* New York: Hastings House.
Wallace, M. (1978). *Black macho and the myth of the superwoman.* New York: Dial.

3

PROFESSIONS OF FAITH

A Teacher Reflects on Women, Race, Church, and Spirit

JOYCELYN MOODY

> We have attempted to separate the spiritual and the erotic, thereby reducing the spiritual to a world of flattened affect, a world of the ascetic who aspires to feel nothing. But nothing is farther from the truth. . . . The dichotomy between the spiritual and the political is also false. . . . For the bridge which connects them is formed by the erotic—the sensual—those physical, emotional, and psychic expressions of what is deepest and strongest and richest within each of us, being shared: the passions of love, in its deepest meanings.
>
> Audre Lorde, "Uses of the Erotic" (1983)

A good friend, a Roman Catholic who is also a colleague at the university where I teach English, and I sit discussing my frustration with the process of writing this chapter. I confess to her, "I am not a holy woman." She has two responses. First, she sits back away from me and nods vigorously, saying, "See, but what does that mean? You obviously

---

AUTHOR'S NOTE: I want to acknowledge the compassion and generosity of two dear friends, Shileen Burke and Frances Wood, who helped me with this chapter. This chapter is dedicated to my parents, George A. and Catherine E. Moody.

have some definition of 'holy woman' in mind when you declare yourself *not* one."

I nod myself, miserably: Her observation does not make my task any easier. After a moment, though, she leans into the table and confides that her partner of many years, a Protestant clergywoman, recently surprised her in a conversation they had had about just this notion. The clergywoman had been marveling at how blessed she felt, for never before had she imagined that her life would be so full of holy women; and she named several of her closest friends, her partner among them. My friend's voice wobbles as she tells me that she'd felt honored but also stunned: "Holy woman" had always seemed a term the clergywoman reserved for members of traditionally black churches.

Later, recalling my friend's use of Audre Lorde's phrase "sister outsider" to describe her estrangement from African American women reared from childhood as Baptists, Methodists, Pentecostals, and so on, I think of Jill Nelson. This witty and urbane author's memoir, *Volunteer Slavery* (1994), taught me many critical lessons with each reading. Luckily for me, the lesson of Nelson's sage subtitle—that there is no such thing as an "authentic Negro experience"—reverberates steadily; it's a lesson I seem to need to learn over and over.

I think of Nelson and remember writhing under a former friend's acrid scorn of Afro-Catholics. Fastidiously Baptist, Davida had no patience with black Catholics. During 1990-91, we were together at a small Midwestern liberal arts college, and throughout the year, she often mimicked the Church's chants and rites, mocked its clergy and laypeople, and derided parishioners' deference to "idols and icons." In short, she was disdainful and contemptuous of Roman Catholics, African Americans most of all.

By the time I met Davida, I had already abandoned any formal religion and taken to proclaiming myself atheist, yet Davida's self-righteousness disturbed me. Her criticisms had been aimed directly at me sometimes, former Presbyterian and former Catholic both, but never yet Afro-Protestant.[1] I thought my disquiet simply another form of my insecurity around members of some traditional Afro-Protestant sects. Often, during my life, I have felt ashamed of having been raised as a black Presbyterian, chagrined by what I judged the incongruent and oxymoronic implications of an "Afro-Presbyterian." I used to disparage my parents' choice of Presbyterianism as a choice against other, "real" blacks, and I boasted my resentment of their choosing it for me.[2] As Presbyterians, we had sung "hymns," not spirituals; we had prayed silently, never shouted or "got happy." So Davida's jeers, especially about the religious music I knew—or rather, those gospel songs I did not know—seemed fair rebuke for myriad ecclesiastical crimes, for my sins of omission. But one lesson of Nelson's astute memoir disputes my fallacious inference and tacitly proclaims Davida's scorn as erroneous as my shame: the idea that my religious background is culturally or racially deficient, is inadequate and inferior, derives from a belief that one (religious) experience—Davida's—qualifies as an "authentic Negro experience." Wiser now, I'd sardonically agree: It's an authentic *Negro* experience, all right. Years later, my guilt transformed to comprehension, I have news for Davida. As my sage colleague Marcia says, "If I'm in it, it's black." Or, to cite Angela Davis's prudent admonition to African American academic women, "We can no longer ignore the ways in which we sometimes end up reproducing the very forms of domination which we like to attribute to somebody or something else" (1994, p. 427).

I remember many aspects of being Presbyterian; other things about that experience, I've forgotten on purpose. Occasionally, I joke with a colleague about our both having grown up Presbyterian. She jests more than I do, as she did after we'd seen *A River Runs Through It*. Our banter about the minister-father's repressed love and elitism, about his wife's quelled pain, her plainness, filled the hollow places that the film delved out of our post-Presbyterian arrogance. But for me, there was no solace in our teasing: I know there's a vast difference between her having been raised Presbyterian as a white girl in Alaska and my having been reared Presbyterian as a black girl in Alabama.

I recently taught Fannie Barrier Williams's "A Northern Negro's Autobiography" (1904/1991) for the first time. Reading its race-proud description of the Williamses at worship among New York whites at the turn of the 19th century, I recalled my own girlhood—from ages 6 to 20—among Southern whites at church. Williams wrote nearly a century ago:

> My parents were strictly religious people and were members of one of the largest white churches in the village.... Ours was the only colored family in the church, in fact, the only one in the town for many years, and certainly there could not have been a relationship more cordial, respectful and intimate than that of our family and the white people of this community. (p. 12)

Struck by what Alice Walker (1983) might call the "contrary instincts" of Williams's pleasurable memories of being nurtured by whites and her tacit resistance to racist tokenism, I retreated behind a mask of deprecation of my own devising. Facing my mostly white students, I quipped, "I can honestly say now that I have forgiven my parents for raising me as a Presbyterian." But inwardly, I believed I might have also said, "I have never adequately thanked my parents for rearing me Presbyterian," for my personal experience challenges Malcolm X's barbed observation to the effect that "eleven o'clock Sunday morning is the most segregated hour in America." Throughout the 1960s, I was the only little black girl in the only black family among Southern whites called Little, Turnipseed, Thompson, Mosley, Shott, and Hart, at the significantly named Community Presbyterian Church. I felt exclusive and protected—but also deceitful and fraudulent. Growing up black and Presbyterian in a white church in the segregated South gave me a profound and a *profoundly false* sense of security and an exaggerated sense of my family's superiority to other African Americans. At the same time, it gave me an irrefutable and ever-encroaching sense of my inferiority to other African Americans, who attended "real" black churches. At my all-black public school, perhaps I wondered whether I was a "genuine" black person. More likely, I had no resources to articulate even to myself such feelings of class distinction.

One of the most enduring memories I have of being young, black, female, Southern, and Presbyterian is of the November Friday that our church youth group (directed by my indefatigable father) attended service at the local synagogue. Actually, I cannot recall anything we *did* among the Jews in Mobile, only that I was enthralled by the velvet beauty and evening shadows of the synagogue at dusk in late autumn. Sans stained glass, sans crucifix, its grandeur seemed to me much lovelier, more exquisite than our own sanctuary's brick-and-board, plain austerity. Looking back, I think the memory looms large for two unrelated reasons. For one, though young, I must have comprehended that, in Alabama, Jews were as anomalous as African American Presbyterians. (Was this a covert lesson my father devised for the white teens and my brothers and me?) And second, perhaps I remember the synagogue because, for me, the sacred has always been intricately bound up with the sensuous, with what poet Audre Lorde (1983) calls "the erotic."

Indeed, in the summer I turned 14, I was saved from sin precisely because of sensuous surroundings. We were at Pinetreat. An expansive retreat camp-resort deep in rural Baldwin County and owned by the Mobile Presbytery, Pinetreat is as fecund and wild and lush a woods as exists deep in the American South. Overrun each June by dozens of youngsters, camp there marked the beginning of vacation. For many

Presbyterian youth, it was also where we first found God. In the halcyon splendor of Pinetreat's natural beauty—its red clay dirt and clearwater creeks, its mummifying kudzu and cavernous ravines—I found God waiting for me like a serene lover. My fingertips felt tender, all my tactile surfaces swollen, for weeks in anticipation. The textures and the redolence of Pinetreat, like those of the synagogue later, established for me a sensuousness and a sensuality now vital to spirituality; from camp and temple, I learned that I could not love or praise God, could not experience God, until—unless—all my senses were engaged in the discovery of God.

I sensed God's presence increasingly less as I came of age at Community. With a Catholic aunt, I often returned to the Afro-Catholic parish where I'd studied during seventh grade while riding out the storm of compulsory busing and school desegregation. Later, lured by the sensual Mystery of the Mass and by my intimacy with Jesuits, I converted to Catholicism as a college sophomore. My Protestant parents were shattered, for they could not comprehend the relief, the release I found in Intercession, Reconciliation, the Rosary. I could not make them understand that, during the 20 years I had practiced Presbyterianism, I had had only two experiences, camp and temple, that I believed genuinely spiritual.

Because it occurred at Pinetreat, I counted my religious conversion from sin to salvation at age 14 as an authentic spiritual episode. Despite my double consciousness—angst, rather—as a black Presbyterian, I did not doubt my salvation or consider it spurious, although it happened when I was among whites only. (At camp that summer, there were two or three African American peers to bear witness. Oddly enough, one of them, my pal Gail, was the Catholic daughter of a Presbyterian mother.) The only time I ever questioned the earnestness and authenticity of my experience of being saved came shortly after camp that summer. My closest white friend, Maggie, had gone home and, as we were all commissioned to do, told her mother of her conversion. Imagining Maggie with her mother, I wince; the scene is so different from the one in which I had sat with my mother in my bedroom, the two of us crying together over the Good News as morning sunlight filtered through my sheer pink curtains. For when Maggie described how we teens, heady with Spirit, some speaking in tongues, had been led to God by a newly ordained, 30-something-year-old pastor with blond panache and a Pentecostal flair, her mother denounced our ecstasy as revelry, orgy, mass hysteria.

"Mass hysteria" is, of course, precisely the phrase the uninitiated use to characterize the rapturous "getting happy" that often takes place in traditional Afro-Protestant churches.[3] Recalling Maggie's sorrowful account of her sharing the (Not-So-)Good News with her mother, I understand that her mother's vitriolic response to our adolescent conversion experience had specifically to do with its show of joy and ebullience, with our virgin zeal and elation. For no matter their private exultation in the Passion, the traditional Presbyterians I've known rarely acknowledge such ecstasy, and they never, never, never condone it in those Christians they find offensive.[4] Ironically, Maggie's mother and Davida, my Baptist associate in the Midwest, share a great deal in common: Whereas Davida criticized white Christians, and the blacks who worshipped with them, for what she judged unauthentic and/or deficient professions of faith, Maggie's mother deemed repugnant the primitiveness and incorrigibility she imputed to her daughter's camp experience. Tainted with racial phobias and religious chauvinism, the perspectives of both women impugn the Gospel. Neither seems to me to emanate from piety or love.

I do not mean to suggest that all Presbyterians or all Baptists are too obdurate or staid or myopic to distinguish between piety and prejudice. Both Maggie's mother and my friend Davida were undeniably devout women, but they seemed to me not to perceive the distinctions between—or better, the convergences of—piety and spirituality. If a pious experience is one in which we communicate with the Divine—even manifest as mortal—with only the finite power accessible to mortals, then perhaps a spiritual experience can be said to be one in which the Divine—even manifest as mortal—communicates with us through our senses, with all the immeasurable power open to the Divine. I do not mean to condemn the limitations of any individual Christian or of any Christian sect. Indeed, I want to acknowledge the religious fulfillment that Presbyterianism, in particular, has provided members of my family. The minister who guided me to salvation in my 14th summer and the campers who found God with me proved to me that an experience can be, is often, both "religious" and "spiritual." Even more, they taught me that the practices of any one denomination are too various, too diverse to generalize about and that that diversity does not pertain to race or culture. Looking back, I see that God was indeed at Community Presbyterian Church during all the years I worshipped there: God was in every earnest act of kindness and generosity that helped foster my childhood security. For that I remain grateful.

Religious chauvinism, however, like that expressed by Maggie's mother, partly provoked my leaving the church altogether after college. And partly I left because of my acculturation in a postbaccalaureate academy terrified, and thus contemptuous, of things mystical or divine. By the time I had completed course work for a doctorate, I had been thoroughly indoctrinated as an infidel. Fully submerged in academe, desperate for all the rights and privileges accorded thereto, I learned to spurn religious persons as primitive, bovine, or asinine, to castigate religion itself as specious and illusory. Moreover, my derision of piety and spirituality ensued from my immersion into second-wave feminism. In the early 1980s, before the advent of today's womanspirit movement, I understood feminism to repudiate Christianity especially for its patriarchal proscription of women's sacred and secular autonomy.

Even teaching among Jesuits, I foolishly refused to accede any place for the sacred in my teaching of literary texts by self-identified holy persons. This resistance necessitated extraordinary manipulation and contortion. I wanted, for example, to transform the curriculum of the college's required course, Masterpieces of the Ancient World, the reputable—and requisite—anthology for which contained only one woman's text, and that one translated into modern English by a male novelist. Researching early women's literature to expand my course, I discovered a number of poignant narratives by women. As an autobiography scholar, I was most captivated by the Medieval life writings of Dame Julian of Norwich and Margery Kempe—but chagrined by my interest because it proved exceedingly difficult (read virtually impossible) for me to separate the two women's spirituality from their literary achievement. As a feminist, I could not read Julian's erudite account of her visions of God as both father *and mother* in *Sixteen Showings* (ca. 1373/1993) without feeling tremendous *theological* excitement. Instead of allowing my mostly Roman Catholic students to acknowledge or debate the mystic's religious convictions, however, I required them to analyze her (translated) prose style, diction, imagery, and so on—an assignment that chafed them no less than me.

Similarly, my pedagogy then permitted only an analysis of the feminist elements of Kempe's remarkable homiletic narrative. Distinctive as the first autobiography written in (Middle) English, *The Book of Margery Kempe* (ca. 1432/1995) was dictated to religious and secular scribes (to men). It details a woman's struggles for sexual and reproductive rights, but also for religious and spiritual autonomy: for Kempe, a mother of 14 who deserted her family to become a "crying" pilgrim, was tried and acquitted as heretic and hysteric at Leicester in

1417. Although her piteous weeping moved me greatly, precisely because it verified the depth of her piety, I restricted my early teaching of Kempe's narrative to its feminism and prose style. I abstained from any examination of these spiritual accounts that would treat as affirming or legitimating any truths about divine or mystical phenomena.

While still with the Jesuits in the late 1980s, I began to concentrate on early African American autobiography in my graduate studies and committed myself to writing a doctoral thesis on the autobiographies of my ethnic foremothers. Specifically, I determined to survey late-19th-century mulatta educators, mixed-race and/or middle-class women including Charlotte Forten Grimké, Anna Julia Cooper, and Mary Church Terrell. One afternoon, however, my dissertation advisor, who had recently reissued three early black women's spiritual autobiographies, suggested that I study the narratives of other 19th-century African American holy women. I resisted blurting my first thought: "No way I will spend the next few years of my life thinking and writing about a bunch of Holy Rollers!" Nevertheless, to develop my knowledge, I read the recommended narratives. And as the song says, "My soul looks back in wonder."

Immediately, I perceived that this newly recovered body of literature would require strategic defense and analysis and that the most critical scholarship might come from womanist professors like myself. After I had completed my dissertation, in a brief article for *The Womanist*, I would explicate some of the imperatives that seem to me implicit in the marvelous works (Moody, 1994). For one, if we are not to risk the loss or suppression of these texts again, we must recognize the verity and the value of the precious oral narratives of 19th-century black women who lacked the skills to inscribe, but not to organize or authenticate, their own experiences. Astute scholars have reasonably cautioned that white amanuenses, well-intentioned abolitionists included, simply could not reconstruct the lives of free and enslaved blacks as they themselves might, had they the proficiency. Yet, if we insist on disregarding dictated autobiographies as suspect or sophistical, then we must relinquish our literary acquisition of hundreds of significant autobiographical accounts. Then we must sacrifice such texts as "Belinda, or the Cruelty of Men Whose Faces Were Like the Moon" (1782/1996). In this petition to the state of Massachusetts for reparations, the African subject describes her abduction at prayer, her enslavement in America, and the misuse of her own and her daughter's labors for the material advancement of an uncaring slavemaster.[5] As Joanne Braxton (1989) writes:

> This "as-told-to" account reflects an African woman's shock at being taken while at prayer and sold into slavery. . . . [and] records, therefore, not just the physical aspects of the capture in West Africa, and the dreaded "middle passage," but the complete disruption of the narrator's emotional and spiritual life and the corresponding loss of her sense of place, both physical and metaphysical. . . . "Belinda" reveals one black woman's early attempts to own her words, her freedom, and most assuredly, her own image. (p. 2)

Through their lacunae, early black narratives implore contemporary scholars to become, as Frances Smith Foster (1993) asserts, "literary anthropologists, looking underneath the stated ideas and events to see what is not shown" (p. 9). Comprehending that the conditions of early African American women's lives were recorded almost exclusively by these women themselves because (white/male) persons with power did not consider them worthy of documentation and chronicle, we must research the sociopolitical contexts of their lives to interpret fully the fragments and codes of black women's life stories. Furthermore, we must acknowledge that our limited access to 19th-century African American women's writings is largely the effect of scholarly neglect and correlates directly with the fact that the subjects were black, female, poor, and illiterate (or poorly schooled)—each attribute signaling their want of suffrage. Moreover, the women's literary disappearance was precipitated by their evangelicalism: Even during the Second Great (Religious) Awakening, their (white) compatriots—precursors of today's academic elitists—often deprecated the sacred experiences of free black and slave women as "primitive" and "African."

Hypersensitive to my own disparagement of spirituality and religion prior to reading these texts, I was primarily concerned that the women's narratives would be dismissed for their Christian agendas. My earliest teachers in the segregated public schools of Mobile County, all of them fiercely proud Race Women, had engendered in me an ardent and enduring love of African American literature, which I continue to cherish for its intrinsic beauty and complexity. Yet I wonder that my progression into academe as a black feminist literary scholar did not once proceed from an eagerness to redress, if not to obliterate, any lingering racial elitism I had developed as a Presbyterian; perhaps I had unconsciously hoped that a professional career of sharing African American literature with others would help me atone for past transgressions against The Race. Similarly, scholarship addressing early black women's conversion narratives would serve as my recompense for what I increasingly hoped was my *former* religious elitism. Now, just as I earnestly regard teaching African American literature as my race work, I regard the scholarly attention I pay to the spiritual autobiographies of 19th-century African American women as my spirit work.

Grave testimony to the need for intellectual investigations of spirituality in the context of African American cultural studies is made by Frances Smith Foster and Chanta Haywood (1995). Their historical essay "Christian Recordings" chronicles the promulgation of Afro-Protestantism and, while commending the 1960s reissuing of many texts produced by and about African Americans in the 18th and 19th centuries, exhorts further study of early black spirituality:

> However, the imperatives of the prevailing hermeneutic, generally known as the Black Aesthetic, encouraged, if not dictated, characterization of any manifestation of Christianity in African-American culture as retrograde, assimilationist or diversionary. . . . In the revisions of curriculum, concept, and literary consumption that have occurred since the institutionalization of African-American Studies, there remain large gaps in our knowledge of the relationships between religion and art, church and community; and considerable ambivalence about much of what we do know continues. (p. 17)

My response to the spiritual autobiographies I first read in the winter of 1989 was hardly "ambivalent." I was awestruck. Ironically, nothing in my experiences of reading such impassioned and eloquent African American autobiographies as *Narrative of the Life of Frederick Douglass* (Douglass, 1845/1996) and Harriet Jacobs's *Incidents in the Life of a Slave Girl, Written by Herself* (1861/1987) had prepared me for the unspeakable power and majesty of these holy works. Some of the narrators had, like Douglass and Jacobs, spent years in slavery, but their incontrovertible faith that they were divinely ordained, each woman's absolute conviction that God had established a relationship with her personally, was more awe-inspiring, more sublime, than the most woeful slave conditions suffered or recorded by either Douglass or Jacobs. Reading the narratives of sanctified women like Julia Foote—the African Methodist Episcopal (A.M.E.) minister whose late-life "throat malady" humbled her and tormented me, it being the more pathetic because she spent her whole life raising her voice in resistance to racism, preaching and protesting, as bell hooks says, "talking back"—reading these narratives I discerned the convergence of the religious and the sensuous. Julia Foote was not Maria Stewart, Jarena Lee, Mattie Jackson; these women were not ascetics inhabiting a world of, in Audre Lorde's (1983) phrase, "flattened affect." Not ascetics, but zealots, their lives bore exquisitely the textures of nap and grain, board and rope. Reading their narratives, in a rush of erotic perception, I remembered the woods in June at Pinetreat.

It is commonplace to speak of black people, African American Christian women especially—the "mothers of the church"—as embodying the integration of the sacred and the secular. Lorde complicates this concept, however, when she writes of the inseparability of the spiritual and the erotic, of the false dichotomy between the spiritual and the political (as cited in the epigraph preceding this chapter). Affirming the erotic as the blessed tie that binds the sacred and the secular, Lorde ameliorates the conventional definitions of the three key terms: *spiritual, political,* and most radically, *erotic*. Applied to the autobiographies of early black women, the new definitions attest to the narrative facility and linguistic authority of even those women ostensibly incapable of inscribing their own texts. For example, an 18th-century woman, Alice, though illiterate, used her voice to establish herself as preacher, historian, and philosopher. As Foster (1993) wrote:

> Hers is the earliest extant example of an African American woman who testified to her experience in this country and thereby tested the ability of language to influence the society within she lived. . . . [Alice] not only freely interpreted the Holy Scriptures but she also presumed to teach about the secular past and to analyze and to judge the present. (p. 7)

I rejoiced especially to read the political details of these women's spiritual narratives. I felt empowered by such accounts as the mid-19th-century writings of Rebecca Cox Jackson, an uneducated visionary divinely endowed with the facility to inscribe her own sacred experiences. When Jackson enumerates such sins as antifeminism and clerical chauvinism, perpetrated against her by her minister-brother, Joseph Cox, upon her determination to preach the Gospel, her pietistic act of writing becomes at once a political transgression against man and a spiritual submission to God. Another woman, Jarena Lee, who became the first woman preacher of the A.M.E. Church, records not only the sexism and other trials she suffered but also the ethnic and religious diversity she joyfully experienced as an itinerant evangelist. Ironically, Lee's own denomination had been born in the early 1800s, after its founders had abandoned the race prejudice and elitism of white Methodist congregations.

The holy women's perspicacious analyses of gender, race, class, and custom help me appreciate more fully the conventions and traditions of Afro-Protestant churches. To invoke a monolithic Afro-Protestantism for the moment, the capacity of the historical black church to effect social and political change is legendary. Sometimes while reading these narratives I am filled with remorse for the ramifications of my Presbyterian youth because I realize how much I was denied by my lack of exposure to that historic force. A vivid memory blends my genuine deprivation and apparent class distinction. I am 10 years old in April 1968. Mrs. Yelding, my beloved fifth-grade teacher, weeps silently and incessantly before the television she has brought to school. All day, she cries without noise, watching the funeral of a man whose name I do not know: Martin Luther King, Jr.

* * *

The most succinct of the spiritual autobiographies I frequently teach and think about is a slender tract called "Memoir of Old Elizabeth" (Elizabeth, ca. 1863/1988). I don't remember the first time I read it; I only know it is the one 19th-century narrative to which I always return. A scant 19 pages, it was dictated around 1863 by a 97-year-old Protestant preacher and details her early life as a slave, her religious conversion, her itinerant evangelism along the Eastern seaboard, and her admiration for the quiet ministry of Quakers. Its actual amanuensis is unknown, but I believe I owe this person almost as great a debt as I owe Elizabeth, the magnetism of the narrative's prose so draws me.

To my astonishment, I find myself reciting from "Memoir of Old Elizabeth" at my doctoral dissertation defense. It is late August 1993. Although we won't know it until afterward, a thunderstorm is gathering while my committee, my parents, and I assemble in a tiny stark and subterranean library in the humanities building at the University of Kansas. As soon as we settle into the German Reading Room, I intuit that we cannot begin the proceedings until we have heard the sermon at the center of Elizabeth's tract. Making my voice as imperial as I have always imagined hers, I recite the sermon that sustains me:

> Thus we see when the heart is not inspired, and the inward eye enlightened by the Spirit, we are incapable of discerning the mystery of God in these things. Individuals creep into the church that are unregenerate, and after they have been there awhile, they fancy that they have got the grace of God, while they are destitute of it. They may have a degree of light in their heads, but evil in their hearts; which makes them think they are qualified to be judges of the ministry, and their conceit makes them very busy in matters of religion, judging of the revelations that are given to others, while they have received none themselves. Being thus mistaken, they are

calculated to make a great deal of confusion in the church, and clog the true ministry.

These are they who eat their own bread, and wear their own apparel, having the form of godliness, but are destitute of the power. (p. 15)

Days later, back at home on the West Coast, I realize that I had felt no trace of self-consciousness as I spoke Elizabeth's words. At the time, they had seemed, quite simply, the century-old "collected treasure" of an insolent but inspired woman, and I her medium, her 20th-century repository—I, who had always been the cynic in my crowd of women friends, to scoff at New Age religions, to jeer at the eerie thanks Alice Walker offers to "everybody who comes" to *The Color Purple* (1982). The doctoral defense had marked the commencement of my scholarship on early black women's spiritual autobiographies. Reciting Elizabeth's words still seems the most proper means I have to revere the African American holy woman whose little book has taught me most about love, self, and Spirit.

NOTES

1. I borrow the term *Afro-Protestant* from Frances Smith Foster and Chanta Haywood (1995) as they define it in "Christian Recordings: Afro-Protestantism, Its Press, and the Production of African-American Literature." Foster and Haywood assert that they use the term to allude "to the argument that African-Americans did in fact create a version of Protestantism unique and fitting to their own experiences" (p. 19). For them, "Referring to 'Afro-Protestantism' is also an intentional exclusion of other religions and other forms of Christianity including Afro-Catholicism, Eurocentric Protestantisms, and other denominations in which African-Americans participate" (p. 20).

2. See Sara Lawrence-Lightfoot's (1994) biography of Katie Cannon, "the first black woman ordained in the Presbyterian Church."

3. Analyzing the therapeutic and cathartic effects of Afro-Protestant worship services, Toinette M. Eugene (1995) details some of the conventions of traditional black churches. In "There Is a Balm in Gilead: Black Women and the Black Church as Agents of a Therapeutic Community," she writes:

> When various members in prayer meetings or revivals pray or testify, the congregation usually shares the account of their suffering with numerous "amens" and "tell Jesus" . . . Choirs and gospel singers also depict the past and present sufferings of Blacks in the rural and urban settings. Not only do the men and women weep at these concerts, but a good number of them also faint, shout, and cry out "thank you" to Jesus for helping them endure. (p. 63)

4. See Katie Cannon's responses to public prayer, as Lawrence-Lightfoot (1994) wrote:

> It was not the petitions to God that caused her to shudder; it was the public display of prayer that she hated. "I thought the Christian thing should be individual. Doing it corporately, collectively, brought on a *vulnerability* . . . To have to say it out

loud, publicly, was horrible." . . . She worried about "letting go," about "where the spirit might take" her if she lost control in prayer. (p. 51)

5. Although Belinda's scribe remains unknown, Foster (1993) notes, "Historian Sidney Kaplan speculates that another black person, possibly Phillis Wheatley, served as [Belinda's] amanuensis" (p. 44).

REFERENCES

Belinda. (1996). Petition of an African slave to the Legislature of Massachusetts. In S. M. Harris (Ed.), *American women writers to 1800* (pp. 253-255). New York: Oxford University Press. (Original work published 1782)

Braxton, J. (1989). *Black women writing autobiography: A tradition within a tradition*. Philadelphia: Temple University Press.

Davis, A. Y. (1994). Black women in the academy. *Callaloo, 17*(2), 422-431.

Douglass, F. (1996). *Narrative of the life of Frederick Douglass, an American slave, written by himself* (W. L. Andrews & W. S. McFeely, Eds.). New York: Norton. (Original work published 1845)

Elizabeth. (1988). Memoir of old Elizabeth. In S. Houchins (Ed.), *Spiritual narratives*. New York: Oxford University Press. (Original work published ca. 1863)

Eugene, T. (1995). There is a balm in Gilead: Black women and the black church as agents of a therapeutic community. In J. Ochshorn & E. Cole (Eds.), *Women's spirituality, women's lives* (pp. 55-71). New York: Harrington Park.

Foster, F. S. (1993). *Written by herself: Literary productions of African American women, 1746-1892*. Bloomington: Indiana University Press.

Foster, F. S., & Haywood, C. (1995). Christian recordings: Afro-Protestantism, its press, and the production of African-American literature. *Religion and Literature, 27*, 15-33.

Jacobs, H. (1987). *Incidents in the life of a slave girl, written by herself* (J. F. Yellin, Ed.). Cambridge, MA: Harvard University Press. (Original work published 1861)

Julian, of Norwich. (1993). *The shewings of Julian of Norwich* (Middle English texts). Kalamazoo: Western Michigan University, Medieval Institute. (Original work published ca. 1373)

Kempe, M. (1995). *The book of Margery Kempe: The autobiography of the madwoman of God*. Liguori, MO: Triumph Books. (Original work published ca. 1432)

Lawrence-Lightfoot, S. (1994). *I've known rivers: Lives of loss and liberation*. Reading, MA: Addison-Wesley.

Lorde, A. (1983). *Sister outsider: Essays and speeches*. Trumansburg, NY: Crossing.

Moody, J. K. (1994). The holiness of herself released. *The Womanist, 1*(1), 7-8.

Nelson, J. (1994). *Volunteer slavery: My authentic Negro experience*. Chicago: Noble.

Walker, A. (1982). *The color purple*. New York: Pocket Books.

Walker, A. (1983). *In search of our mothers' gardens*. Orlando, FL: Harcourt Brace.

Williams, F. B. (1991). A northern Negro's autobiography. In H. L. Gates, Jr. (Ed.), *Bearing witness: Selections from African-American autobiography in the twentieth century* (pp. 10-22). New York: Pantheon. (Original work published 1904)

PART II

Research Processes
Giving Voice

4

WHAT DO WOMEN KNOW?
... AS I WAS SAYING!

CHRISTINE OBBO

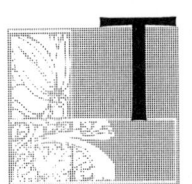T he lives of the women in this chapter cover the different epochs of modern Ugandan history: beginning with the advent of colonialism (accompanied by Christianity, formal schooling, and the market economy) at the turn of the century, the political independence era, the lost years of state violence and anarchy, to the present when women seem to bear the brunt of structural adjustment programs for economic reforms imposed by the World Bank (WB) and the International Monetary Fund as conditions for further loans for economic development.

The writing of this chapter coincidentally started on August 30, 1995, the day the largest nongovernmental organizations (NGOs) forum opened at Huairou, a town 53 km from Beijing, where the United Nations (U.N.) World Fourth Conference on Women was to open in

---

AUTHOR'S NOTE: Except for Leya, who long ago allowed me to use her name, all names have been changed to protect the identities of the informants and also their families who are not the subject of this chapter.

5 days. The first conference, which took place in Mexico City in 1975, was a celebration for women from all over the world of the U.N. declaration of that year as the International Women's Year, and 1975-1985 as the Decade for Women.

Each of the four conferences has revealed changes in women's priorities. At Mexico City, Western women's primary concerns were with equality, which was regarded as the sine qua non of the women's liberation movement; women from Eastern Bloc countries stressed peace as their priority; and women from the South saw development as indispensable to improvement of their status. The second conference, in Copenhagen, revealed the growing pains of global sisterhood when Southern women repudiated their junior status to Northern women and claimed the right to articulate their concerns, priorities, and problems. The third conference, in Nairobi in 1985 to mark the end of and to assess the achievements of the Women's Decade, showed that women still had a long way to go before achieving equality, development, and peace. The U.N. General Assembly, in December 1985, endorsed Resolution 40/108 (the Nairobi recommendations) as the plan of action suggesting women's education, health, employment, and equality as minimum targets for the year 2000.[1] The Convention on the Elimination of All Forms of Discrimination Against Women was eventually adopted by the U.N. General Assembly in 1979, and it became an international treaty in 1981. The convention establishes an international bill of rights for women and an agenda for action by countries to guarantee those rights. Despite the fact that, by June 1990, most countries in the world had acceded or rectified the convention, women's rights as an aspect of human rights have yet to capture the political will of leaders and policymakers. The official Beijing Conference was opened by a male politician who cataloged what the Chinese government had done for women and the final plan of action, which strongly reaffirmed women's rights as human rights, particularly in the areas of education, health care, and employment. This was not a re-enshrining of new recommendations, but rather a reworking of those from 1985. They were also nonbinding, and governments could ignore them. The 2,500 or so NGOs made a difference in creating space for women to express themselves. As was the case in Nairobi, the NGO delegates were subject to harassment by a host regime that felt threatened by women's increased commitment to change existing gender power relations.

This chapter is a modest exercise in giving expression to women's voices and in rescuing their perceptions and experiences from being mere murmurs or backdrops to political, social, and cultural happenings. Women's voices have been devalued by male chroniclers of cultural history even when the men acknowledge female informants; they are overshadowed by the voice of male authority and ascendance in society.[2] Most often, women's views are dismissed with smirks or disparaged as nonsensical in the apparent belief that men talk and have discussions on serious matters but women gossip. This attitude is not limited only to men in societies we study; until recently, professional academics, too, had problems taking women's utterances seriously. (Still, some continue to regard the exercise of paying attention to gender issues as ideologically motivated.) In anthropology, Edwin Ardener (1972) was the first to expose the professional concerns that prevented scholars from writing about women. He pointed out that one exchanged anecdotes about women in the situations studied, presumably at parties, but that writing about them would cause one to be laughed at. Even women anthropologists regarded writing about women only after producing their professional magnum opus. Ardener located the problem in the Western intellectual baggage that anthropologists took with them to the field and that guided how materials were presented to academic audiences. Men, on the one hand, talked about such things as marriage and kinship in universalistic terms, which made generalization and theory building relatively easy. Women, on the other hand, responded with particularistic detailed answers that were seen as a hindrance to making order out of the collected data. The current debates and divisions in anthropological discourse concern the problem of generalizing while at the same time representing areas of deviation from the presumed norm as articulated in the privileged voices of those in social ascendancy by virtue of their gender, education, wealth, age, and so on.

The title of this chapter invokes two attitudes that I have found prevalent when issues of gender or the cultural division of roles, privileges, and resources become the central focus of research. Questions are raised about women's cultural, political, social, and general economic knowledge. Of course, since the late 1970s, women's studies programs or departments have been accepted as reality in U.S. academe. But old habits die hard. In 1977, I was the first student at the University of Wisconsin at Madison to get a doctorate (from the Department of Anthropology) written entirely on women, and to my knowledge there has not been one since. I had considered myself a student of the problems of change as they affect relationships between men and women. I saw my study as framed by the dominant discourse at the time in the area of women's struggle for social, sexual, and economic autonomy in the context of the economic changes that were taking place in Uganda in the 1960s and 1970s. In 1981, when I went for an interview to teach African anthropology, one of the male interviewers asked me, "How did you do it?" I indicated that I did not understand what he meant, and he spelled it out for me: "Get a doctorate on women in anthropology?" I knew he was not suggesting that the Madison Department of Anthropology was unusually conservative but that my perspective on women somehow weakened my grasp of anthropological and African issues. I deliberately committed a faux pas by asking the interviewers generally, "What makes people think that men are the custodians of knowledge all over the world?" Needless to say, I did not get the job, but I was glad that I had had the courage to say what I felt then. I learned later that the job had been earmarked for an inside candidate and that we, the short-listed candidates, were being interviewed to satisfy university regulations that required a search.

I bring up this incident because it reminds me of the moment in 1971 when I decided that the understanding of social and cultural dynamics was too important to be left to men only: It is important to pay attention to gender issues in research (see also Warren, 1988). I was in the office of a city official in Kampala, and as I told him about my research on women, he looked through his wide window overlooking the low-income area where I worked and asked, "What do women know?" In 1990, I encountered the same elitist and chauvinistic attitude at the Kampala Food and Agricultural Office (FAO). While interviewing a male employee for a paper for the FAO on "the constraints and achievements" relating to women and agrarian reform in Uganda, he decided to tell me instead what FAO had done recently. Peasants had been taught to waste less grain by plastering cow dung to winnowing baskets. Peasants were being encouraged to mulch their banana groves to reduce time spent on weeding. As I listened to the catalog of achievements, I realized that these were reports by male field officers who preached to women what they were already practicing. I told him about a paper I had recently read that was commissioned by FAO on Rwanda and that was written by a social scientist whose main area of research was Nepal (in Asia). The expert had concluded that, to increase food production, the farmers (women) would have to learn to plant bananas with other crops to have extra food and to reduce soil erosion and that cropping patterns should shift from the relatively labor-intensive legumes to sweet potatoes, which are drought resistant. My Ugandan colleague and I laughed because we knew that bananas have always been intercropped with legumes, herbs, and vegetables; that sweet potatoes were as labor-intensive as beans; that both crops were often intercropped; and that potatoes grown in drought were often rejected as food suitable for humans. I suggested that the achievements he had just told me about were similar to those of the expert who disregarded local knowledge. He admitted that women have always plastered baskets and houses and mulched banana gardens.

On the other side of the question "What do women know?" by men is the often demure, sometimes resigned, and occasionally impassioned phrase, "As I was saying . . ." During my first fieldwork, I learned the many ways in which men managed to dominate every discussion and how, at the end of each episode, some woman would say, "As I was saying . . ." to indicate that the discussion would continue when we were alone. Still others would step on my foot or signal in some other way that they were not going to be able to put in a word as long as a man was holding forth on the matter. Once among the Akamba of Kenya, a man joined a group of women telling me about female circumcision and immediately took over as the expert informant. After 15 minutes, the collective silence of the women told him that something was amiss and he shut up. The women continued, "As I was saying . . ." and we talked all night, only leaving to let out the animals in the morning and feed the children and husbands before leaving for the gardens and market.

Even in societies where women's public discussion is not restricted, men still assert their mastery over cultural knowledge on public occasions. This was brought home to me while doing research among the Kenyan Luo of East Kano District. When the body of an unmarried mother and the last born of a widow was repatriated from the city, her paternal uncle insisted that her body should not be brought into the house that his late brother had built; to do so would bring misfortune (*chira*). An impromptu "court of death" came into session, with him presiding. He was opposed by one of his sisters. Everyone expected the widow's grown sons to enter the fray, but they kept a dignified silence. The widow who had been getting the house ready stepped out and addressed the uncle, "You were saying . . . ?" It was not really a question because, in the same breath, she asked that her daughter's body be brought inside her house. The uncle went away in a huff and even boycotted the funeral. The widow wept and between singing hymns repeated, "As I was saying, we are a Christian home and the very man who appropriated our cattle and did not lift a finger to help me or the children after I was widowed is telling me that my daughter should lie in the outerhouse!" The point I am driving at with all these examples is that women are not totally inarticulate on any issue on which they themselves or their children and husbands are involved: We researchers must create the space in terms of appropriate times and ways to enable women to say, uninterrupted, what they want to say. *Uninterrupted* here does not mean that only one person speaks at a time (as is common in Western practice); indeed, it is common to have, at any given time, three or four people speaking at once. *Interruption* here means assuming to know the truth and explaining away or even dismissing women's attempts to describe knowledge and perhaps suggest a theory or two.

METHODOLOGY

I begin this section with the issues that commonly crop up in relation to native (African) researchers writing about African societies. Fieldwork is assumed to be much easier for us than it is for foreigners. There may be some grain of truth when one considers the many behavioral clues and sociocultural sensibilities we share as Africans. I also hasten to add that the need for asking people questions and hearing their answers and living with them cannot be overemphasized. One misconception that we educated people have is that we know what ordinary people think and want simply because we go home for some weekends or employ some poor relative in our households.

The gap between what the elites think they know about the poor and the peasants is often farther from their lived reality. This was poignantly exposed by the failure of the so-called development decade to improve the welfare of the masses, and the upward struggle faced by AIDS intervention programs. Developers had ignored what people already knew or their reservations about the new techniques being proposed. AIDS control programs assumed that controlling the spread of HIV was an epidemiological issue that required just public health intervention with the technology of the condom. In AIDS research, two camps of reporters developed: (a) "Those of Us Who Know the Culture," purporting to offer the emic view even without in-depth interviews with the people and (b) those who wanted to give the people voice to explain what was going on. In 1990, a colleague asked me why I spent so much time in the village and slums when I already could write the answers without leaving the university. I told him I needed to hear, see, and smell what was going on out there, rather than imagine it or construct it from incomplete information. For example, I found that sex workers who were the target of much public discussion and intervention programs because they had been identified as a "risky group" in AIDS transmission were deflecting attention from themselves as prostitutes by defining their sexual partners as *mikwano* (friends) rather than as *baqanzi* (lovers). They were distancing themselves from the word *baqanzi* because of its sexual connotation and asserting the right to have friends like everyone else. Again my colleague, who shared the same language, was unaware of this language deconstruction and shift in usage and assumed that either I misreported or the women misspoke by referring to their sexual clients as *mikwano* instead of *baqanzi*. It was a while before people were asked about their sexuality in a manner that would even begin to inform public policy.

Once, a professional acquaintance asked me whether the women I write about are my relatives. On another occasion, I had to disappoint a friend who, as an editor for a major publisher, was editing a book on women and African agriculture, because one of the reviewers wrote, "This is a very bad chapter. Why does she not write about Uganda where she is from and would know most!" I was very grateful that the editor sent me a copy of the reviews. I declined the book editor's offer to rewrite my chapter when I told her that I was pressed for time and would not be able to change it. Two points are at issue here. First is the assumption by my colleague that native scholars just sit around with their relatives whom they know well, thus "doing research" without effort. Second is the hidden territorial claims by the manuscript reviewer who did not want me to write on Western Kenya where I, like her, had done research although not in the same district or location.

I take my anthropological training very seriously. I went through the same rites of passage that foreign researchers go through, and I have never done research in my "own community" of any description (e.g., village, ethnic group). This situation may change, but hitherto I have worked in communities in Kenya and Uganda (and visited for extensive periods some communities in Tanzania), where I had to learn everything and was the outsider although my skin color was indistinguishable to a casual observer. The anthropological method of participant observation requires that one should live and interact with the people one is studying. This deep immersion in a different African society can produce culture shock in an African, as it does in a foreigner. An educated African, by virtue of missionary education and exposure to foreign theories and often lifestyles that are different from those of the ordinary people, may not find it so easy to do participant observation. Many of us never return to the villages, and if we do so, the wearing of suits and high heels ensures that we will not be made to sit on low chairs or mats. So a self-fulfilling situation develops whereby the educated people are expected to behave like important people and are disparaged when people think they are not living up to expectations. When I have gone to study problems and issues in villages or in low-income urban areas, my acceptance is crucial to the data I collect. I have not hidden the fact that I am educated or that I am a foreigner. I like wearing comfortable clothes, and I like walking barefoot whether I am in the field or not. In two instances, I was told at the end of my stay that I had been watched carefully and that it was decided I was not putting on an act of going native. Twice I have had my published findings presented to the people by a third party and the reaction even several years later is: "Thank you first for having come to us and for listening to us." Apart from my personal comfort and professional training, I had been socialized very early on by my educator father to make it my business to blend in different situations.

    The five women in this chapter constitute five generations of relatives between 22 and 94 years of age. The presentation of each woman's views and observations is followed by a discussion that summarizes the main issues. The information was collected through participant observation and unstructured conversations with each woman individually or with the others (as we worked, feasted, mourned, and so on) over 25 years. Sometimes the views were told in a matter-of-fact way, often what was said was influenced by performance for an audience (a visiting neighbor or friend and even a relative), and occasionally deep personal pain or pride in accomplishment resulted in unsolicited confessions. I select the issues that each woman persistently returned to in our meetings. The views of some of the women were contested on the spot or, in their absence, by the other women. Through participant observation, I recorded silences, sighs, as well as words.[3] I met a challenge of listening to several people speak at once, and the success of my data collection depended on mastering it. This often happened when the topic was interesting or when people wanted to contest what was being said. (Once, I gave seniors in an anthropology methods class the exercise of recording a conversation of three people speaking at once. They hated it and said it was disruptive and abnormal. Conditions in the field do not always correspond to what we think is normal.) Last, I never set out to collect oral history. I merely listened to these women as part of my anthropological research on ongoing social change.

Leya

Leya was born in the last decade of the 19th century and died in 1984. She bore two daughters, Mary and Debora, and a son, Miko; and had 10 grandchildren, 32 great-grandchildren, 61 great-great-grandchildren, and 10 great-great-great-grandchildren. Her father died when she was a baby, and she was raised by her mother, who was a professional singer, with the help of her paternal uncle, who was a clan leader. When she was about 10 years old, her guardian took her to live at the court of one of the most prominent chiefs. The practice of fostering children with well-off families was and is still widespread. In Leya's case, the uncle hoped that if she was at the chief's court, she might one day come to the attention of the king, become one of his wives or mistresses, and thus give the clan leaders access to the palace court. She was baptized and trained by the chief's official wife into the etiquettes of a good Christian woman.

> I saw my mother often because she used to come with other singers and musicians to the chief's court to perform on important occasions. She would tell me about their performance at the palace and how much they had been paid. This income was taxable. She never remarried because she said, "I will never starve as long as I can hold a hoe and sing!" I was happy most of the times in my adoptive home. The other women in the household, two wives and three relatives, worked very hard, compared to the official wife for whom I became handmaiden. There were many other children who had been fostered like me. We collected firewood, water, swept the house and yard (*luaava*), and washed the plates and dishes. In the afternoons, we girls would relax by learning to weave mats and baskets while the boys played games of wrestling and some learned to read the Bible. Each person had a specific job assigned to them: Mine was to pass around hand-washing water at the chief's table before and after meals. I was also responsible for his drinking water pot: I cleaned it, filled it with water, and scooped the water from it when he desired to drink. Important men lived in fear of being poisoned, so being entrusted with the drinking water storage pot was a big burden.
>
> The women at court wore cotton clothes, but peasant (*bakoci*) women still wore bark cloth wraps without sleeves. Each woman had a working dress (*kadde*) made of coarse, heavy material and a Sunday dress made of light white material with tiny flowers—they were called *siiti*. Working men's uniforms were short-sleeved tunics that reached their knees to facilitate hoeing, made from unbleached cotton called *american*. Important men wore ankle-length tunics and coats, as well as shoes and fez caps when going to church or the palace. At home, they wore wooden sandals brought in by the Arabs from the coast. These sandals were used by the chief and his official wife for wearing after taking baths in the evenings so that their feet would not get dirty. Women did not wear shoes like men.

My mentor at court told my mother that I was so beautiful and well behaved that she would suggest to the chief that their second son, who was in England, should marry me. One day, she even paid a singer, not my mother, to praise my beauty.[4] I hated it. This was near the time that the son was due to return. One night, after dinner, the chief asked me to take him drinking water in his room. He had union with me that night because he said that my breasts looked ready. The official wife suspected what had happened because next day I was in pain and walking in what she called a funny way. She bathed me with herbs and I felt better. But the chief continued to demand that I take him water at night, and each time he united with me. I was ill for a very long time, and the result was that I gave birth to my first daughter. I was now the chief's third unofficial wife. The son returned and soon after became mad. We do not know whether it was due to his experiences in England or whether it was something that happened after his return. He insisted on wearing tennis clothes, wooden sandals, stayed most of the time in his room, and read the Bible.

The chief died 20 years later. The children of the official wife had been well educated, compared to the others; they also inherited most land upon his death, and as a result his prominent descendants today are from that branch of the family. But because he had a lot of land, the other wives and their children were allocated land in different parts of the country. I moved here with my children, and I supported them by farming. My eldest daughter married the son of a former chief and friend of her father. Her family has done well: Her four children were all trained in professional jobs here and abroad, and she lives well. My second daughter married a neighboring farmer, but the marriage broke down after 15 years, and she has lived here with me ever since. My son and youngest child settled within shouting distance after marrying a stunning beauty from nearby. I have not talked to them for 19 years. His children were forbidden to visit me, but my other grandchildren stay with me frequently—in between their schooling and marriages. I am always concerned to have sufficient food. Until 1956, when a missionary-trained midwife settled in this village, I delivered most of the children in the surrounding four villages. So now you know when you hear people call me *Jaiia* (grandmother). I delivered my second daughter's two children and two of my son's four children. In each case, they had prepared for hospital births, but the babies came at night and we had no way of getting them to the maternity. We have a good maternity here named after Mary Stuart, and one of my brightest granddaughters works there. My daughter-in-law had a difficult second birth, and she ended up with a paralysed right leg. She accused me of bewitching her, but no one in these parts believed her because they knew that I was the best midwife and a good Christian. Her negative feelings against me started when I took my son to court to stop him from selling all our land from under us. He was a long-distance lorry driver for an Asian businessman in Kampala. He took to drinking and smoking bang; he accumulated debts and raised money for repayment from the land sales. I would go to work on my land, and there would be someone threatening me that it was trespassing on their land. I was always in court over land. I recovered quite a lot of land back and earned the enmity of my son and his wife, as well as the people who lost court cases. People used to say, "How can a mere woman take you to court, leave alone defeat you?" I told them that I was a chief's widow.

Discussion

Leya was a remarkable woman, just as her mother had been. She never knew her mother's name, partly because women were usually addressed as mother of so and so as a sign of respect, and partly because she was also just known as "singer." Anyhow, women professional singers could not have been common. In a 319-page book on customs of the Baganda Kagwa, the leading chronicler in the vernacular who acknowledged assistance from women informants devoted exactly 20 words on women singers—under the subject of taxation (Kagwa, 1905/1952, p. 164). This seems to have been the only profession that offered women an independent source of income and the only women on record to pay taxes in precolonial Buganda.

The possibility of being poisoned by jealous rivals is still a real fear among successful men. And with the improvement of the means of violent assaults by hired gunmen, arranged car or plane accidents are also causes of worry.

Leya had many women friends because she gave them advice on looking after themselves during pregnancies and helped them deliver and nurse their babies in health and illness. Barren women always got advice on where to seek fertility help. As a result, when Leya was too old to dig or do her own laundry, there were always village children sent by their mothers to help her. Most men hated her, partly because women who had marital problems often stored their treasured things with her, and partly because they thought she hoarded land and relentlessly prosecuted those who encroached on her land. Two local men blamed her when her daughter denied them access to children they had fathered. She never remarried because she claimed that she could support herself. She also thought that, having been raised and married in an elite family, the peasants were not good enough for her.

The salient points in Leya's reminiscences have also been repeated by other women. An example is the fact that men had a head start in adopting Arab- and Western-style apparel. Even today in very poor homes, a man might have shoes, whereas the wife has none. One just has to stand by the roadside on market days to see that the majority of women walk barefoot, whereas men manage to wear shoes, some made from recycled car tires. Again, men had a head start in literacy and therefore education because boys were encouraged to read the Bible during their leisure time, whereas girls were trained in homecraft. In fact, when girls started school, they were predominantly trained in home economics subjects that would make them appropriate wives for educated Christian men.

Parents and guardians continue to foster children with well-off relatives, friends, and teachers in the hope that they will get opportunities and benefits, particularly education, and lead better lives than their parents. Foster children have always been and continue to be exploited and abused. Even when the accounts of abuse are fictionalized, the incidents sound as real as accounts by victims. Macgoye, in "A Freedom Song" (1977, pp. 34-35), a poem about an 8-year-old Kenyan Luo girl called Atieno, highlights and dramatizes the fate of poor relatives who are indispensable to elite families, yet expendable: Atieno cooks, cleans, and minds the children at her uncle's home while his wife sews to generate income and even manages to further her studies. Atieno is not paid yet, when she is accused of ingratitude, envy, and jealousy of the children's clothes, shoes, and beads. She is left to be fair game to staying male visitors, she gets pregnant, and she dies of postpartum bleeding at age 14. More meat and sugar than she ever had in her life are lavished at her funeral. She is soon replaced.

Although Leya always referred to the rape at age 13 by her guardian as a union, she always, even in her 80s, had tears in her eyes. Her language is a triumph of Victorian linguistic prudery, which the missionaries brought to Africa. This has emerged more recently when AIDS researchers decided that, because HIV transmission was predominantly through sexual intercourse, there was need for unambiguous sex education and they would try authentic vernacular words to describe *coitus*. They found that the respondents preferred the innocuous words *kweaatta* (to unite) or *kulabaaana* (to see each other) or *kuziina* (to dance a woman) to the word they described as rude, *kutomba* (to fuck). When people talked about chastity and fidelity, they often said, "The missionaries stopped us from dancing." This phrase referred to the virtual banning during colonial times of dances that were suggestive of sexual activities. As one respondent said, "The missionaries condemned local dances as obscene. In 1985, at the International Women's Decade Meeting in Nairobi, our dancers stopped traffic and policemen and ordinary people going home when we performed. People's tongues were hanging out as dancers twisted their hips padded with colorful clothing."

Debora

Debora married a typist at the county headquarters who also farmed on the weekend. He was one of the first people to build a corrugated roof house because a British missionary had told him it was foolish to have books in a thatch house because they would be vulnerable to fires. So in colonial jargon, he was a progressive man. Debora then had married well. She managed his farm and was assisted by an agricultural worker. After 10 years of marriage, she bore a daughter, followed by another 2 years later. The children resembled two local men—a teacher and a market trader-shopkeeper. People gossiped, and a few years later she deserted her husband and came to live with her mother as an independent woman (*Nakvevombekedde*).

> What I remember most about my childhood before my father died is that there were always visitors. My mother told me that they all came to eat well, and they particularly liked the new drink of tea, milk, and sugar. There have been many changes in women's lives in my lifetime. I did not wear shoes until the day I got married. We had bought a secondhand pair, and my feet hurt all day but I looked smart. They became my Sunday shoes. The 1950s were years of prosperity: Food was plentiful, and coffee brought wealth to everyone. It became the custom for women to expect their husbands to buy them the latest fashionable fabrics for dresses to wear at Easter, Christmas, and when they bore a child. This is really what led to the decline of polygyny: Men could not afford to dress more than one wife. A woman who was not given dresses for celebrations had grounds for deserting her husband. The first question a woman was asked when she visited her relatives was whether the husband looks after her well—that is, dresses her. Bright-colored clothes became fashionable because they were easy to care for and women felt that they looked better in them. Women found many ways of buying clothing from travelling Arab and Somali traders and selling small amounts of coffee a time to middle men who went around the villages. In the 1950s, many women also invested in china (porcelain) cups and plates.
>
> My sister always wore gum boots to work in the garden. In 1960, when I bought my first pair, I became the talk of the area as other women envied me. When I left my husband, I built a corrugated iron house with a cement floor and chalked brick wall. I was well-off, and we had land so that, unlike other independent women, we did not have to sell food or to brew beer. My mother was opposed to alcohol because it is forbidden in Christianity and she thinks that beer drinking attracts smokers and adulterers!
>
> From the mid-1950s, many Kenyan men—Kikuyu, Akamba, and Luo—came to this area. They were running away from the Mau Mau war in Kenya. Two wealthy men built private schools so that the migrants could continue their secondary schooling. They hired anyone who could read to

teach and charged high fees. It seemed to me that the students taught themselves. The school owners built large tiled houses, hired drivers to take them around to their offices in Mercedes Benzes. They bought small Morris Minor cars for their children to ride to the good mission schools. They were all the time dressed in suits. Their homes had guard dogs. Renting rooms became another source of income for many families. We built a four-roomed house and had four lodgers who stayed in them for at least 10 years. The lodgers provided us with security because with prosperity came robbery with violence. Kenyans were feared because of what we heard the Mau Mau were doing. People used to lie awake worrying about their doors being kicked in, knocked down by large stones. These robbers were known as *bakondo,* or brakers of locks. When caught, they would be beaten to death or buried alive. The detectives and police could never get anyone to talk, and so the causes of such deaths were never solved. Prosperity also fueled envy. Neighbors might hire robbers to attack a rich person or personally commit arson on thatched houses. The guns that a few World War II veterans returned with were used as models to make homemade guns to rob or to kill. The authorities used to confiscate them and prosecute the owners if caught.

We lived in fear of others, but each person wanted to prosper. I remember one man in the next village who was accused of practicing witchcraft so as to prosper at the expense of other people. He was rich. His wife was beautiful and dressed well. Her mother was equally gorgeous despite her smallpox-scarred face. She was an independent householder (*Nakvevombekedde*) and lived in this village. She sold beer, and wives suspected her of enticing their husbands. She was accused of murdering a lover by serving him beer laced with ground glass, and of burning down a neighbor's house. Whenever women had sick children or suffered miscarriages, the diviners always identified her as the source of the problem. The villagers hired a gunman to kill her son-in-law, who survived but was hospitalized. Many villagers visited the hospital, and one day when the doctor went to discharge him, he was found dead. His family migrated from the area.

I sent my eldest daughter, Malyamu, to stay with my sister Mary because she was near some good schools. I befriended a teacher who agreed to accommodate and tutor my second daughter, Bitulesi. But fostering children produces a lot of misunderstanding. The children work hard and have little time for schoolwork, so they do badly. The host family feels that they deserve being served in return for food and lodging. My mother has had to look after Mary's daughter and even granddaughter who got pregnant in school but wanted to finish their education. They came here to save Mary from shame, and the children grew up here without problem. They exploited us and did very little work, but mother felt that the important thing was to encourage them to finish school. Today, many unmarried mothers lack the extended family support system, and their education is cut short, and they live in grinding poverty. Malyamu became the second wife of a government minister in 1964, and she died in childbirth after a difficult pregnancy that forced her to be confined to bed most of the time. Bitulesi went to live with a policeman, but despite my mother's expertise and visits to fertility experts, she does not have a child. I have no direct grandchildren, but our home is always filled with our children. My sister says, when I fret, that I am being punished for denying the children their true birth rights. Mother and I agreed that I had made a mistake befriending a Catholic foreigner, and a Muslim, but that to acknowledge their suspicions of paternity was preposterous, given our status as Christians (Anglicans) and chiefly background. My husband was sterile; for 12 years I tried but could not conceive. I would have stayed with him, but he could not bear to look at the children as my enemies' rumors and gossip fueled his hurt pride.

Discussion

Debora's observations underline the changes brought about by the colonial administration, missionaries, market economy, and changes in interpersonal relationships. Formal education was provided by missionary schools. Boys had a head start in education and, hence, in formal wage employment. Debora's husband was a typist, which indicates that he could read and write. In the 1930s and 1940s, educated Africans could be teachers, missionaries, chiefs, or clerks (typist-secretaries). Hitherto, clerks had been white women and Asian men. Asians employed men to peddle sewing machines, and thus for many years tailoring was dominated by men. African men served in Burma during World War II as the Carrier Corps of the King's African Rifles battalion. Among other things, the guns they returned with were copied by craftsmen, thus increasing the level of violence. Debora shows the underside of prosperity created by the market economy: The increase in robberies and envy motivated attacks on persons and property. What she said is worth repeating: "We lived in fear of robbers and envy yet everyone wanted to prosper."

The 1950s prosperity from coffee production stimulated rural entrepreneurship that generated independent or supplementary incomes for individuals and families. Schools were built for students who, for some reason, wanted to prolong their student status: foreign men who would be deported as Kenyan war fugitives or local students who had failed to gain entry to certified government and missionary schools. These students became a source of additional rental income for families. Quack doctors providing door-to-door injection treatment made lucrative incomes from people, particularly in rainy seasons, when transportation was difficult and when people knew deaths were common. Medical personnel made supplementary incomes by illegally selling drugs to these "doctors." Midwives obtained licenses to open rural maternities but used underground means to stock them with essentials.

But some entrepreneurship activities were looked down upon by the Anglican Christian majority in the area. Shopkeepers and butchers, who were predominantly Muslims, were despised as earning money "dishonestly." Independent women who sold beer were seen as immoral and as husband snatchers by the majority of married women and Christians who had been taught by the Church Missionary Society emissaries to be sober in all ways, including avoiding alcohol. Although tea became commonplace in the 1950s, before then it was a prestige drink to be had at the homes of chiefs and white people. Even today, the best gift one can give to poor people is a packet of tea and milk, if possible. Women decided through their spending power to wear bright-colored clothes, rather than the somber, muted colors that missionaries preferred.

Debora and Leya were subverting the cultural tradition that children belonged to the genitor. Her husband declined to be the pater or social father to the children because there were no provisions in the cultural expectations for him to mask his infertility by raising children who resembled his village mates. And whereas mother and daughter took the high moral ground of being opposed to adultery, Christians, and from a chiefly family as sufficient reasons to deny a Muslim-butcher-shopkeeper and a Catholic-teacher foreigner their children, the local people saw them as hypocritical. Debora had not only cheated on her husband, which was against Christian teaching, but the two women were justifying their ethnic and religious prejudice after relieving the poor men of their money, pride, and progeny. It was thought that they gave Christianity a bad name, and the frequent premarital pregnancy of the granddaughters was further proof of this. Leya simply said that what went on in her family was nobody's business.

Gertrude

Gertrude is Leya's granddaughter and daughter of Mary. She is a trained nurse-midwife, has been "married" twice, and is the mother of two children—a boy and a girl. She spent much time with her aunt and grandmother.

> I became socially mature during the 1960s. Those were giddy years. The country became independent. It looked like anything was possible. A lot of taboos were being challenged. Many women began to eat eggs, which was healthy. Reluctantly, educated Muslims, Catholics, and Protestants began to interact and even to marry. When Miria, an educated Muganda

woman, married the prime minister, who was a Lango, then many parents and girls saw it as all right to marry foreigners. The new independence politicians were from all over the country. They drove Mercedes Benzes, had drivers, and wanted educated girls as mascots. When I was training at my hospital hostel, nearly everyone had a politician or civil servant for a boyfriend. Needless to say that abortions were common. My brother, who was at university, constantly complained that the women there all had these rich boyfriends from outside. Many bad marriages were made. One woman we knew well did not want to date foreigners. She had a boyfriend who, like her, was a Muganda, but he was a drunk and was already beating her and womanizing. She became pregnant and married him. A few years later, she committed suicide.

In the '60s, everyone wanted to prosper. Some of my colleagues used to sell medicines to "doctors" who went around the villages, dispensing injections. This was illegal, and since the 1950s, there had been detectives to curb the practice. The spread of the primus stove was a bonus because many actually boiled needles or held them over the flame. But I must say that I was impressed that many people used hospitals. Women, except in emergency births, sought to give birth at maternity centers in increasing numbers.

It was been painful to see things deteriorate in the 1970s. We had a really ignorant leader, who was against family planning. I and other women organized an underground network to smuggle the pills in and to distribute them to women. You cannot imagine the high demand for them. Women were willing to pay anything for them to avoid pregnancies or abortions. At the same time, many school girls died of complications from illegal abortions. Even though some of them even had mothers who were nurses, they confided in friends and risked their lives! I took several girls to a friend of my grandmother who performed risk-free abortions with a soft weed that had a gel in it.

My young sister, also a trained nurse, became the second wife of a politician in the 1970s. She is beautiful and spent a fortune bleaching her skin to look like grandmother, who hates her reddish skin. She had many boyfriends, but she was ruthless in abandoning them. She liked the fast life—boyfriends with fashionable Mercedes Benzes and lots of money to spend on her. She was involved in a car accident and is now in a wheelchair and has become a born-again Christian. My daughter is a doctor, and my son is a lawyer. We had to bribe the university officials during the 1970s to admit them because they had actually failed. So if you hear her hectoring on her title and science, be sympathetic; she is insecure about her training. I am amazed at how poorly our children were trained in the 1970s. My son is married to a lawyer too. She and her friends have been trying to educate women about their legal rights, but I feel that whether they lecture or give workshops, they never really connect with the women. The Pajero vans they arrive in, the expensive clothes, the high heels and jewelry, puts them up there. They hardly notice that the women still speak less and sit at the back during public meetings unless they are defined as important.

> If ever there had been a women's movement in this country, I would have joined it. Women here have to put up with a lot. We hear of what women elsewhere have achieved. Here, each regime ushers in men and women followers who accrue benefits and come to believe that all of us are making progress.

Discussion

When African countries became independent, many Northern countries brought in money that they called Development Aid. These were loans to countries but had strings attached to them. Interest loans were to be paid after a certain period, and materials for funded projects had to be purchased from the lending country. The monies were regarded by the new politicians as personal coffers to travel, build fancy houses, enable their families to acquire education abroad, and their wives to shop in Paris, New York, or London; and always the justification was, "We must live, eat, dress, and travel comfortably if we are to be respected by our former colonial masters." The pattern continues: Expensive houses, lavish lifestyles, including cars and "society weddings" for daughters, overseas education, and foreign capitals shopping are *de rigueur* for elites in power.

Perhaps this year's women's meeting in Beijing has come too late for women like Gertrude to have an input, but the women's rights issues they are concerned with have not gone away: access to family planning, safe abortion, women not being mascots for those in power who flaunt borrowed economic clout, and above all women having real say in politics rather than sitting in the back and nodding in agreement at whatever men say.

Elizabeth

Elizabeth is Leya's great-granddaughter and daughter of Mary's grandson Gabriel. She works for an international nongovernmental organization and travels a lot. Her husband is an agricultural officer. They have three children.

> Women have made great progress in this country. They hold important jobs, and they are making their mark in politics. I know men will elect women on character more than they would do if the criteria was party membership. We are really a model for the whole of Africa. We tell women what their rights are, but some are reluctant to take our advice. But we are making progress.

You know it is going to take a long time before men in this country allow women the same rights as they themselves enjoy. Women are just there to serve them. My women friends are always complimenting me on how well I look when I return from my trips. It is because I have not had to worry about the responsibility of managing my household. I always find things in disarray although we have domestic help. My friends who never have a respite say they find married life tedious. It is no wonder some women decide not to marry. Some of the customs we have now are retrogressive as far as I am concerned. My young sister who is a teacher got married recently to a university lecturer. At the city reception in the garden of a hotel, suddenly an armed chair was brought and her groom installed himself in it. She had to kneel before him and feed him cake. She had to repeat the process with at least 20 guests from the groom's side who were sitting at the VIP table. She smiled, but I know that it was not easy to kneel and get up, kneel and get up in a long dress and high-heel shoes on a hot day. At the reception in the village, again, she served the first plate to her husband, on her knees, as older women advised her to obey and to serve her husband always. I overheard her whisper to her husband, "I hope you are not taking old women's talk to heart, dear," but his wide smile showed that he was enjoying himself very much. The cultural fundamentalists in this country feel that women have gotten out of hand and need to respect and obey men. I say that no amount of publicly induced kneeling on wedding days is going to make women do what they do not want in a marriage.

Women in Parliament have had to deal with the majority of men who do not want them there. In the recent elections (1994) a woman who has been in Parliament for about 5 years faced strong opposition from the local churches which collected money to fund her two male opponents. She won by the skin of her teeth because women realized at the last moment what was happening. One of my colleagues who tried to run found that her opponents managed to convince the people that women have no business in politics because it encourages them to neglect their husbands and children. Whenever one of the most outspoken women in Parliament addresses an issue, male Parliamentarians murmur or even heckle, "I thought she was here to talk about women's issues only!" Eventually, women in politics will get their act together. Meanwhile, we try to do something for the uneducated women.

Discussion

Elizabeth represents women who are currently active in political, social, and legal issues in Uganda. Her seemingly contradictory stance is also common. On the one hand, she lauds the progress that women have made, primarily through the efforts of elite women to educate the ordinary women about their rights and the fact of women's political representation. On the other hand, she reveals through her close personal experience that women have taken two steps forward and two behind. Women politicians are disparaged by their male colleagues who do not engage in fair play. (Women in the 1960s faced similar opposition from men who thought and openly said that women's place was in the home, looking after their children and husbands and not in Parliament.) The revival of cultural practices, such as kneeling, that emphasize women's submission to men cannot be lightly dismissed when even educated women are being forced to submit to them. It is important to add here that the practice has been invented even in groups that did not have them before the 1970s. Last, Elizabeth suggests that as long as married life is subject to women waiting on men all the time, women will seek and enjoy spaces, such as travel or bachelorhood, that free them from stultification. Elizabeth and her colleagues may genuinely believe that they are doing something to improve the lot of Ugandan women, but as long as "they" are doing things for "them," there is still a long way to go before sisterhood is realized and real change in women's lives occurs.

Margaret

Margaret is Leya's great-great-granddaughter and great-granddaughter of her son Miko. In 1992, she had just finished school and was looking for another office job as a secretary, perhaps, because she was tired of being messenger and tea maker. She had recently left home and moved to live with her boyfriend in the capital city, Kampala.

> I am lucky to be working. Most of my childhood playmates rebelled against schooling in the 1970s, and they are now regretting it. I see some of the boys here roaming the streets, offices, and shops and generally living on their wits, what is popularly called *bavave*. They are nomadic, eating and sleeping wherever they can impose themselves on acquaintances, family friends, or relatives (however remote the connections are). Whenever they return to the village, people get anxious because of their dubious lifestyles, which may involve stealing. I remember that, at one time, a group of them argued that it is wrong to steal from your family but not from elsewhere; but now even family members complain that cash or valuables disappear when a *muvave* visits. Some lucky ones do find jobs as casual workers at factories or other businesses. The girls are lucky to get jobs. No one wants to work as a domestic servant, but it is probably better than sitting all day in the sun selling sweets and cigarettes or hawking food. It is difficult to describe the poverty these women suffer. Some live alone, but quite many I know live with boyfriends who do not support

them and their children because they do not make enough money, or the little they occasionally earn goes to support other girl friends. Once I met an old classmate who worked as a porter at a factory and told me that he had two "wives"; but from what I could see, he could not even support himself. Many girls hope against reality that their boyfriends are one day going to earn enough money to support them in comfort, so they tolerate unfaithfulness and even physical abuse. I grew up hearing my aunts say that as long as a woman can work, she did not need a man to lord over her because that was being a slave of a poverty-slave. Now my friends say that these are difficult times, it is better to have a man!

Men say that the reason there are so many women working as hawkers, street sweepers, etc., is because they have AIDS, and men are afraid of marrying them. My boyfriend is so scared of AIDS that he has been using condoms. I guess I am lucky. Two of my best girlfriends died of the disease, and at my office I was hired because the previous tea maker had succumbed to the disease and could no longer come to work; the accountant is just hanging on, and the deputy manager was known to have died of AIDS. The city is full of what we jokingly call the living dead (*enquli*): Many take it with good humor when addressed as such. AIDS deaths are so common that no one can afford to be prejudiced against victims.

Discussion

Margaret's narrative captures the flavor of the lost generation that grew up in the 1970s. Their lack of education condemns them to live marginal lives and to endure grinding poverty, especially the women who end up as unwed mothers. Marriage, which in most cases is elusive, is seen by women as a refuge where they hope to get male support and protection but are often shamelessly exploited. The climate of restricted employment opportunities, exacerbated by the IMF and WB structural adjustment programs, has laid down conditions for correcting past economic mismanagement as conditions for future lending. These economic reforms have left many people vulnerable, and women bearing the brunt of grinding poverty.

This cohort of 15- to 29-year-olds who have no scruples about exploiting relatives and friends also comprise the group that is most affected by AIDS deaths. So describing AIDS as a disease of poverty appropriately describes their condition because they cannot afford to use condoms on a regular basis.

Last, Margaret's observations about how AIDS patients are supported and tolerated in the workplace has been the remarkable feature of the epidemic in the areas that have been badly affected for the last decade or so.

SUGGESTIONS FOR TEACHING ORAL NARRATIVE RESEARCH

A collector of oral narratives must attempt to familiarize him- or herself with three things: *rapport, listening,* and *writing.*

The quality of the data depends on the rapport the researcher establishes with the informants. Good rapport (friendly relationship) makes collecting data relatively easy because it makes for access to the many situations that constitute the informants' lives. This is useful in enabling the researcher to check on the information of the informants' narratives by listening to other people's reactions and also to see how and when and which details of the narratives change or remain constant. This is natural, as all knowledge is socially constructed, and oral narratives involve performance for an audience (the researcher alone or in the company of others).

Listening to what informants say requires that one learn the language. It is impossible to do oral narrative research through translators because even when they are very good, they unwittingly edit out the nuances that are transmitted through tone of voice and body language. Of course, with good rapport, one can introduce a tape recorder or even a video camera to capture, for later analysis, "all" that goes on in the research situation. But there is no substitute to interacting on the spot as the informant narrates because it shows that the researcher is not a passive listener, but rather understands what is being said by, for example, seeking clarification on points.

One of the best research habits to acquire is writing. Except in situation where it may be physically or situationally awkward, it is important to take notes for future reference. Even with a good memory or recording devices, written notes are indispensable in keeping the record straight.

NOTES

1. Nairobi Forward-Looking Strategies for the Advancement of Women, Kenya, 15-26 July 1985.
2. Kagwa acknowledged two wives of chiefs and women from two former kings' courts and princesses of a former court (1905/1952, pp. v-vi). Ordinary women, who were all around him, including his wife, are ignored as possible informants and yet they lived the culture he describes as restrictive to women.

3. Peek (1994, p. 477) has urged researchers to pay more attention to the acoustics of African worlds—their sounds, silences, elaborate alterations, and the denial of human speech.

4. Leya had a cinnamon-colored skin, which is known as red. Singers glorify it as similar to a red, smooth-skinned fruit that grows in swamps—*etunaulu*. Many women, including her grandchildren, use skin-bleaching creams to look "red"—beautiful.

REFERENCES

Ardener, E. (1972). Belief and the problem of women. In J. S. La Fontaine (Ed.), *The interpretation of ritual*. London: Tavistock.

Kagwa, S. A. (1952). *Ekitabo Kye Empisa Za Baganda* [The customs of Baganda]. London: Macmillan. (Original work published 1905)

Macgoye, M. O. (1977). *Song of Nyarloka and other poems*. Nairobi: Oxford University Press.

Peek, P. M. (1994). The sounds of silence: Cross-world communication and the auditorial arts in African societies. *American Ethnologist, 21*(3), 474-494.

Warren, C. A. B. (1988). *Gender issues in field research*. Newbury Park, CA: Sage.

5

YOU HAVEN'T SEEN ANYTHING UNTIL YOU MAKE A BLACK WOMAN MAD

ARLENE HAMBRICK

GREAT BEGINNINGS

The students were settled in the classroom. Attendance had been taken, lunch money collected, homework handed in, the pledge recited, D.E.A.R. (Drop everything and read) completed, and now it was time for my favorite subject—math. It was initially my intention to review; after all, it was the beginning of school, and I just wanted to find out how much the students had retained over the summer. I called several students to the chalkboard and gave them each a problem to complete. "I hate math," said Charles. "I just don't understand it." I couldn't believe what I had just heard. How could this student fix his mouth to say he didn't like math? I just loved teaching it. Didn't he understand that math was the foundation of all there was? Didn't he understand that black people were the creators of math? How could he say such a thing?

I immediately began to get on his case. "How could you not like math? Black people invented math. You've got to be good in math. We invented it, designed it, and continue to be the designers and innovators of it." And I went on and on and on, telling the stories about all the things that black people had invented.

"Well, what about women?" Angela asked. "What did black women invent?" I was really stunned by this question. I knew the names of lots of black women heroines of my own life—Harriet Tubman, Sojourner Truth, Nannie Helen Burroughs, Zora Neale Hurston, and Maya Angelou. I've had many intimate consanguine historical moments with African queens—the Queen of Sheba, Cleopatra, Nefertiti, Tiye, Makeda, Hatshepsut, and Nzingha—but I couldn't honestly say that I knew of anything specifically and tangible that black women had invented. "Well," I said, "if anybody has ever invented anything, I know that black women were in the midst of inventing too." The reality was that I had absolutely no idea of what black women had invented, but I was just as sure that they had invented something.

I had been challenged by the students, so choosing a topic was more a mandate than a choice. I knew that finding black women inventors was the way. What I didn't know was where to go next. There was no dearth of information on black women scientists or inventors. The only thing I knew was to ask family, friends, and coworkers whether they knew of any names. Most people knew as little as I did. However, one of my coworkers and friends gave me a list of black inventors that she had been using to write her master's thesis. From this list, I obtained several names of black female inventors—Miriam Benjamin, Sarah Boone, Sarah Goode, and Clatonia Doriticus. From this list, numerous ERIC searches using various descriptors resulted. When each search produced zero entries, I solicited the librarians at Boston University and Harvard University and the University of Massachusetts. These solicitations produced nothing. The librarian at Boston Public Library concluded that there was no such topic. Although extremely upset, I became more determined to complete this project.

Searches for usable information among patent archives followed. I located patent drawings and patent narratives of each inventor's work. Patent narrative information led to census records and city telephone book searches. I obtained addresses, occupations, how many persons lived in the households, whether one was married or single, a renter, a boarder, a homeowner, and so on. I took four trips to Washington, D.C. My last search took me to the U.S. Patent Office. There I was referred to Patricia Ives, who had self-published a book on black inventors. As we spoke, I asked why all black women inventors were dead. She told me that was nonsense, that Mildred Austin Smith was alive and living right there in Washington, D.C. If I wanted to talk with her, all I had to do was call her up and she would consent to an interview. Mrs. Ives gave me Mrs. Smith's telephone number, and that was the beginning of this oral history project.

WHY ORAL HISTORY, ANYWAY?

I was totally awed, knowing that I would have the opportunity to really meet and talk with an important black woman. I had spent so much of my life trying to tell others the importance of the lives of various black women, and now finally I would have an opportunity to hear the real story of what it meant to be a black female inventor. To date, everything I knew of my inventors was what I had dug up through archival searches. The voices the women had were voices I had given them. Now, I was about to have the opportunity to allow a black women to speak for herself and tell her own story.

Story in the black community is important. Here we can recollect and renew ourselves and our creative genius. Burrison (1989) says that "people have always loved a good story. The narrative impulse—the need to tell of or listen to experience and imagination structured into plot—is one of the traits that makes us human" (p. 8). Until recently, historians, genealogists, social scientists, and others have concentrated their efforts of establishing paradigms of human characteristics on male models of story and what it means to be human, while ignoring and underrating women's experiences (Jordan & Kalcik, 1985). Historically, life experiences were talked about in terms of male structures. These structures were thought to be the epitome of human existence. Women's experiences were totally ignored; better yet, they weren't even thought about as alternatives to comprehending human existence. Although scholars of women's studies have made impressive strides in integrating and broadening the story of women into American history, they still ignore or give only token attention to "women of color" (Winkler, 1986). The void in theoretical frameworks for studying women of color, and black women in particular, continues. Therefore, the stories and life experiences of black women remain invisible in women's studies scholarship. Black womanism (not to be confused with feminism—for we must have our own thing) had to discover, through much hurt and pain, that a book in the bookstore about women was synonymous with white women and did not include us. Today, progress has been made, for every now and then we can find a book, article, or other work about women that includes a sentence, word, or chapter about us. One chapter, however, cannot possibly capture the experiences of black women. We need whole works about our experiences so that those expressions can be documented, recorded, analyzed, and integrated into the general genre of American historical scholarship.

As I embarked on this project, I began to understand better why research, particularly oral histories, has been a handicapping issue when it pertains to black women. Research is expensive. I found this type of research to be very expensive. First, one has the general womanpower spent in doing the research. Then, one has to account for the many trips to Washington, D.C., Chicago, Virginia, North Carolina, and Connecticut; housing, transportation, food, and intracity travel must also be considered. All of this had to be done while I held down a regular 9-to-5 job or during vacation times. This meant, of course, that I got no vacation.

Also, black female scholars need to be taken seriously. Not only has it been denigrating to acknowledge the invisibility of information on black women, but it is even more discouraging when, as a black female scholar, one cannot get one's work into print. When I began my research on black women inventors, I received several offers for publication, but the authors wanted to use my work and give me credit in the footnotes. All the stories my mother had told us—on summer evenings, sitting on the front porch—of the degradation that black women took from slave masters and their wives came back to my memory. Rage began to build in me as I remembered how black women were exploited and raped and made to feel less than human. Here we are, 300 years later, still being exploited and raped, just on a different level. In fact, I have found little understanding or support among academicians concerning my topic. Professionals have chosen to focus on my concern about science education, but not on my major emphasis—the lives of the inventors themselves. This is just another ploy to make black women invisible—if we don't acknowledge work about them, we can continue to pretend they don't exist. In juxtaposition, if they don't exist, then we don't have to acknowledge them. This work is the result of what happens when you make a black woman mad.

A BLACK WOMAN'S INVENTION

When I began my initial project, I simply wanted to create role models for young Afro-American princesses while giving voice and visibility to a group of Americans who had been silenced by the annals of historical inaccuracy. The genesis of this research was my collecting archival information on black women inventors and giving voice to their stories. Ellen Eglin was one such woman.

Ellen Eglin, who lived in Washington, D.C., in the 1890s, is the first known black woman inventor. She was a member of the Women's National Industrial League, and she invented a clothes wringer. Ellen never patented her invention, but sold it instead, in 1888, for the sum of $18. The wringer was a great financial success to the buyer. When Ellen was asked why she sold the invention so cheaply after having invested months of study in it, her reply was simple:

> You know I am black and if it was known that a Negro woman patented the invention, white ladies would not buy the wringer. I was afraid to be known because of my color. I am, however, working on another invention, and when I'm finished, I will have the money to push it after the patent is issued to me. This invention will be known as a black woman's invention. I will place a model on exhibition at the Women's International Industrial Congress to which women of all colors are invited to participate. (Hambrick, 1993, p. 142)

To Ellen Eglin, I did not have to give a voice. She very capably left her own. Today, we find black female inventors who are alive and more than able to speak for themselves. These were the next voices I attempted to resurrect. Sojourning into this new episode demanded that I use new methodologies; simply investigating archival records would not be enough. This adventure would traverse a variety of professional boundaries, crossing bridges of ideas, designs, theories, and paradigms that could add a deeper dimension to work already begun. I also expected that I would find more answers yet undiscoverable. My tenacity in continuing this sojourn despite the rejection and attitudes that insist I become silent came only to satisfy the hunger for knowledge about my topic that forced my scholarship—studying the unstudied and attempting to discover why it had never been studied—to proceed. I had to try to make the invisible visible by bringing these women from the margins of scholarship to the center (at least my center) of scholastic concerns.

The exploration of archival research on the women only whetted my appetite to learn more. I hoped my dream of interviewing living women would lead to allowing black women to verbalize and give voice to their own lived experiences. Besides serving as role models, studying Afro-American women's lives and experiences would, I was convinced, add a new perspective on historical, sociological, and psychological information derived from traditional white male, white female, and black male images in all disciplines. I could also invent with credence the legitimating of black women's lives and work.

Research Processes: Giving Voice 69

This was not to be the first oral project that I had worked with, however. C. Eric Lincoln and Lawrence H. Mamiya (1990) wrote *The Black Church in the African American Experience*, for which I was trained to solicit and collect data. I was attending seminary at the time, and Dr. Lincoln had come to participate in a black history lecture series. While there, he sought persons interested in working on this project with him. The work for me consisted of contacting potential interviewees; setting up a mutual date and time for meeting; interviewing, including completing a lengthy forced-answer and open-ended questions questionnaire; and returning completed ones to the team leader. I interviewed A.M.E. pastors from the greater Chicago area. We met for approximately 90 minutes, talking and filling out the questionnaire.

Although this was my first real encounter with research methods and oral history, it was not my first introduction to it. Arnett A.M.E. Church in Chicago first introduced me to oral history research. The church was preparing for its 50th-year anniversary and wanted to produce a historical document. Although I was a young person, I remember members of the church soliciting other members to go into their closets, attics, and basements and bring to church pictures and other memorabilia to be placed in the upcoming book. I remembered this experience and knew the necessity of preserving the histography of the church. Consequently, at every church that I have pastored, I have attempted to collect its history, much of it through oral historical narratives.

BLACK MAGIC IN THE MAKING

This work is hardly meant to be a comprehensive study of black women or black women inventors. It is just a beginning. I chose to follow Mrs. Ives's suggestion and telephone Mildred Smith. She gladly agreed to an interview. We set one up for the next day because I was not planning to be in town long. We met at her church because she was director of the flower committee and needed to get flowers prepared for an upcoming program. We met, we talked, we shared, we ate, and she extended an invitation for me to meet at her house the following morning because she wanted to give me a copy of the game Treedition, which she had invented. I spent that evening buying a tape recorder and tapes because I didn't want to miss anything she said. I also spent time formulating questions that were important to me. Mrs. Smith told me about her sister, Mary Beatrice Kenner, of Williamsburg, Virginia. Not only were they sisters, but she was a mistress inventor as well. I interviewed Mrs. Kenner at her home later that same summer.

Chicago is my hometown, and that is where all my family lives. While on vacation there, I decided to look in the telephone book to see whether I could find one Marjorie Joyner, the inventor of a permanent wave machine. I really didn't expect to find her in the book, but when I called and she answered the phone, I became even more convinced that this project was coming to fruition. Dr. Joyner invited me to meet her first at her workplace—the *Chicago Defender*—where she headed the newspaper charity committee and ran the Bud Billiken parade (the largest black-sponsored parade in the state). Later, she extended an invitation to meet with her at her home so that I might see, know, and experience the story of her life. The ironic part of this was that each woman had an opportunity to meet with me in a place other than her home, yet each chose to allow me to enter the labyrinth of her sacred world and share from this perspective.

Being new at interviewing, I naturally wanted to elicit as much information from the inventors as I could, but I needed to do it from a personal perspective. The interviews began with an introduction of myself and what I had hoped to gain from talking with them. I tried to create a relaxed atmosphere. I'm not sure whether that was for me or for them. I think it was for both of us. Over the years of talking with and listening to black women, I have discovered that the more relaxed the atmosphere, the more intimate I'm able to become with them and the more open each becomes about her story. I wanted to understand their stories vicariously from their personal perspectives. I poignantly acknowledged the rules of objectivity in research, but I didn't want to be objective. I saw no reason for neutrality. Here we were, black women, lives intertwined, needing to weave our webs adroitly, bringing truth, enlightenment, and healing to ourselves and future generations. We were black women—mentoring, truth telling, sharing, healing, creating black magic. I wanted to experience their stories as they experienced them. I knew that I would always be an outsider; after all, I wasn't an inventor. But I was black and I was a woman and I did care. The women responded with depth and courage—I had gained their trust—as they told their stories. Sometimes I asked questions; most of the time they talked.

Writing It Down Ain't All That Easy

Talking is so different from writing. I soon discovered this phenomenon as I attempted to construct interviewing transcripts. I didn't have the financial resources to hire anyone to type a manuscript, so it was left to me to get the job done. I was in for a real surprise. When I started, I had no idea of the complexity of the issues while transposing from one mode of communication to the other. Spoken vernacular is quite different from written, especially if you are black and conversing in an informal manner. Initially, I wrote word for word what was on the tapes. When I read the hard copy, it was unreal. I found repetitions, interruptions, incomplete sentences, and fluency problems. I left the manuscript as it was until I sought examples for this writing (I wasn't sure whether exact words were sacred gods). I refined anyway. The written language didn't capture the tonality, emotional expression, or gestures the women used. To remember these items, I placed in brackets a description of the gesture or an indication of sighs, laughter, and smiles, with appropriate terminology.

From time to time, I found myself drawing on my personal experiences to elicit and/or draw responses as needed. Initially, I would use this method to establish rapport. Marjorie (see Photos 5.1 and 5.2) knew that I was a schoolteacher, and this is how we made one connection.

Author: I love that picture (pointing to a picture hanging over the fireplace). It's just so glorious. How old were you when they took it?

Marjorie: Maybe about 45. You see I'm 95 now.

Author: Your hair is all white. Had it turned by 45?

Marjorie: I was born with all white hair. My hair has been white all my life (using both hands, she starts from the top of her hair and moves her hands down the entire length of her hair).

Author: I have an aunt whose hair was like that. I mean she had white hair all my life. I never saw her with any other color.

Marjorie: Well, that's the way it was with me. My father said that my mother had white hair when she married him. I was the only child who came out of 13 that had white hair. My hair has been white all my life. I thought it was a color. It never dawned on me that it was white. Then after someone had said, "What's that old gray-hair woman doing in our class?" the teacher turned and said, "That ain't no old woman. She ain't no older than you all. But she was born with white hair." They couldn't get over that. Then I started tinting it . . . Also, after I was married, my husband didn't want me to do that. He said, "That's why I married you, because I liked your hair. It was white." So that's when I knew that it was a color. But before that it was hair.

Photo 5.1. Marjorie Joyner, with black hair (at age 23).

Author: Nobody had ever said anything about your white hair before then?
Marjorie: If they did, I didn't pay them no mind. I was in class. So maybe that's why they said it.
Author: The kids never teased you about your hair?
Marjorie: No. I guess they didn't do that in those days. They behaved themselves.
Both: [laugh]

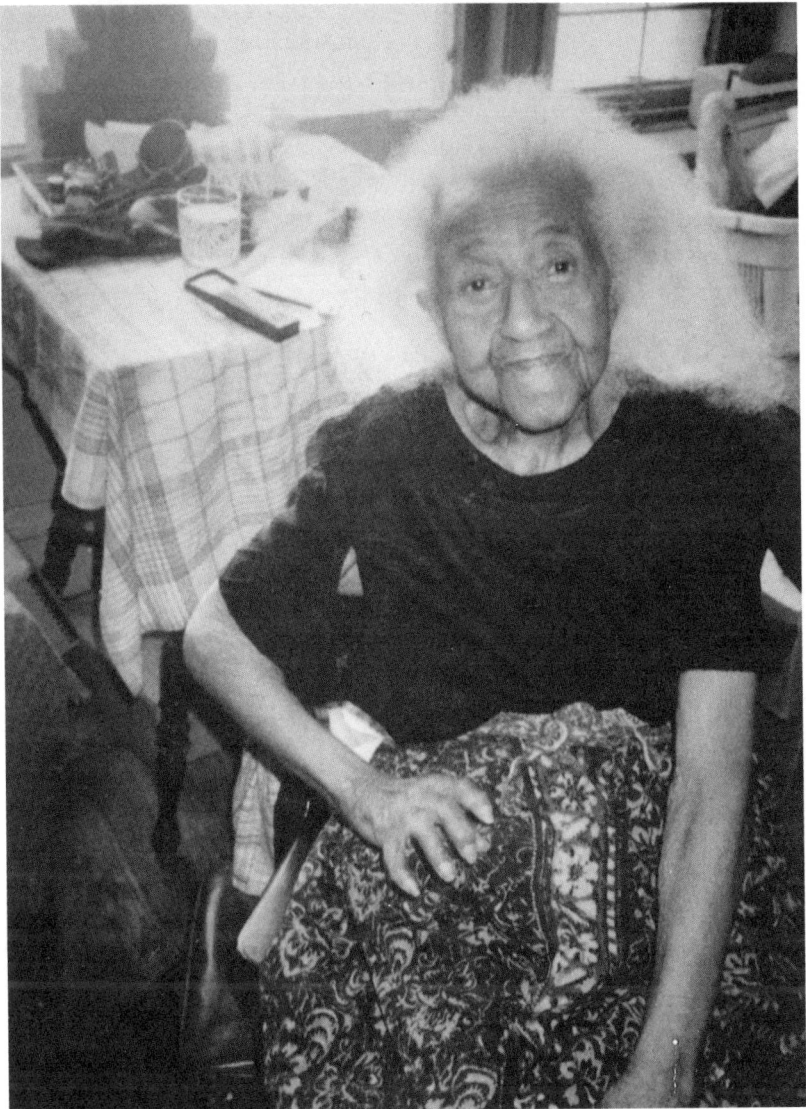

Photo 5.2. Marjorie Joyner, age 95 (seated in front of her kitchen table).

A Harmonious, Intoxicating Aroma of the Characteristics of Black Female Inventors

How does one justify analyzing the interviewing process on such a small sample sizing? Simple. This project began as an opportunity to hear personal stories of black female inventors, not as a data-gathering event for historical purposes. Therefore, the analyses that I offer here are personal, intuitive reflection on similarities noted among the women. A diverse body of similar and dissimilar entities was discovered. The limited scope of this work, however, insists that only a few be disclosed here. The similarities discussed were chosen simply because I was amazed to find these same similarities in my own life and took this as an opportunity to explore these issues in greater detail in lives that were not my own.

Salvaging Selfhood

Invisible dignity: a term coined by Katie Cannon (1988), an Episcopal priest, succinctly describes the life experiences of black women, female inventors in particular. Loosely defined, it means finding and maintaining a feistiness about life that nobody can wipe out despite the amount of suffering inflicted on you. When Ellen made her decision to sell her invention for only $18, she had to choose between (a) becoming apostate in the midst of misunderstanding and attempts to destroy her dignity in the face of white coeval pantheon perceptions of who she was as a black woman and (b) giving humanity her invention and maintaining her dignity and self-worth although she may never get credit for the legitimacy of her work.

Beatrice Mary Kenner (see Photo 5.3) understood those experiences of degradation and invisibility and denial of her personhood as she stood at her front door, expecting joyous news of having sold her patent, when what she got instead was looks of contempt and disdain because of the blackness of her skin:

> When I was 18 years old, I got my first patent. That was a calamino pad and device for certain times of the month. I got two patents on that. You used a belt inside. I made that, too. Kotex Company was interested, but so was a company in New York called San-A-Nap-Pack Company. They were very interested. They had gotten so interested that they talked money to me. Of course, I built all kinds of houses and had bought all kinds of cars. Anyway, they made an appointment to visit me in Washington, D.C. That Sunday morning, I was so excited, I was driving everyone else crazy. Then, they drove up to the house in a large limo and knock on the door. When I went to the door that did it. They were so shocked. The representative didn't expect to see me—a colored woman. They stayed and talk a little while, then they left. They never spoke money, contract, or anything. That company tried to manufacture the calamino pad anyway, but I held the patent on it and they couldn't. That was an experience that I have never forgotten.

Photo 5.3. The author and Beatrice Mary Kenner (from left).

Marjorie Joyner, inventor of a permanent wave machine, learned how to salvage her self-worth and maintain her dignity with integrity as she discovered that her acceptance into beauty school was hers alone to experience, certainly not to be shared with her black sisters.

Author: Was Madame Walker the first person you worked for?
Marjorie: Yes. But I knew how to do hair. I went to a white school before meeting Madame Walker. But you see, a white school don't know to tell you about a black nothing. So I called myself doing my mother-in-law's hair. I did it the white way. I brushed it and I combed it. And I brushed it and combed it some more until it started getting dry and began to s-w-e-l-l. I didn't know how to get it back down. She said, "EOh-o-o you ruin my hair! Why did you do that?" I said, "I just shampooed it and dried it." During those days, we used Dandareen on the scalp. It was a liquid. That's like putting some more water on it. It s-w-o-l-l-e-d up bigger. So she said, "You just don't know how to do colored people's hair." I said, "Well, what's the difference?" She said, "The difference is now look how you got my hair. I know a lady who is coming to town to different storefronts and teaching people how to do black folks' hair.

It cost $17.50. I'm going to invest $17.50 in you and send you there." (We laugh.) So she gave me $17.50, and Madame Walker was a glad teacher. She saw that I was an energetic person and wanted to do things if I just knew how. So she showed me how to straighten that hair right out. Then we worked on put that pressing comb on the hair and pulling that hair out. After I had gotten it all straight, something said to me, "Put a wave in it. You know how to wave. Put a wave and a curl." I put a wave and a curl, and Madame Walker was just as surprised as I was with that hair that I didn't know what to do with. She said to me, "You want to travel with me? We can teach them how to straighten and how to put a wave in it." I said, "No, I just got married, and my husband won't let me go nowhere." So she said, "I've never seen a thing like that." Everybody around me wanted to learn. So I said, "I'll take you down to the white school, where I went to learn." When I took about seven or eight to the white school, the school said, "Oh no. Seven or eight Negroes. Oh no." They shut the door in our face and wouldn't let us come in. I knocked on the door again, and this time when they answered I asked them to explain why they had let me go to their school. "We took you in because there was only one of you, but we could never take in this many. We would lose all of our white students if we did that." They shut the door in our faces again.

Mildred Smith discovered that she must learn how to affirm her own worth without scampering for white people's or male validation to find meaning for her life even under the most despotic circumstances:

> My mother never worked. She was an artist. She spent most of her time writing poetry and painting. She did much sketching and occasionally wrote stories, none of which were published. During those days, if you were black and wanted to publish something, you had to do it yourself. White publishing companies were not interested in publishing anything that black people had written.
> Music was what I really liked in life. As a teenager, I sang with my sister and brother in a group we had formed called Perry and His Sisters. We had an opportunity to sing with Arthur Godfrey and his showcase, but my father wouldn't sign the contract for us to do it. Perry and Beatrice were old enough to sign for themselves, but I was still underage and my father said no. His argument went something like this: "What would the community think if I, the preacher, allowed his children to sing and get on stage and do all those kinds of things? I raised church children." Singing was in my blood. Singing was something I felt that I had to do. So I sang. I entered Howard University School of Music and majored in voice.

Invisible dignity as exhibited by these women meant living through the suffering of being black and not allowing the wrong to stop or overwhelm them. Although the world had chosen its own nomenclature to name black female existence, these women, through their own stories, have chosen not to call their experience "invisible" because they have understood its existence and have invisibly fought back by totally renaming their reality. This renaming allowed them to salvage their selfhood. Using invisible dignity, these women have learned not only how to survive but to do it with integrity. Finding themselves between a rock and a hard place, they moved beyond the societal dictates of their day by looking at the world with a new pair of eyes, through demythologizing societal legitimacies and acting from a perspective that was invisible to the world but right for them.

Black Women Are Courageous

The voices of these women have not talked about their courage. Incorporated within their stories, however, is the sense of how they have celebrated life and all its offerings despite the deprivations in their lives. The courage they have amassed and faced the world with has been an inaudible voice within each that has facilitated inward peace and healing, although the outward life saw no peace or healing. As each told her story, I could not be mistaken in the capacity of black women inventors to survive, endure, and even celebrate life under conditions that would ordinarily have driven others to suicide long ago. The women have shown steadfastness and fortitude in the face of rejection and prejudice. They have demonstrated the ability to hold on against all odds, ever striving for personal and communal freedom. Black female courage is watching whiteness not win.

Courage is Mildred Austin Smith never giving up on her dream of patenting her game that would bring freedom and connectedness to the lives of black boys and girls as they learn about their heritage. So although the patent office and patent attorneys told her that her idea was bunk, she held on anyway. She didn't just grin and bear it and leave it alone. She held on, believing that one day her dream would become a reality. And it did:

> Having contracted multiple sclerosis really truncated my work in the music field. At first, it wasn't so bad, but eventually it got worse, and it was just impossible for me to stay in school and to keep up with my music. I just couldn't do it. So first I dropped out of my program at Howard. When

I became confined to my scooter chair, I gave up singing but I continued to play now and then. It was during one of my major attacks of the disease that I had the idea for my invention. I was just lying in bed when it came to my mind. I reached over to my night stand and began to work out the details. I tried twice to obtain a patent for this game. The first time I tried, the patent office told me that the game wasn't valuable and therefore was not worth patenting. Discouraged, I allowed the idea to drop for a while. However, while recuperating from a serious bout with my disease, I again decided to tackle the problem. This time with much persistence, I did obtain a patent. Not able to find a manufacturer, I borrowed the money from my sister. I have done well in selling my game. I recently contacted the company that printed the first edition to get a second edition done. The company sent out a person of Dutch descent to speak to me. When he got to the house and saw that I was black, he acted like the company couldn't do anything for me. The only thing this man did was to give me many excuses about why the company wouldn't reprint the game. Finally he left. I was glad. But the company has not seen fit to contact me since. I will get my game out in a second edition. That's what it means to be black. We don't step back for anyone or anything.

Courage is the staying power of black female inventors. It is the ability of black female inventors to find personal fulfillment in the basic push-pull ambivalence of the do-it-yourself-if-you-want-it-done mentality. It's about learning how to grasp the affirmative side of life amid a system of brutalization and self-aggrandizement. Courage is Marjorie Joyner traveling more than 1,000 miles on a boat to obtain for herself and others the right and privilege of learning what the world had to offer in hair culture:

Author: How did you get to Paris?
Marjorie: Well, in my going around, I had also met and known Dr. Bethune. She was out trying to get money for opening her school. Dr. Bethune realized that I was very down because I couldn't get the white school to let the others in. So Dr. Bethune asked me where the white ones learn to do hair. "Oh," I said, "They learned it in Paris, France." They went to Paris and were taught the Marcelle method; that's the French way of doing hair. She said, "Well, you go to Paris, France too." I said, "That would be dumb. You really mean for us to go to Paris?" "Well, why couldn't you go?" she said. Dr. Bethune then turned around to me and said, "You buy cars, don't you? You bought a house and you buy clothes. If you can do all those things, then you in turn can do something else." Sure enough, I called myself getting together a group to go to Paris. When I turned around, I had 196 people signed up. In those days, you didn't have credit

cards. So when everybody got their money together, I went down to the United States Oceanliner Nashbe Ship and plunked $20,000 on the counter and told them I wanted to buy some tickets to Paris, France. Boy, were they surprised.

Black womanists, as seen through these inventors, have shown themselves to be more than just a defensive reaction to the devastatingly oppressive circumstances of anguish and desperation whose etiology emanates and is perpetrated by Western cultures. It's an attitude—an attitude that carries out a pragmatic philosophy of life that refuses to be bound in any manner to what others think they ought to do or think. Beatrice Mary Kenner was not about to allow the United States government to tell her how to spend her pension money that she drew down when she quit her clerical job because she could not get promoted because of her race. Marjorie Joyner refused to define herself as a beauty culturist who was inferior to white beauty culturists. So she fought for the equity of all beauty culturists to take and pass the same examination instead of two dissimilar exams based on white perceptions of what one "ought" to know because of the color of one's skin. For each of these women, it took courage to move steadily and continually toward individuation and personal self-expression.

Throughout the annals of black women's existence in the United States, black women have used their creativity to silently carve out living space within multilayered opposition to their "being." It has been proved repeatedly that black women have been denied their rights as citizens in the United States, but they have never stopped being involved in a continuous search for equal status. In this oral history project, one cannot help but notice that each woman has had to develop a pragmatic lifestyle that superseded traditional paradigms of womanhood. It has been difficult, at best, to analyze, interpret, and bring comprehension and definition to what it means to be a black female inventor. The traditional images of womanly stature just didn't fit well. Yes, of course, they are female. I know that. But these woman had not experienced life like many of their counterparts. I needed to search for themes or issues that stood out and made black women's life different from traditional female images.

Bulldog Tenacity and God Too

Bulldog tenacity is certainly one of those images. Bulldog tenacity—you're right and you know that you're right and you intend to stand your ground no matter what hand life has dealt you—seen in their prayers and spiritual attentiveness was one such factor. Each inventor was active in her respective church. Each inventor has testified to the importance of being "bulldogeristic" about her faith and belief that God has called her to share her gifts from the Giver with the world. Powerful stories have been shared by the women expressing or showing how the power of prayer and faith in God has impelled each to continue striving and resisting temptations that would keep her from her calling. These black women have heard the higher calling and have used it as a guiding force to help find meaning in their lives and to create something where others believe nothing was. Mildred Austin Smith stated:

> God has been my guiding force throughout my life. When I wasn't traveling for concerts, I work as a choir director. I played for the choir at Ebenezer Methodist Church and for the young people's choir. I lectured at senior citizens events, school events, and church functions. Although I am in a wheelchair-scooter, I continued using my creative talents by running a flower shop for Shiloh Baptist Church. I believe that people should follow the dreams that God gives to them. I followed mine as long as I could. And I encourage all of you to do the same.

Beatrice Mary Kenner had another story to tell:

> You have to have one adventure that you feel started your journey with God. Mine was when I was almost burnt to death. My story began near Christmas when I was a little over 5 years old. I was sitting on our front porch when I heard my mother tell my brother, Sugar Boy, that if he raked the yard, Santa Claus would be good to him. Well, I wanted Santa to be good to me too, so I jumped off the stairs, grabbed an armful of leaves, and ran to put them on another pile. By the time my mother noticed I was on fire, she put the baby down, snatched his blanket, ran down the stairs, grabbed me, knocked the burning leaves away, and wrapped me in the blanket. The white doctors said that I was burnt too badly for them to do anything. The doctors at the black hospital—Good Samaritan in Charlotte—had no idea of how to handle burn victims. My mother and grandmother, being country women, had experienced many hardships before. They never gave up on me. These two great black women sat in a rocking chair in front of the fireplace and held me to their chests for 6 weeks. My going through that experience has been the inspiration for my life and has directed my living and my relationship with God. The accident burned my lips so badly that they grew down to my chin. You can imagine what hell I went through growing up. The kids called me "burnt face" and didn't want to play with me. People used to say, "She ain't never goin' to be nobody." Yet the more I heard statements like those, the closer I would

draw to God and the more determined I became. That fire burned my body but not my soul.

This was one of the most precious and intimate magical moments in the whole interviewing process. As she spoke, all the painful pointillist, didactic memories of being told that I was less than everyone else were evoked. Here I became connected. Here I discovered that I was not the only one who had been discarded by sociological dictates. Only those who truly loved me stayed near. A gentle peace and calm encompassed my being as I began to understand that many of my life experiences were part and parcel of my ethnic and cultural historical legacy. Life became more livable. My will to survive despite all life's atrocities energized me. The magical moment of Mrs. Kenner's story brought out the joy of being a black female. I would wish the uncovering of this ecstacy to be experienced by everyone. So try this and see whether you, too, can find wholeness:

First, think about this question: If you were to interview someone your senior, what do you think you could learn about yourself? Use your imagination to creatively explore what this meeting would look like. Whom would you be talking to? What relation, if any, is he or she to you? Why did you pick this person? What did you expect to accomplish? What are you talking about?

Now that you have some insight into what's possible, choose someone to interview who fits this picture. Look everywhere. Don't just stop at family members, neighbors, or church members. How about that person who has always had a transubstantiate presence in your life? Before meeting with this person, you really should have an idea of what you want to know. Develop a few questions. Keep them broad. You want to give your speaker lots of latitude. Listen carefully as the speaker tells his or her story. Compare and contrast this person's story with yours. Experience self-healing by discarding stereotypes imposed on you by the world. Find yourself by comparing, analyzing, and appreciating similar holistic experiences. Take time to share your story, share your story, share your story.

REFERENCES

Burrison, J. A. (Ed.). (1989). *Storytellers, folktales, and legends from the South.* Athens: University of Georgia Press.

Cannon, K. G. (1988). *Black womanist ethics.* Atlanta, GA: Scholars Press.

Hambrick, A. (1993). *Biographies of black female scientists and inventors: An interdisciplinary middle school curriculum guide—"What shall I tell my children who are black?"* Unpublished doctoral dissertation, University of Massachusetts, Amherst.

Jordan, R. A., & Kalcik, S. J. (Eds.). (1985). *Women's culture.* Philadelphia: University of Pennsylvania Press.

Lincoln, C. E., & Mamiya, L. H. (1990). *The black church in the African American experience.* Durham, NC: Duke University.

Winkler, K. J. (1986, April). Scholars reproached for ignoring women of color in U.S. history. *Chronicle of Higher Education, 32*, p. 8.

6

ORAL HISTORY

Louisiana Black Women's Memoirs

GEORGIA W. BROWN

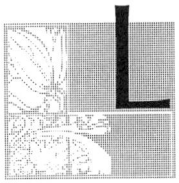ouisiana black women's memoirs take up a wide range of both past and contemporary experiences of Louisiana women. The black women of Louisiana have an incredibly strong, rich, and sensitive history. Most have lived full lives replete with both joys and sorrows. Recording these histories is of utmost importance to present and future times.

Oral history is defined as historical information that is obtained through interviews with persons who have led significant lives. Oral tradition (African American) dates back to storytelling in ancient times. Some of these stories were gathered and recorded by using interviewing techniques and classified as oral histories. Oral history began to gain popularity in the 1960s, and today the need still exists to collect oral accounts of history, especially those of women.

Oral history is a valuable tool for stimulating interest and motivating students to do research and learn of past and present accomplishments of black women. Through this medium, knowledge can be expanded by recording and highlighting the changes that took place and discovering what did and did not work in the lives of these black women. In addition, one can discover how women viewed themselves and how this view affected the choices they made. Oral history will provide students with pictures of women at different stages of life and help them examine the culture and traditional images of black women. As well, the division of household chores, childhood games, and original expectations of parents, friends, and communities are explored. These histories can make history lively and more interesting than books.

Black women have traditionally been the caretakers in our culture. This particularly holds true in Louisiana, where women for a long time were mothers, domestic workers, teachers, nurses, and helpers in many other areas. This chapter deals with the methodology used to collect, research, and preserve oral narratives of the black women in Louisiana.

The goals of the project are

- To develop a picture of black women
- To examine the culture's traditional images of black women in Louisiana
- To develop a clear picture of how society viewed and treated black women
- To expand women's view of themselves and their choices
- To provide students with pictures of women at different life stages

Oral histories of black women from diverse walks of life and from various parts of the state are being gathered and recorded. In many instances, this oral history project has allowed women to express memories they might not otherwise have had an opportunity to do. Women are being selected by age, educational background, and economic and social levels. The narratives are edited from the interviews and arranged by subject matter in chronological order by age of interviewee, occupation, and so on.

Oral histories of the black women of Louisiana point out how they adapted to some unique circumstances of life in Louisiana, particularly during the eras of the Depression and segregation. Some discussed how members of their families migrated from Louisiana as a means of achieving social and economic mobility that they thought was not possible in Louisiana. In some instances, it was apparent that some of the women interviewed were reluctant or appeared to want to hide their real feelings about certain topics. Some were either ashamed or pained because of the nature of the subject matter. Others were able to discuss freely the issues of racial discrimination in survival and work situations. Some, after opening up, stated that this was the first time they could really say how they felt about whites, especially those who had been their employers. One woman related a work experience she had while in high school, where she had been employed to baby-sit and later was assigned more responsibilities. She was asked to go out on a ledge on the second floor of a house and wash the outside of windows. Ironing family clothes was another job added without any additional pay. This, she said, made her more determined to stay in school and go on to college.

Persons conducting interviews should be aware of this reluctance so that they may identify the kinds of situations that elicit these feelings and use approaches that are less threatening or intimidating. Recording and compiling an oral history is an excellent way of preserving and passing down one's family history. Memoirs can be recorded when engaging in a long talk with a parent, grandparent, aunt, uncle, or other relative. Students can be encouraged to record during family activities and to collect old photographs, have relatives identify them, and give some background information on the subjects in the pictures, such as time, setting, and anything they can remember about the persons.

Oral histories can be easily integrated into the curriculum. An oral history curriculum must include information that will enable students and facilitators to better understand the process. Measures must be taken to ensure that they become acquainted with participants and that provisions are made to assist students in learning to conduct interviews. They should be taught to become sensitive to the hopes and fears of persons being interviewed, as well as to their own. This can be done by having students begin learning about their communities.

Some resources, materials, and equipment that will prove useful in conducting or teaching oral history are the interviewer, participants (persons to interview), tape recorder, video recorder, tapes, quiet accessible meeting place, transportation, pad, and pen.

Activities that can be used in teaching oral history include the following:

Conducting discussion groups

Asking the class to share some stories told to them by their older relatives

Reading articles on subjects useful as background preparation

Compiling a list of questions based on information desired from interviewees

Showing films on women's history, followed by discussions on contents of the films

Having members of the class conduct oral history interviews; reviewing and discussing techniques used, their effectiveness, or weaknesses and strengths; discussing specific topics selected and why

Careful preparation for a scheduled interview is of the utmost importance. As the interviewer, you should assemble all equipment, making sure that each piece is in proper working order. Have a clear idea of the purpose of the interview and do some background research.

Interview skills can be learned with practice. Following are some suggestions to help facilitate the process:

PREPARATION

1. Begin by defining the historical problem you wish to investigate. Only then can you decide whom to interview and questions to ask. Select a subject who will cooperate with your purpose. Be sure the person understands your purpose.
2. Be aware of your own cultural assumptions, values, and attitudes; this awareness avoids the danger of interviewer bias. An interview does not call for an impossible neutrality, but it does demand special self-awareness and self-discipline.
3. Be objective. Do not let your personal biases and assumptions influence your questioning techniques.
4. Do some background research about the subject and the environment of the person selected.
5. Make notes of the proper names and correct spellings of places and organizations.
6. Select a respondent who is able and willing to provide the information you need. Respondents may be chosen because they have special knowledge of or occupy unique positions in a historical event, movement, or institution.
7. Explain the purpose of the interview, either in writing or in person, to the respondent. If you are conducting the interview for a class as well as for your own research, be certain that the respondent understands this dual purpose.
8. Draw up an interview guide listing the topics of specific questions to be explored. If you are doing the interview for an organization or school, it would be helpful for you to discuss this guide in advance with the persons concerned.
9. Become thoroughly familiar with your recording equipment before the interview. Note names, dates, and places on all tapes. Number them in sequence. Choose an interview setting that is as private and nonthreatening to the respondent as possible. Set up your recorder matter-of-factly and show no awareness of it after the session begins. During the interview, note proper names, places, and organizations. At the end of the session, confirm spelling. At the time, you should have the respondent sign a legal release form indicating any restrictions on

the use of the interview. This form transfers copyright privileges to you, the organization, or the school, making it possible to deposit the transcript and tape to you or the organization/school for use by others.

THE INTERVIEW

10. Interviews may be autobiographical or topical. In either case, begin at a point in time previous to the central events you want to explore. For all interviews, include basic socioeconomic information regarding family, geographic origins, and class.
11. The degree to which you control the course of the interview depends on its purpose and the nature of the questions you pose. In general, seek a balance in which you allow respondents to express the logic of their lives as they understand them, while at the same time maintain control over the overall direction of the conversation and frame questions so as to elicit information that is relevant, reliable, and valid. Listen carefully. Do not be afraid of silence. Allow the respondent time to think and to continue after a pause. Critically evaluate the flow of information so that you can ask for clarification or elaboration where the respondent's statements are evasive, superficial, or unclear. Take notes that will remind you to ask such questions or to return to a topic from another angle, rather then interrupt the respondent's train of thought. Introduce new topics so as to guide the conversation in relevant channels.
12. Avoid leading or prejudicial questions. Your questions should be open-ended; they should not supply a list of alternative answers. They should be direct and to the point: Avoid asking several questions in the guise of one. Frame questions within a language and context understood by the respondent.
13. Memory is most fallible regarding previous attitudes and feelings. Seek concrete examples from which you can infer subjective orientations. Focus on behavior but try to understand the meaning the respondent attaches to his or her actions. Develop facts and events first and then explore feelings and values. You may need to stimulate the respondent's memory or reduce chronological confusion by supplying facts learned from background research.
14. It may be helpful to arrange the sequence of topics so as to postpone until last those questions that may be threatening or challenging to the respondent. Within each topic, it may be helpful to begin with a broad question and then to ask successively narrow and detailed questions as they prove necessary.
15. When a respondent seems unwilling or unable to provide certain information or provides false information and rationalizations, approach the topic from another angle, indicate contradictory informa-

tion that you have from other sources, or wait until later in the interview to return to the topic.
16. Ordinarily, an interview session should last no more than 2 hours. Be alert to signs of fatigue, distraction, or boredom. Conduct a long interview in several sessions. It is often helpful to interview the respondent again after you have analyzed the content of the interview and as your understanding of the research problem evolves.

PROCEDURES

17. Immediately after the session, listen to the tape. Evaluate both your own behavior and the content of the interview. Only by such self-criticism can you learn from your mistakes and acquire interviewing skills.
18. Check all names for proper spelling and include a brief introduction to the interview. This introduction should contain a description of the context of the interview and anything you consider significant about the goals and setting.
19. After the interview has been transcribed, send a copy to the respondent to be edited for accuracy and clarity.
20. Once the interview is done, "history making" begins. The interview is raw data that must be tested against, and used in conjunction with, other evidence.

Oral history starts with the collection, transcription, and preservation of interviews. But its goal is historical synthesis and interpretation.

Suggested questions to be used in collecting oral histories are as follows:

Family Background

Name

When and where were you born?

What was your father's name? Your mother's first and maiden name?

What did they do for a living?

What were their levels of education?

What were their occupations?

What are your siblings' names, birth order, and levels of education?

What chores did you have to do as a child? How were chores divided among your brothers and sisters? Were you paid for this work?

Who of your family members (including extended family, if appropriate) most influenced or inspired you? Why?

What was the most important thing you learned at home?

Describe your community/church.

Early Education

Where did you go to elementary school, and how large was the school (one room? graded?)?
If you did not attend school, why?
Who were your best friends? Why?
What were your favorite subjects?
What extracurricular activities were you involved in?
Were any of your teachers especially influential? Why?
Where did you go to high school, and what was the size of the school?
What were your favorite subjects? Why?
What sports did you participate in? What did you get from these activities?

College Education

What college?
Why did you decide to go to college? Why did you choose to attend this college?
What did you hope going to college would do for you?
Did many of your friends or relatives go to college, or was your attendance unusual?

Financing

Was sending you to college a financial hardship for your parents? If so, why did they do it?
How did you pay for college? Where did you work while a student?
How did you find work? Whom did you work for? What were your duties? What were you paid? Did you learn anything valuable from this work?

Campus Living

Describe your first day on campus.
Was there any hazing of freshmen? How did you and/or others respond?
Where did you live? If not in the dorm, how did you find a place to live? Who were your roommates? Did you know them before, or were they chosen for you? Describe them.
Describe your dormitory room.

Academics

What was your major, and why did you choose it? Did you change it? If so, to what and why?
What was your favorite class? Why?
What was your most memorable class? Why?
Who was your most memorable professor? Why?

Rules

What rules applied to dormitory living—housekeeping, quiet hours, lights out, closing hours, visitors, and so on?

For women, describe the closing hours, sign-out procedures, dress codes, and any other specific regulations for women.

Who made these rules, and how were they enforced (by residence assistant, a student-run dorm council, university administrators)?

What were the penalties? Can you recall any specific example of someone breaking these rules? What happened to this person?

How did students feel about these rules? If there were differences in the rules for men and women, how did you feel about this?

Extracurricular Activities

What activities were you involved with (e.g., student government, honorary and professional clubs and societies, service clubs, theater/music groups, newspaper or annual)? What were the major activities of this group?

Describe fellow members and any faculty or administrators who were involved.

What sports, if any, did you take part in? Who was the coach? How were teams selected? What was the most prestigious sport? Why?

Social Life

Dances—dress, drinking? Bands—black? Chaperons? Sponsors? Frequency?

Dates—activities, frequency?

Describe concerts, theater, other cultural activities sponsored by your school or available in the city in which your school was located.

Was there riding with boys? Were there rules about this?

Sorority/Fraternity

Did you belong to a sorority or fraternity? Why or why not?

Describe rush. By what criteria were pledges chosen? Why did you choose the sorority/fraternity you did?

Describe your house or meeting rooms.

Describe initiation. Was any hazing involved?

Describe other activities, ceremonies, and so on.

What was the role of sororities/fraternities on campus?

Which ones were most prestigious? Why?

Did sorority/fraternity affiliation affect whom you dated?

Student Leaders

Who were the most popular and/or influential students? What offices did they hold? What fraternities/sororities did they belong to?

Who was Homecoming Queen, Sweetheart of _____, and so on, and how were they chosen?
What was the greatest contribution of your college experience to your later life?
What do you wish your college had given you that it didn't?

An interesting oral history subject in Louisiana is Mrs. Dorothy Early Davis, an educator at Southern University at Baton Rouge. With her permission, an annotated transcript of her interview is included here.

Q: What is your name?
A: Dorothy Early Davis.
Q: When and where were you born?
A: February 26, 1932, Scotlandville, Louisiana.
Q: What was your father's name? Your mother's first and maiden name?
A: Jessie Early and Clara Thomas.
Q: What did they do for a living?
A: My father was a laborer at Standard Oil Company, and my mother was a homemaker.
Q: What were their levels of education?
A: My father had a second-grade education, and my mother completed the fourth grade.
Q: What are your siblings' names, birth order, and levels of education?
A: 1. Jessie, elementary; 2. Earlean, 2 years college; 3. Gladys, B.S.; 4. Zenolia, high school; 5. Almeana, B.S.; 6. Florida, M.S.; 7. Georgia, B.S.; 8. Richard, high school; 9. Geraldine, M.S.
Q: What chores did you have to do as a child? How were chores divided among your brothers and sisters? Were you paid for this work?
A: Housework, gardening, farming, milking cows. Chores were divided by interest and ability. There was no pay.
Q: Who of your family members (including extended family, if appropriate) most influenced or inspired you? Why?
A: My mother and her sisters, as well as my father's sister influenced me in homemaking ambitions. My older sisters were role models in educational and social situations.
Q: What was the most important thing you learned at home?
A: The value of family as a support system. The value of honesty; hard work. The importance of faith in God. Education was highly valued

in our home, second only to religious activities. In fact, if one of us were reading, studying, or pursuing an educational activity, he/she was exempted from work for that time. Books were purchased as much as possible. Although my father had limited formal education, through self-teaching he was able to do involved calculations.

Q: Where did you go to elementary school, and how large was the school (one room? graded?)?
A: Scotlandville Rosenwald School, later South Scotlandville Elementary School; four-room school, grades first through seventh.
Q: Who were your best friends? Why?
A: Daisy Cosey was my best friend; because we had similar interests: studying, writing, art.
Q: What were your favorite subjects?
A: Reading and music.
Q: What extracurricular activities were you involved in?
A: As I recall, there were not many organized extracurricular activities. I was active with the Girls Reserve Club [part of the YWCA].
Q: Were any of your teachers especially influential? Why?
A: All teachers were influential; they demonstrated dignity, industriousness, success. I was most influenced by my home economics teacher because of her personal appearance, good grooming, and the ambience of order and beauty in her classroom. Her name was Beulah Moore. My principal, the late Anna T. Jordon, impressed me with her gentleness, fairness, and intelligence.
Q: Where did you go to high school, and what was the size of the school?
A: Southern University Laboratory School; about 200 students.
Q: What were your favorite subjects? Why?
A: My favorite subjects were English and social studies.
Q: What sports did you participate in? What did you get from these activities?
A: Intramural basketball; I acquired appropriate skills and enjoyed interaction with others.
Q: What college did you attend?
A: Southern University from 1948 to 1952.
Q: Why did you decide to go to college? Why did you choose to attend this college?
A: My parents made the decision before I was born. They moved to the Baton Rouge area because of the college.
Q: What did you hope going to college would do for you?
A: Provide an opportunity to find good employment and enhance life.

Q: Did many of your friends or relatives go to college, or was your attendance unusual?
A: All who had the ability to go to college went.
Q: Was sending you to college a financial hardship for your parents?
A: Yes.
Q: If so, why did they do it?
A: They valued education highly.
Q: How did you pay for college?
A: Parents and my library salary. My parents provided most of the money.
Q: Where did you work while a student? How did you find work? Whom did you work for? What were your duties? What were you paid? Did you learn anything valuable from this work?
A: I worked in the library at Southern University for 4 years. My pay was $.30 per hour. I performed many duties, including simple cataloging, filing, shelving, inventory, and acquired necessary skills. My sister, an employee of Southern University, recommended me for work.
Q: Describe your first day on campus.
A: Since I had gone to high school on the Southern University campus, I was familiar with the campus but was impressed and excited about meeting people from all over the world. Registration was puzzling.
Q: Was there any hazing of freshmen? How did you and/or others respond?
A: Only boys were hazed by hair shaving. We found their bare heads amusing.
Q: Where did you live? If not in the dorm, how did you find a place to live? Who were your roommates? Did you know them before, or were they chosen for you? Describe them.
A: I lived at home.
Q: What was your major, and why did you choose it? Did you change it? If so, to what and why?
A: English education was chosen because I always loved it.
Q: What was your favorite class? Why?
A: English composition.
Q: What was your most memorable class? Why?
A: World literature. It was so broadening; the teacher was interesting.
Q: Who was your most memorable professor? Why?
A: Dr. Jessie Snowden, because she allowed for creativity in writing assignments.

Q: For women, describe the closing hours, sign-out procedures, dress codes, and any other specific regulations for women.
A: No bare legs, no pants, no extreme bareness, i.e., short skirts or midriffs exposed.
Q: Who made these rules, and how were they enforced (by residence assistant, a student-run dorm council, university administrators)?
A: The dean of women provided them.
Q: What were the penalties? Can you recall any specific example of someone breaking these rules? What happened to this person?
A: No.
Q: What activities were you involved with (e.g., student government, honorary and professional clubs and societies, service clubs, theater/music groups, newspaper or annual)? What were the major activities of this group?
A: The student newspaper—writing articles. Pledge Club of a sorority—social and civic activities.
Q: Describe fellow members and any faculty or administrators who were involved.
A: The student newspaper advisor was encouraging, resourceful. He took students on appropriate trips and brought speakers to the campus.
Q: What sports, if any, did you take part in? Who was the coach? How were teams selected? What was the most prestigious sport? Why?
A: I was involved in modern dancing.
Q: Did you belong to a sorority or fraternity? Why? Why not?
A: I pledged Delta Sigma Theta Sorority, Inc.
Q: Describe rush. By what criteria were pledges chosen?
A: Rush was a general party where young women learned via talks, skits, etc., about the sorority. Pledges were chosen by popularity, grades, and acquaintances.
Q: Why did you choose the sorority/fraternity you did?
A: I chose Delta Sigma Theta because of its popularity and prestige on campus and because of the high standards this sorority observed.
Q: Describe your house or meeting rooms.
A: Meeting rooms were usually a dorm room decorated in the colors and symbols of the sorority.
Q: Describe initiation. Was any hazing involved?
A: Initiation is a secret.
Q: What was the role of sororities/fraternities on campus?
A: Social and civic activities and to encourage high scholastic achievement.

Q: Which ones were most prestigious? Why?
A: Delta Sigma Theta and Alpha Kappa Alpha.
Q: Did sorority/fraternity affiliation affect whom you dated?
A: No.
Q: Who were the most popular and/or influential students? What offices did they hold? What fraternities/sororities did they belong to?
A: The Student Council president, football players, all fraternities, sorority and fraternity presidents, fraternity sweethearts.
Q: What was the greatest contribution of your college experience to your later life?
A: The development of interests and skills in English (writing) and library science.
Q: What do you wish your college had given you that it didn't?
A: A broader-based education; encouragement to seek fields of study other than education; an awareness of other options; formal teaching of creative writing.

CONCLUSION

There is so much to learn about the proper techniques and approaches in gathering oral histories, such as how to select subjects, how to conduct interviews, and what questions to ask to provoke the best responses. There are many opportunities for creativity. The approach can determine the success or failure of an interview session. Several methods have been applied by the Women's Studies Center at Southern University. Some have included note taking, tape recording, and videotaping. Regardless of the method selected, it is important that the interviewer exercise patience and sensitivity.

When I began collecting oral histories, I had little or no experience in organizing and recording oral narratives. I only knew that this was an important and neglected area of women's history. I asked the advice and assistance of historians and consulted printed literature on the subject before embarking on the project. After doing this, I became more comfortable and began conducting interviews because of valuable information and assistance obtained from the staff of the T. Harry Williams Center for Oral History at Louisiana State University and Agricultural and Mechanical College. As a result of these interviews, my knowledge and appreciation of the plight of black women in Louisiana were enhanced beyond belief. Their thirst for knowledge, dedication to family, and struggle for equal opportunities became painfully clear.

PART III

Research Processes
Health and Well-Being

7

TALKING ABOUT SEX AND HIV

Conceptualizing a New Sociology of Experience

RENÉE T. WHITE

> Zora [Neale Hurston] was a cultural revolutionary simply because she was always herself. Her work, so vigorous among the rather pallid productions of many of her contemporaries, comes from the essence of black folk life.
>
> Walker, 1983, p. 89

> To gain an effective point of view, I spent many hours on the streets, talking and listening to the people of the neighborhood.
>
> Anderson, 1990, p. ix

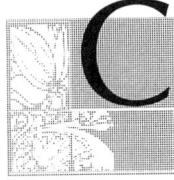apturing the essence of life, in all its complexities, is a challenge that can be answered by ethnographic research and oral narratives. Learning how to ask questions and listen to those in our communities and neighborhoods is a method of study that is still new to many

AUTHOR'S NOTE: All names used in this chapter are pseudonyms.

in the social sciences. Understanding the way people live their lives can result in a greater understanding of how the social world functions.

Field research enables the search for more personal, "everyday" meanings and explanations of the social problems with which we often find ourselves identifying. For example,

> Some ethnographers have constructed their accounts almost exclusively through the first-person narratives of their informants. The strategy can be a powerful one. In the hands of a skillful author, the resulting text can appear as a vivid and privileged reconstruction of the speaker's experience. A variety of narrative accounts can provide a shifting point of view: a kaleidoscope of contrasting or complementary perspectives is provided through a variety of voices. (Atkinson, 1992, p. 24)

Field research, ethnography, and other qualitative methods are effective in the development of research questions that can be addressed with large-scale surveys. Although such methods may not confirm or conclusively explain the existence of social phenomena, oral narratives, by encouraging people to represent their own life experiences, can certainly shed light on how and why the social world affects their lives.

Determining how to use oral narratives within an ethnographic project can result in a new set of methodological, ethical, and ideological questions. As a sociologist, my training prepared me for a quantitative and meta-theoretical world. What was I to make of the one I was to encounter through fieldwork? This chapter is informed by the years spent collecting data in New Haven, Connecticut, for a project on AIDS, race, and teenage females' sexuality. Reflecting on field notes concerning both the process and outcome of field research has provided the framework for this chapter, which draws on specific quotations to develop each section.

This chapter focuses on the theoretical and philosophical issues that emerged as a result of using an exploratory research process. This also requires reviewing the process of data collection. Such a process includes developing strategies for entry and access to key individuals in the field, sampling from the available adolescents in the community, generating methods for data collection and recording, and interpreting/analyzing findings. Ultimately, revisiting the field points to some of the personal and scholarly benefits of narrative studies.

"IS THERE EVEN A SLIGHT POSSIBILITY THAT YOU'LL FIND OUT SOMETHING NEW?": THE UNIQUE VALUE OF NARRATIVE STUDIES

Social scientists are often received with skepticism outside disciplinary circles. This is a result, at least in part, of the way research is conducted and the results are interpreted. In the case of research on black women's sexuality and AIDS, both the generation of hypotheses and data collection have been rife with problems and controversy (Winter & Brekenmaker, 1991). Sexual behavior and related outcomes are so often interpreted within racial-ethnic parameters that it is assumed that race determines or explains what is found.

Traditional ways of confronting and addressing sociological questions appeared to fall short of providing truly revelatory accounts of why so many men and women of color in certain urban areas were living with and dying from AIDS. The fact that black women and Latinas are living with HIV is not an explanation of how or why or to what extent this is true. Claiming that racial differences in rates of infection are explained by race and class in statistical modeling cannot answer a difficult question: Why?

The body of research on AIDS and sexual behavior usually falls into three categories: (a) tracking the incidence of infection and the rates of sexual activity; (b) measuring AIDS/STD knowledge, and (c) identifying cultural differences in sexual behavior and attitudes (Chavkin, 1990; Herz & Reis, 1987; Winter & Brekenmaker, 1991). These three areas of research rely on surveys, epidemiological data, and interviews. They do not include the long-term investigation of participants' lives. Consequently, none of these approaches can capture the range of societal factors associated with black women's risk of HIV infection.

Confronting a complicated yet imperative question such as the association between AIDS and race necessitates shifting the analytic lens from the phenomenon or behavior being studied to the "subject" or "actor." We can confirm that race is a relevant factor in the study of AIDS, but can traditional social science methods get beyond this to the real world in which our subjects/respondents/participants/informants live? These methods identify the *what*, but not the *how* or *why*.

Using a method inspired by ethnography and drawing on sociological theory, I was able to illustrate how people develop their sexual identities within specific social contexts. In this particular project, using field methods was essential because the issue of interest was the interaction of socioeconomic and sociocultural factors in the *lives* of young women. Such an intricate issue could not be comprehensively studied with a survey or questionnaire.

"BUT WHERE'S YOUR HYPOTHESIS? WHAT ARE YOU GOING TO PROVE?": POSING QUESTIONS WITH FIELDWORK

Ethnography is open-ended and exploratory. You do not need any preconceived notions about what you will find. For example, social scientists as diverse as Clifford Geertz (*Negara*, 1980) and Joyce Ladner (*Tomorrow's Tomorrow*, 1973) have used ethnography to explain or better understand social phenomena. In each of these cases, social processes were studied in longitudinal projects. Instead of starting with a range of hypotheses to test, these social scientists generated the data and then developed social explanations for the social facts the researchers observed.

The methodological focus of the research centers on developing concepts through observation and in-depth interviews. As such, the results are time- and context-specific. This specificity is extremely valuable when one is interested in clearly understanding the social space or context in which attitudes are formed and acted on by individuals. Concern for generalizing findings, though relevant, does not diminish the usefulness of this approach.

Although I had a clearly defined interest, as well as some broadly outlined expectations (in terms of the in-depth nature of the information I sought), the method I used had to introduce me to the social practices among teenagers, which eventually could be used to develop hypotheses, if necessary. The query and hypothesis stage is very different when you use fieldwork, ethnography, or oral narrative. Rather than state that race and class explain the association between race and HIV infection among adolescents, I wanted to ask a question.

The goal was to investigate why young women of color were (and still are) overrepresented among those at greatest risk for HIV infection. My main assumption was that a variety of social and material elements influenced this decision-making process. Thus, the goal was to determine whether and how these elements affected decision making. Although surveys and interviews can generate data concerning correlations and associations among variables, these methods do not always provide insights into why people behave as they do.

Many ethnographic, life history, and narrative studies use grounded theory because this inductive approach highlights potential associations and recurring patterns in the recorded life histories. By using grounded theory, a study begins with a general topic, which is addressed by the empirical data (field notes), and then ends in developing hypotheses and concepts (Burawoy, 1991; Kaplan, 1964). Extracting general principles from particular observations provides the foundation for theorizing the existence of social phenomena. It does not start with rigidly defined associations among elements, factors, or variables. "Proponents of grounded theory insist on approaching research without preconceptions—that is, hypothesis. . . . For others, there is acceptance of . . . articulated problems or questions that may guide research. This may or may not result in the formulation of specific hypotheses during the research or at the completion" (Yow, 1994, pp. 8-9). Instead, this type of investigation assumes that discovering and uncovering the interesting and unexpected is an end in itself.

By combining ethnography and oral narrative with other methods, I gained a more complete view of what young black women encountered on a day-to-day basis and how their sexuality and sexual behavior fit into this overall picture. Sex and sexuality are among the most private facets of our lives. For adolescents who sometimes believe that their entire identities are connected with sex and dating, talking about these issues can be even more challenging. Gathering such sensitive information requires trust between the young women and me, which can only occur once we have developed relationships and they feel comfortable enough with me to be honest about their experiences.

Conducting extensive, open-ended interviews (narratives) incorporated ethnographic strategies because I had to spend as much time with the young women in their real-life contexts as they would allow. This was not, however, akin to the ethnographies done by Leon Dash (1989) and Betty Lou Valentine (Whitten & Szwed, 1970). In those instances, the researchers gained greater access to their "subjects'" public and private lives and sometimes witnessed their most private moments.

My project was somewhat different from these. Because the girls' parents were not included in the study, my exposure to their home lives was somewhat limited. In many cases, I was able to see their homes and meet some of their friends. These moments were informative precisely because I remained a silent observer of the young women's daily experiences and interactions. The study had ethnographic elements because, having lived in New Haven for many years before initiating the project, I had a reasonable understanding of the city and was able to observe interactions among adolescents in public spaces over a long period of time. The insights emerging from these observations were to contribute to my sensitivity to the needs and concerns of young women in the project.

This approach enabled me to spend long periods of time with these girls in both structured (controlled) and unstructured settings. By becoming acquainted with the girls, I learned about their sexual behavior and decision-making processes, as well as the impact of their sexual identities, poverty, and perceptions of family and motherhood on these processes. Using such a flexible and adaptable method for primary data collection provided a comprehensive picture of the experience and meaning of adolescence in the 1990s. The ultimate benefit of this approach is that these young women had the opportunity to personalize the findings in literature on sexuality and sexual behavior. After some time and encouragement, they provided insights into adolescence that can only come from personal interaction.

"THE THING IS, HOW DID YOU GET MY NAME, ANYWAY?": CONFRONTING THE SAMPLING QUESTION

By requiring frequent and extensive contact with young women, the sample size had to be limited. At the same time, it had to be large enough to highlight possible trends in behavior and attitudes; the findings could definitively either challenge or confirm existing research. In addition, the sample had to be demographically representative of other young women in the city; in this way, the findings could arguably represent, or at least reflect, the experiences of other adolescent females.

An additional selection requirement was that I approach white and other nonblack female adolescents. Although black women were the focus of the project, contact with other young women would help illuminate what issues were common to all racial-ethnic groups and which ones might be influenced by racial-ethnic or cultural differences. Ultimately, I wanted to oversample the number of black teenagers—having a group that was 70% to 80% black. The target number of participants was a minimum of 20 and a maximum of 40 young women. My goal was to contact organizations and programs that attracted various kinds of teenagers from different racial-ethnic groups, neighborhoods, educational levels, socioeconomic backgrounds, and households.

My selection process was largely nonrandom, in that I approached any young woman who expressed interest in this project. At the same time, however, I remained cognizant of the importance of generating a group of discussants who reflected various social, economic, educational, and ethnic backgrounds. By using a snowball selection process, a few participants introduced me to additional friends who were included in the sample; in turn, these girls introduced me to their friends and acquaintances.

To minimize sampling bias in my nonrandom selection process, I approached four organizations for participants. I relied on youth-oriented groups because of the time constraints involved with meeting teenagers on an individual basis. In deciding which programs to approach, I required that (a) they include participants who, in addition to being residents of New Haven, were representative of the background characteristics in which I was interested; (b) the administrators and outreach staff express enthusiasm for the topics I wanted to study; (c) an educational or outreach component be part of the program; (d) the group meet at least once a week; and (e) discussions include sexual behavior and/or dating.

The groups I selected differed in composition, organizational structure or administrative style, operating philosophy, and prerequisites for participation. One was an academic enrichment program. Another was a pilot project, initiated in a local high school, that addressed cultural differences. The last two were affiliated with local health clinics. Three of the four programs were coeducational, and one attracted preteenagers as well as teenagers. Participation in the study depended on whether the young women were comfortable and was therefore completely voluntary. I offered no financial incentive for participating.

It should be clear that this is not a random or anonymous sampling process. Although variance is sought, it is also important to find participants who will ultimately tell their stories. Even if there is less heterogeneity among the participants, the potential wisdom and insight to be gained from their stories still remains. What has to change is the way this information is used. We cannot expect to conduct narratives in a social vacuum; participants, if they are from the same community or neighborhood, may know each other and will probably talk about some parts of the interview process. This sharing would be highly problematic if one were using other methods; such contact would skew how people respond. In narrative research, however, interactions among participants might stimulate thoughts and memories they wish to share with you.

"I'D LIKE TO INTRODUCE YOU ALL TO . . .": MAKING CONTACTS WITH ORGANIZATIONS IN THE COMMUNITY

Many organizations in New Haven focus on youth issues. They use a number of techniques to deal with the problems and needs of teenagers from a range of racial-ethnic and socioeconomic backgrounds. In addition to addressing sexuality, contraception, pregnancy, and AIDS education, these programs often include components that address the day-to-day existence of young adults. This inclusion became relevant when I was determining which organizations to contact and how to gain access to and acquaint myself with female participants. To make an informed decision, I had to collect information on as many groups as I could find and then contact program directors.

Initial efforts to speak with concerned individuals prepared me for later contacts with organizations. First, I had to confront the political terrain in which the social issues of adolescents were located. Each individual or organization involved with teenagers envisioned him- or herself or themselves as having the definitive view of what teenagers in New Haven require for healthy social and sexual development. As a result, there appeared to be ideological, political, and policy boundaries that they would not cross when addressing social issues. It was necessary that I understand what and where these divisions were early in the research and interview process so as to minimize the risk of alienating the people I contacted.

Second, I had to learn how to communicate effectively with youth professionals and the teenagers. Contacting the professionals involved learning the language that social workers, health care providers, educators, and other youth advocates use on a regular basis. Most of this language was removed from the discourse found in social science theory. Recognizing this language enabled me to eventually prove myself aware of general adolescent issues, as well as those issues more specific to black teenage females in New Haven. In contacting the teenagers—as an adult, who is therefore by definition removed from teen popular culture—I had to remain receptive to and undisturbed by the occasional communication gaps that might challenge my interactions with the young women.

Inclusion in the project depended on the willingness of case managers, outreach workers, and administrators to introduce me to the young women and to encourage ongoing interaction among us. Before this was feasible, I had to establish a strong relationship with as many of the professionals as possible. In addition to reading about the programs, I met with the support staff connected with each program and always brought articles or other literature I thought might be of interest to them.[1] Essentially, it is always important to value the time of the people being contacted and to adopt a collaborative, rather than an authoritarian, demeanor. In the early stages of the project, I always emphasized that my primary role was as a researcher who was also interested in and committed to contributing to the organization in whatever ways they deemed most appropriate. I presented myself as willing to learn from and report on their experiences, as well as those of their peers and clients.

This acknowledgment points to the continuing ethical debate about how forthright a researcher should be about her intentions. The ethical demands are different in any type of study in which researcher and participant have any sort of contact. In field research, this is particularly true because self-disclosure and one's very *presence* within a setting can have long-term effects on participants and nonparticipants alike:

> In field research... the variables are legion and uncontrollable, and long-term consequences of a project cannot be foreseen. [Joan Cassell of the Institute for Policy Research] proposed instead that field researchers be guided by the principle of treating people as ends rather than means—an idea that contains the obligation to do as much good to subjects as possible, to be open and honest, and to share any benefits with them. (Holden, 1979, p. 540)

"ARE YOU SERIOUS ABOUT ALL THIS? WHAT ARE YOU REALLY DOING WITH ALL THIS STUFF?": TRANSFORMING AND CHALLENGING MY ROLE AS RESEARCHER

Most of my early professional contacts expressed frustration and mistrust because they believed they worked in agencies and organizations that had been overstudied, especially by nonminority social scientists.

These studies, though sometimes brief and generally noninvasive, were nonetheless viewed as intrusive and uninformative. Some of the observations made by these professionals clarify the tension between the academic and local advocates' communities:

> I have developed a reputation as unapproachable with people doing research because I make it difficult for them to just swoop down and study my kids and then swoop back to their ivory tower without leaving us something in return.
>
> Look, you folks haven't a clue about what the real issues are. Those of us who work on the front lines have to deal with real life, while academics merely think they know what's going on. Over the past few years, students have approached me, claiming to be truly committed to this or that, and what happens to them? After they get the minimum, they disappear!
>
> I don't like sociologists. Even black ones. I think you have sold out, which is more dangerous than the white ones.

Racial-ethnic conflict mingles not only with issues of informational and experiential territory but also with cynicism about the proper role that researchers should and do play in the community. "Gatekeepers, sponsors, and the like (indeed, most of the people who act as hosts to the research) will operate in terms of expectations about the ethnographer's identity and intentions" (Hammersly & Atkinson, 1995, p. 77). I suspect that, as a black woman, I encountered more skepticism from these early contacts precisely because of this "town-gown" tension.

My presence had to be ambiguous because I was a black woman like them, yet one who seemed to enjoy certain privileges. Many saw my status as a reflection of an elite lifestyle—one shaped by my membership in an exclusive Ivy League social club that was perceived as anti-black, anti-working class, and ultimately anti-New Haven. As such, how else could I have been regarded? If people saw me as actively participating in a social reality that fundamentally rejected them, by extension this meant that my own racial-ethnic-gender identity had to be compromised. There also was the issue of my research status. Any involved, intimate kind of project presumes some sensitivity and commitment to the participants. If my presence is, at best, questionable, then my integrity as a researcher will also be questioned.

These conflicts are well documented in the works of Patricia Hill Collins (1990) and bell hooks (1990) and in the emerging literature on ethnography in sociological research (Burawoy, 1991; Yow, 1994). A basic tenet of social science research is to be clear about one's status in the group under study. As a black woman, I was part of the racial group of interest in the study, but as a representative of a major university, I represented the mainstream (nonblack society).

Even though my contacts expressed support for the project, they also needed reassurance that I retained a strong enough ethnic identity and sense of community that I would not ask questions or interpret findings without any cultural sensitivity. They also needed to see that I was not isolated from New Haven (as exemplified by the "ivory tower quotation" above). Sometimes, this involved my showing that I was acquainted with businesses and neighborhoods not traditionally frequented by members of the university community. At other times, this involved articulating my research interests in whatever was perceived as race/class-appropriate language. After passing what were clearly meant as tests, being black clearly became an asset in further contacts with the advocates, most of whom were black women or Latina. They considered me both an outsider and an insider. Having links with the university was no longer considered a drawback or a problem, but a potential resource.

When first meeting with the young women, I faced their curiosity and resistance. I was usually introduced during the first meeting by whoever facilitated that day's discussion. I was always introduced as what I was—someone interested in researching their attitudes, beliefs, and experiences by documenting their memories and daily experiences. As expected, they were very cynical concerning what I could offer them. Most were uncomfortable with the idea of talking about personal issues with a stranger. Some said that I could not be interested in them, that my interests had to lie in sensationalizing teens' sexual behavior. As one girl said, "What's up with this sex thing? Don't you educated types know about it?" In only one instance did a young woman immediately ask to take part in a systematic project with me.

At first, I remained an observer, noting which young women were particularly vocal or were treated as peer group leaders. My silence was important because I had presented myself as someone who wanted to learn from them, who did not have all the answers. The extent of my participation was determined by the professionals. Sometimes I merely handed out materials and helped set up before the meeting. At other times, I was included in staff planning sessions during which they solicited my input.

Once my presence was less intrusive during group meetings, I began to initiate conversations with different girls concerning popular culture issues of interest to most adolescents—music, clothing, and sports. I initially approached only those who had made efforts to talk with me or who allowed me within their personal space (this was usually expressed by saving me a seat, letting me play with their children, or smiling at me). During these discussions, I reiterated that I was interested in learning about their experiences and opinions of popular views of adolescence (by *popular*, I mean media representations, as well as academic ones). Among the factors I expressed a wish to explore were dating, sex, and male-female relationships. Anyone who appeared interested was invited to participate in group discussions on any topic of interest to them. This participation constituted the initial focus group discussions. I purposely left topics undefined because I wanted the participants to believe that they had some control over this process and that I had no negative, predetermined motives.

The transition from visitor to observer and then associate was often subtle. My role must have been confusing for many of the participants. I was not a teenage participant, I did not hand out a questionnaire and then leave, and I was not a program director or case worker. It was easy to make myself available to them in an attempt to gain their trust. Using these structured settings as the sites of my first encounters with them, however, actually made it more difficult for them to see me as someone they could spend time with on other days. Because the downtown shopping mall was one popular social spot for many teenagers, I had to spend hours there, sometimes alone, sometimes speaking with one or two young women I might see who knew me. I had to create circumstances and environments outside the boundaries of the programs in order to see them in other social settings.

Not all the participants appreciated seeing me during their off-time. As one teenager told me, "There is no need to shadow me like that. You must have something else to do." Ironically, I was running errands of my own and was not engaging in active research collection. This incident raises the liability and benefit of living among the individuals one interviews. On the one hand, it is often difficult to separate the researcher and "average person" roles for all those participating in the project. Can there be moments of social contact when data collection is either warranted or expected? On the other hand, living in this kind of social space enables the researcher to even engage in "passive" modes of data collection through simple participation in the rhythm and flow of the community.

"YES, I HAVE HEARD ABOUT WHAT HAPPENED": DEVELOPING A RAPPORT

The transition in the reception of one's presence is simultaneously slow and enlightening. Because collecting these narratives required first developing trusting relationships, I had to let the young women dictate the paths this process might take. Reading the cues that indicate their willingness to delve into personal issues is usually difficult and requires having a working knowledge of the teenagers' personality styles. Once I had permission from them to include them in the study, I entered this new phase in our relationships: juggling for control and testing each other's truthfulness/trustworthiness.

Having preexisting knowledge of a range of relevant issues (from both personal experience and the initial interviews) prepared me for the different kinds of tests to come. As the personal narrative process was to emerge out of group discussions, much of the testing I faced occurred within groups. In one case, a group of Latina teenagers were talking about their day. They used "Spanglish," a hybrid of Spanish and English. None of these teenagers was willing to speak with me in the beginning. They would slip between Spanglish and Spanish when speaking to each other; they had assumed I knew no Spanish and thus could be excluded from their discussions.

In most conversations, these young women would not translate their comments for others in the group, or when they did, it was obviously inaccurate. I "showed my hand" one day by laughing at a joke one of them told in Spanish. Even though this reaction was not completely self-conscious, it did facilitate the relationship I was to develop with one young woman. I had indicated that I knew Spanish, that I was not going to chastise them for things previously said, and that I had a sense of humor.

In another case, young men devised dramatic stories to test my sensibilities. They wanted to prove their sexual experience through telling shocking stories. One time, Dexter, a 14-year-old, talked about his relationships with women 30 years old and older. Each time, his version changed and his friends responded accordingly by laughing and glancing at me. When I asked him to explain why the two women in question kept changing in his recounting of the encounter, he said, "Hey, my sister, I'm the undercover lover . . . I don't need to lie. I'm hype." In another example, Angel tells me that he created a drug and named it after himself: "Heard of angel dust? I did that. Now I'm rich, and the ladies love me." I told him that, by coincidence, I had heard about another drug of the same name that existed before he was even born. He laughed and said, "You know about that? How would a lady like you know that?" Obviously, preconceptions about researcher and participant roles will, on some level, affect personal interactions.

Working within groups where people know each other involves both benefits and drawbacks. On occasion, participants would serve as screeners or fact-checkers: If one person misrepresented information, another might interject and challenge her. Having grown up together also meant that some young women already felt comfortable with each other. As a result, they would either protect each other from seemingly invasive questions or maintain a sense of camaraderie, thus creating a safe discussion environment. These dynamics placed a great deal of control with the participants. They could choose to either actively include or exclude me from their inner sanctum.

After a few weeks, some teenagers started to meet with me individually. Initiating this stage required being sensitive to the ways each young woman expressed herself and how private she had seemed in previous group discussions. Willingness to delve into personal life issues is as varied as can be imagined. Some people will volunteer personal experiences; others need encouragement. After a few meetings with one young woman, I wrote about facing a stone wall:

> I do not know what to try next. Marlene is friendly, but so guarded. Her answers are complete but lack the depth I had expected. Maybe I need to push her less, but I'm frustrated. What has left her so careful about things? Even talking about what I thought were mundane sorts of things is hard. Remember to raise something about her cousin. If what Susie says is on target, that's a way to open things up. Otherwise, I think we're stalling.

This process is time-consuming because it involves individualized attention. Each participant is her own person and has her own boundaries. Discovering what these are may take trial-and-error. This approach is often discomforting for those with formal training in data collection who are used to more stable and predictable timetables and reliable research formats.

Determining how and when to guide individual interviews involves an element of openness. Both preliminary literature review and early interviews should shape what general topics are to be addressed, but it is also important to allow flexibility within discussions. You never know exactly where a conversation or commentary will take you.

Written guidelines help in organizing discussion topics, but they are only that—guidelines. Seemingly unrelated discussions may eventually touch on the heart of the research question (this may become immediately apparent, or only after reflection). The strength of narrative is that the participant's life is the resource, and she is your intermediary.

For example, one young woman was describing a move her family had made to a different street. This was the seventh move in about 2 years. In reality, this conversation ended up highlighting the kinds of social isolation that teenagers might experience and the dangers of having an adult exploit this fact. In Cathy's case, the result was sexual assault:

Cathy: . . . then we went to unload and finish. . . . The move was pretty difficult because I missed my girlfriends, and you know.
RTW: You didn't see them after moving, or did you?
Cathy: Well, sometimes, but I wasn't into school so much, and missed a lot and didn't see them. Taking care at home, I guess. And things. I had those two sisters, like I said, and they young. But I also just wanted out of the house, like always.
RTW: What do you mean?
Cathy: Okay, so I wanted out. No big deal. Just tired of packing and unpacking and packing again.
RTW: You wanted out of . . . packing?
Cathy: But also home things. All we always got is each other, and that's not always so good a thing.

After an extended discussion of how much we both disliked moving, Cathy shared this account:

> I was crying 'cause I just wanted to stay one place, and he came over and told me it was okay and that it would get better and he came from behind and hugged me and touched my breasts. . . . He's disgusting, and I won't let him near those girls so he'll have to make do with me.

Allowing the narrator to guide some of the discussion can be unexpectedly fruitful and thus requires some intuition, or reading within and between the lines of discourse.

There is no way to predict when and how enough intimacy will have developed for a participant to relate her own memories as truthfully as she can. This will be a mutually determined moment, one emerging from possibly many months of interactions. Because narrative research involves sharing the most personal elements in a person's life, any number of strategies may be needed. In many cases, asking participants to describe their neighborhoods and what their homes look like opened up the discussions. Some others preferred staying close to a preset script of questions and then extending to a variety of related topics. Still others wanted more control over the path that conversations would take and explicitly dictated where we would start.

"OK, WHAT DO YOU DO WITH ALL THIS INFORMATION?": RECORDING AND PRESENTING NARRATIVES

In most of this chapter, I refer to conversations, discussions, and field notes. Shifting from a record of what people said to a set of conclusions requires a few stages. Obviously, the first stage involves the actual collecting and recording of data. In the second stage, field notes have to be reviewed and analyzed (what I call the presentation stage). Finally, all these reflections have to be formally reported. During this representation stage, one has to decide what findings are relevant and why. To some extent, judgments and evaluations must be made. Each of these stages is especially complex because most one-on-one interactions are open-ended (unstructured) interviews, and not unguided monologue. The issues that guide the questions also shape how responses are recorded during the interviews.

The question of recording and taking notes is a complex one. Because life histories are the focus, it is imperative that they be recorded as completely and accurately as possible. Ideally, this imperative points to tape recording during interviews. Not all people are willing and interested participants. For some, this is a violation of trust or a potential violation of privacy. "What do I do if someone hears what I say? Who's going to be able to do the explaining then?" asked one teenager. The leap from willingness to participate to willingness to do so on the record can seem insurmountable. This is where the issue of trust is relevant, for if the narrator believes that you are going to protect her privacy, she is more likely to agree to some form of record keeping.

If an individual refuses to be recorded, the solution is clear: Do not tape her. This will raise a few problems for the researcher, but arguably it is more important to protect the connection between researcher and participant than to record data verbatim. This is a qualified claim because, ultimately, the goal of a field project is as accurate a rendering of individuals' lives as possible within the existing constraints. As with other stages of research, this is a trade-off. Tape recording may or may not be feasible, but field notes are necessities. They can fill in the gaps in interview notes, add commentary to previous observations, and encourage self-reflection. Being self-conscious of one's presence within a community or group is an important part of collecting data. Writing down and reviewing what happened during the course of that day will facilitate what bell hooks (1990, 1994) recommends: self-interrogation. Reviewing notes is part of the analytical process as much as creating them.

The level of detail in field notes largely depends on how much time one has to engage in their construction and reconstruction. Eventually, they will be a combination of in-the-moment perceptions, after-the-fact elaborations, and down-the-line interpretations. Obviously, this process can be problematic if interpretation obscures presentation. Going from recording to presentation to representation involves the interpretation of narratives. Collecting field notes occurs in the first stage of investigation—recording information—and will be instrumental in the second stage, in which you analyze what you have noted. When you are deeply involved with a person or group and the social role of researcher appears fuzzy, it is easy for interpretations to replace the narratives themselves. The mediator of the author's story, as the expert in social sciences, becomes the true storyteller in this sense—and thus the narrator's experience becomes lost. One possible solution, which was effective in this project, is to check for accuracy by sharing small segments of field notes with the narrator.

CONCLUSION: REFLECTING ON THE UNEXPECTED IN ORAL NARRATIVE STUDIES

There is much more to this story than can be shared here. Working with young women in the construction and presentation of their life histories affected me on many levels. Embarking on this project required studying and learning about a method of research previously unknown to me. Although I had read narratives and analyses of them, I had not learned how to engage in narrative and ethnographic research in a systematic way. As a result, parts of the process were more experimental than I had anticipated.

Working in the community where I lived was ultimately a self-revelatory process. In addition to gathering descriptive information that illuminated more than I had hoped, the method also forced me to question my role as objective researcher. The period of becoming acquainted with these young women also involved assessing how my presence would affect their lives. This is not an example of professional egocentrism; it is merely an eventuality.

Any social contact with another person has to affect the two of you. In narrative research, one engages in very personal, in-depth, and often sensitive territory. The simple exercise of reflection has to affect a participant. In other situations, women may find themselves confiding things they have never confronted before. This disclosure leaves the researcher with a moral dilemma, particularly when the confidence concerns something in the present. What do you do if someone tells you something that is placing her at risk? In such a case, the "objective" researcher confronts the "subjective" confidant. You may not be a close friend, but you have certainly been entrusted with intimate details of a woman's life. As a friend, you want to intervene, which is tantamount to tampering with the research setting—but only in the most literal sense. There is no one solution. How we respond has to be situation-specific.

As these issues illustrate, for black women concerned with the lives of other black women (or for any individual investigating the experiences of someone with whom an alliance is shared), self-interrogation and self-consciousness are ongoing processes. The data collection, recording, and analysis stages will involve reflection, analysis, reinvention, and discovery. In my case, I found that my perceptions of myself as a black woman changed. More important, I came away from this project with an ever-growing respect for the resilience and innovation that I encountered among young women living in sometimes difficult, compromised, and challenging circumstances. By using oral narratives, we have the opportunity to both contribute to the depictions of black women in our disciplines and expand our social, political, professional, and personal selves.

SUGGESTED EXERCISES

Teaching about any qualitative method, especially ones requiring extended and extensive contacts, should encourage a great deal of experimentation and trial runs. Because so much of this method involves developing skills to respond to situations as they happen, strategies including role play (one participant has been given a script, but the other one has not) are effective. In addition, learning how to document and code notes is often left out of the learning process. In the light of these facts, a few projects can be very enlightening:

1. *On-the-Spot Interviews:* What would happen if a researcher simply approached a randomly selected person and asked her to participate in the collection of oral narratives? Which strategies are more effective and appealing? Devise a mini-project that requires the collection of information from strangers. This includes how one should introduce him- or herself, what sites are most conducive to receptiveness, how to develop a trust relationship quickly, and how to deal with rejection. Naturally, this method is far from appealing or effective, but it is important to know how to handle more difficult scenarios and how to conduct "cold" interviews.

2. *Open-Ended Interviews:* In family studies classes, this method had proven popular and especially insightful. Select two or three relatives, trying to include at least one with whom you are close. Identify a topic of interest and develop both a theoretical model and a flexible interview schedule to use during the interviews. Try to record the interviews and reconstruct them with field notes after each interview is completed. Learning about how easily one can reinterpret and forget information is but one benefit of this exercise. In addition, interviewing participants who already have a relationship with you raises challenges and rewards. In comparison with the first exercise, you as a researcher should gain a stronger understanding of how bias can function in either situation.

3. *Note Taking 1:* During any conversation, take notes on anything that transpires. This includes nonverbal events as well. Be as detailed as possible. Do not look at the notes for at least 2 days. On reviewing them, try to determine to what extent they allow you to recapture details from the conversation. Was anything unclear? Could you remember anything that was not included in the notes? Show the notes to the other person and have her evaluate how accurate she thinks they are.

4. *Note Taking 2:* As an extension of Note Taking 1, conduct more focused discussions with one or two people (at least three mini-interviews per person). Incorporate some personal questions into the

interviews. If the interviewees agree to be taped, compare the recordings to your notes. In this experiment, conduct one set of interviews in which notes are taken during the conversation, and then conduct other interviews in which notes cannot be recorded until after the interview.

REFERENCES

Anderson, E. (1990). *Streetwise: Race, class, and change in an urban community*. Chicago: University of Chicago Press.
Atkinson, P. (1992). *Understanding ethnographic texts*. Newbury Park, CA: Sage.
Burawoy, M. (Ed.). (1991). *Ethnography unbound: Power and resistance in the modern metropolis*. Berkeley: University of California Press.
Chavkin, W. (1990, Spring). Women, AIDS, and reproductive rights: Preventing AIDS, targeting women. *Health/PAC Bulletin*, pp. 19-23.
Collins, P. H. (1990). *Black feminist thought: Knowledge, consciousness, and the politics of empowerment*. Winchester, MA: Unwin Hyman.
Dash, L. (1989). *When children want children*. New York: William Morrow.
Geertz, C. (1980). *Negara*. Princeton, NJ: Princeton University.
Hammersly, M., & Atkinson, P. (1995). *Ethnography: Principles in practice*. New York: Routledge.
Herz, E. J., & Reis, J. (1987). Family life education for young inner-city teens: Identifying needs. *Journal of Youth and Adolescence, 4*, 361-376.
Holden, C. (1979). Ethics in social science research. *Science, 206*, 537-538, 540.
hooks, b. (1990). *Yearning: Race, gender, and cultural politics*. Boston: South End.
hooks, b. (1994). *Outlaw culture*. New York: Routledge.
Kaplan, A. (1964). *The conduct of inquiry*. San Francisco: Chandler.
Ladner, J. A. (1973). *Tomorrow's tomorrow*. Garden City, NY: Doubleday.
Walker, A. (1983). *In search of our mothers' gardens*. Orlando, FL: Harcourt Brace.
Whitten, N. E., & Szwed, J. F. (1970). *Afro-American anthropology*. New York: Free Press.
Winter, L., & Brekenmaker, L. C. (1991). Tailoring family planning services to the special needs of adolescents. *Family Planning Perspectives, 1*, 24-30.
Yow, V. R. (1994). *Recording oral history: A practical guide for social scientists*. Thousand Oaks, CA: Sage.

NOTE

1. From these interviews, I generated a list of two health clinics, two community centers, two local AIDS education and support programs, three national service organizations, and four family planning/HIV counselors who worked with different agencies. I repeated the same information-gathering process with this group of contacts and was aided by being able to name as references people I had already interviewed. What distinguished this process from the earlier one is that the intended outcome was direct contact with a sample of these professionals' female clients and participants.

8

METHODOLOGICAL ISSUES IN TRIANGULATION

Measuring Weight Control Behavior of African American Women

JACQUELINE A. WALCOTT-McQUIGG

AFRICAN AMERICAN WOMEN AND HEALTH

Despite the impressive growth in health research, very little work has been conducted on African American women's psychosocial or physical health issues. An intensive literature review revealed that African American women are given only tangential attention in the health literature and are conceptualized as a monolithic group, rather than as women with substantial differences in backgrounds, lifestyles, and dwelling places (Cope & Hall, 1985). In addition, African American women in the lower socioeconomic groups tend to be the most frequently studied. Findings from studies with lower socioeconomic African American women are consequently extrapolated to all groups of African American women. Although I have been expressing these statements since 1989, the full extent of their meaning was not realized for me until August 1992. In August 1992, I was interviewing for a faculty position at a prestigious college of nursing in the Midwest. After I had

---

AUTHOR'S NOTE: This research study was partially supported by the American Nurses' Association Ethnic/Minority Fellowship Program and the Alpha Lambda Chapter of Sigma Theta Tau International Honor Society for Nurses.

presented my data on middle-income African American women, a well-funded Caucasian researcher suggested that my sample was unique and asked me when I planned to conduct research with African Americans who are more representative, such as those with lower income status. I responded by suggesting that because only one third of African Americans have earnings below the poverty guidelines and two thirds above, the term *representative*, when referring to African American women in lower-income groups as representative, was a misnomer. Incidents such as this support the need for the presence of ethnic minority researchers to educate the research community, as well as the community researched, about factors affecting the health and well-being of ethnic minority populations.

I chose a triangulation methodology in which both qualitative and quantitative data are collected to investigate the domain of weight control behavior (diet control, weight management, exercise) in middle-income African American women. In this chapter, I delineate the importance of triangulation methodology in the investigation of factors influencing weight control behavior. I accomplish several aims: (a) to characterize a specific group of women in terms of the factors that self-presentation theorists suggest are relevant to diet and weight control behavior, (b) to explain the actual behavior and the relative value the women place on the attractiveness of selected images, (c) to describe how they use behavior to claim images, and (d) to describe their judgments of efficacy and their self-concept in relation to the behavior. In addition, I attempt to give the reader a blueprint for using the triangulation method in his or her own research.

Literature Review

Obesity is a problem for African American women across all socioeconomic strata (Kumanyika, 1993). Summaries from national nutrition and health surveys indicate that although women of low socioeconomic status have the highest overweight prevalence, controlling for socioeconomic status does not eliminate the obesity prevalence difference between African American women (48.6%) and Caucasian women (32.1%) (Kuczmarski, Flegal, Campbell, & Johnson, 1994). African American women in the highest income or education classes have age-adjusted mean weights higher than Caucasian women in the lowest income or education classes (Kumanyika, 1993). The findings that obesity occurs differentially by race may implicate both genetic and environmental influences (Croft et al., 1992; Flegal, Harlan, & Landis, 1988; Kumanyika, Morssink, & Augurs, 1992; Meyer & Stunkard, 1993; Williamson, Kahn, & Byers, 1991). Researchers have identified several sources of environmental influences—for example, higher caloric intake among African Americans, comparatively lower physical activity, reproductive or lifestyle variables that predispose African American women to excess weight gain (Kahn & Williamson, 1991), and inability of African American women to lose weight or maintain weight losses— related to food preferences or other cultural elements (Allan, Mayo, & Michel, 1993; Kumanyika, 1993; Walcott-McQuigg, Sullivan, Dan, & Logan, 1995). Furthermore, feelings of unhappiness with body size do not negatively influence other aspects of African American women's lives (Thomas & James, 1988).

Psychosocial elements that influence weight control practices of African American women have been little studied. Studies with primarily Caucasian samples indicate that self-efficacy to diet and exercise (King et al., 1993; Rossi, Rossi, Velicer, & Prochaska, 1995), stress (Foreyt et al., 1995), and self-concept (Mintz & Betz, 1986) influence weight control behavior. The study I present here used a triangulation methodology guided by the self-presentational approach to explore selected psychosocial factors that may influence weight control behavior of a group of middle-income African American women.

CONCEPTUAL FRAMEWORK

A self-presentational conceptual framework guided this research effort. The narrative of self-presentation theory (Schlenker, 1980) was modeled and adapted (Figure 8.1) (Walcott-McQuigg, 1992) to examine weight control behavior of African American women. Self-presentation theorists suggest that people seek to associate themselves with desirable images and to avoid undesirable images. Because our behavior, as human behavior, has social consequences, it may be used to control and maintain images that other people form of us. Other people observe our behavior and make inferences about who we are. We can also serve as an audience to our own behavior. How important our behavior is to self and how important behavior is socially is a basis of our self-identity.

A social or self identity consists of a set of relevant images. A variety of images are relevant to weight control behavior, and these vary in terms of their perceived desirability or attractiveness to African American

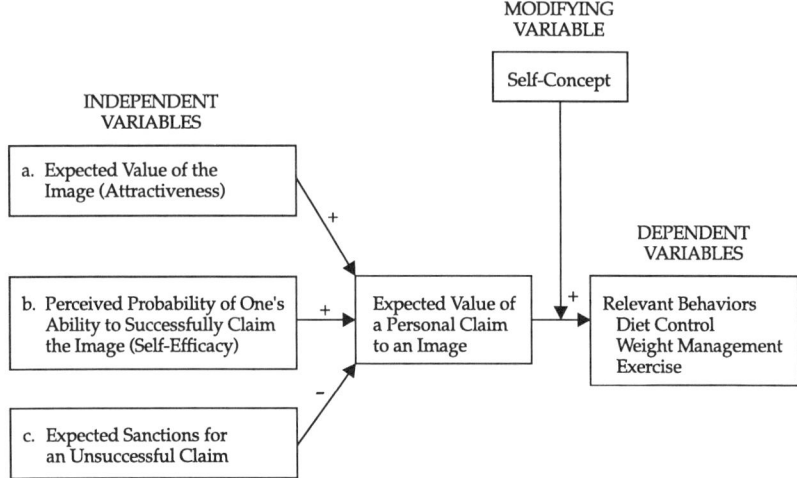

Figure 8.1. Self-Presentation Model of Weight Control Behavior
SOURCE: Based on narrative in Schlenker (1980).

women and the degree to which they facilitate or hinder weight control behavior—for example, the image of monitoring one's diet and weight or the image of serving lots of tasty food. Both are relevant: One probably hinders, and one probably facilitates. When people engage in certain behavior associated with relevant images, they are interested in being perceived by others or themselves as persons who have certain qualities that the images imply or in claiming those particular images (Schlenker, 1980). The image of importance in this study was that of a diet- and weight-managing individual. The behaviors involved in claiming the image were diet control, weight management, and exercise behavior. Women who engaged in various combinations of these behaviors were claiming various levels of the image. No matter how desirable or attractive an image is, a woman may not claim it. The expected value of the claim is a function of several components: The attractiveness of the image, judgments of efficacy to engage in the behavior needed to claim the image, and likely sanctions associated with an unsuccessful claim, together predict a person's likelihood of engaging in the behavior or of claiming the image. This expected value of the image, in turn, is what predicts the likelihood of engaging in the relevant behavior to claim the image. A woman's self-concept influences the strength of the relationship between the expected value of a claim and participation in the relevant behavior. The higher the self-concept, the stronger the relationship.

METHOD

Sample

I conducted a descriptive correlational study with 45 middle-class African American women, primarily from four traditional black sororities, in a large Midwest metropolitan area. Criteria for inclusion in the study were age of at least 21 years, membership in a sorority or similar characteristics as a sorority member, and some college education. To obtain a purposive sample of women who met the inclusion criteria, I contacted the chairpersons of the health concerns committees of four sororities to request that they describe the study to the members and ask them to either contact me or release their telephone numbers for investigator contact. Using the snowball technique, women outside the sororities who had characteristics similar to those of the sorority members were referred to me. *Snowballing*, or network sampling, involves asking respondents for names of other women who have similar characteristics (Burns & Groves, 1993). I called the potential respondents, described the purpose of the study, and requested a meeting at a time and place of their convenience.

The age of the women ranged from 25 to 75 years, with an average age of 40 years. The majority of the women had earned a baccalaureate or higher degree; were employed full-time in professional, middle management, or higher-level management positions; and earned $30,000 or higher. Forty percent were married and living with their spouses, 32% were never married, and 28% were divorced, separated, or widowed. Fifty-eight percent had at least one child. All the women belonged to at least one professional organization, and 91% to at least one personal organization, such as a woman's church group. A select few of the women belonged to a combined total of eight organizations.

Triangulation Methodology

Both qualitative and quantitative data were gathered by using a triangulation methodology that included both face-to-face, in-depth interviews and a structured questionnaire. Triangulation as a research strategy represents a means of more accurately depicting the phenomenon under investigation (Cowman, 1993). There are four types of triangulation: data, investigator, theoretical, and methodological (Denizen, 1989). A *triangulated study* is any study that has several different data sources, or involves multiple investigators, or tests multiple competing hypothesis, or as in this study, combines two or more kinds of data collection methods. This between-methods triangulation (Denizen, 1989), combining qualitative and quantitative data collection techniques, increases confidence in findings (Duffy, 1987; Knafl, Pettengill, Bevis, & Kirchoff, 1988) and is essential to furthering nursing science (Carr, 1994; Myers & Haase, 1989).

Data Collection

Data were collected over a period of 7 months by audiotape using a semistructured interview guide and administration of a questionnaire measuring stress, self-concept, and self-efficacy to diet and exercise. Table 8.1 lists the measurement linkages between the conceptual model elements and the study instruments. Additional data collection included body weight, height, and a wrist measure to calculate small, medium, or large body frame based on information in the Metropolitan Life Insurance Table (Metropolitan Life Foundation, 1983). Although the weight calculation is only an approximation, it is an acceptable measure of the magnitude of fatness for public health field studies (National Institutes of Health, 1985).

Interview Guide

An interview guide was developed to measure social, cultural, and image-relevant factors that influence diet control, weight management, and exercise behavior. For instance, to obtain women's unstructured ideas and perceptions of stress, women were asked, "What would you say are the major stressors in your life?" and "What would you say are the major stressors on your job?" To assess cultural factors, women were asked, "Do you think there is anything about being African American that influences whether diet and weight management are important to you?"

The interview process was pilot-tested on three respondents prior to the implementation of the study. The interviews, ranging in length from 1 to 4 hours, were conducted primarily in respondents' homes. Each audiotaped interview was transcribed verbatim. *Constant comparison*, the act of moving back and forth among data sets to identify patterns and to determine the presence, variation, or absence of patterns (Lincoln & Guba, 1985), was used. An analysis matrix (Miles & Huberman, 1994) was constructed to assist with the comparison process; col-

TABLE 8.1 Linkages Between the Conceptual Model Elements and the Instruments

Conceptual Model Element	Instrument
Expected value of a personal claim to an image	
Expected value of the image (attractiveness)	Interview guide, Importance of Images Scale
Perceived probability of one's ability to successfully claim the image (self-efficacy)	Self-Efficacy Scales for Diet and Exercise Behavior
Expected sanctions for an unsuccessful claim	Interview guide
Self-concept	Tennessee Self-Concept Subscale
Relevant Behaviors	
Diet control	Interview guide
Weight management	Interview guide
Exercise	Interview guide, Questionnaire

umns represented categories, and rows represented units. The Ethnograph (Version 4.0) computer program (Seidel, Kjolseth, & Seymour, 1995) was used to organize the transcribed data set into 78 common units by categories. Table 8.2 lists the 10 categories, the definitions used to assign data to categories, and an example of the type of information that was used in the matrix to determine how units of data were assigned to categories.

To validate my conceptualization of the coding system, the categories and one randomly selected verbatim transcript were given to two women's health researchers. The reviewers examined the transcripts to determine whether the units and categories accurately described the information. For instance, the weight management category described two types of weight management. One unit, health weight management, was one reason why women managed their weight, to remain healthy. Another unit, other weight management, was descriptive of other reasons why the women managed their weight, to "look good and fit in their clothing." Agreement between my coding of the transcripts and the women's health researchers was 90% and 95%, respectively.

Structured Questionnaire

Several instruments were combined to measure stress, self-concept, self-efficacy to diet and exercise, and demographic data. The questionnaires were administered after the interview, in an effort to obtain

TABLE 8.2 Ethnographic Categories, Definitions, and Examples

Category	Definition	Example
1. Diet control	What activities do the women engage in to control dietary intake?	Reduce/eliminate fats, sweets, meat
2. Weight management	What types of efforts are associated with weight loss, weight maintenance?	Enrolled in a weight-loss program for health reasons
3. Weight impact	What factors influence responses to information about body weight?	Determinants of ideal weight
4. Exercise activity	What factors are associated with exercise?	Types, duration, length of exercise
5. Importance factors	What types of things are important to the women?	Family, friends, career, health
6. Health promotion	What types of activities do the women practice to "keep healthy"?	Regular self-breast exam
7. Family history	What is the family history of disease processes?	Disease processes and family members who have had them
8. Stressors	What are the various stressors that may affect weight control behavior?	Life stressors, occupational stressors
9. Health issues	Are the women experiencing any health problems and finding sources of health information?	Woman's major health problem and where she gets health information
10. Other issues	Do other issues affect women's participation in weight control behavior?	Effects of the presence or absence of social support

unbiased data. I waited while the women completed the questionnaires, to ensure a high return rate (100%). Questionnaire data were analyzed by using SPSS (a comprehensive integrated system for statistical data analysis) for mainframes (Norusis, 1990).

Combined qualitative and quantitative data were analyzed through conceptual analysis of all the significant data available. Results from the qualitative data were used to help confirm results of the quantitative data in this *confirmatory*, or conceptual validation, approach. This approach involves a search for logical patterns of relationship and meaning between the variables measured by either or both approaches (Mitchell, 1986).

Measures of Conceptual Model Elements

Expected Value of Images

An image importance scale (Walcott-McQuigg, 1992), developed especially for the study, was used to measure the importance of various images, including the diet and weight management image. It consists of 22 statements, 11 of which query the respondent about the importance of having others view her as a person who engages in certain behaviors, and 11 of which query her about the importance of viewing herself as a person who engages in the same set of behaviors. The respondents rate each image statement on a 5-point Likert-type scale from *not at all important* to *very important*.

Twenty-two items comprised the initial importance scale. I used a principle components factor analysis with varimax rotation to reduce that number to a smaller number of underlying factors (Carmines & Zeller, 1979; Nunnally, 1978). To interpret the orthogonally rotated matrix, I selected items whose absolute weights were greater than or equal to .50 on the selected factor and less than .50 on any other factor. Five factors with eigenvalues of 1.00 or higher explained 67.5% of the variance.

Some images were directed primarily to other persons as an audience. Other images were directed primarily to the woman herself as the audience. And still other images were directed to both self and others. Factor 1 was indicative of a Social Diet and Weight Management Image. Six of the seven variables involved the importance of others' opinions regarding the respondent's diet control, weight management, and appearance. This factor accounted for 22% of the variance. Factor 2, Self-Diet and Weight Management Image, accounted for 13.6% of the variance. These four variables identified the importance of the respondent's own opinions regarding involvement in the health behavior. Factor 3 consisted of four variables that were a combination of self- and others' opinions regarding healthy children and serving lots of good food. Named the Parenting and Hostess Image, this factor accounted for 12.5% of the variance. Factor 4, the Healthy Eating Habits Image, was comprised of three items that accounted for 10% of the variance. It consisted of the importance of others' opinions related to the serving of nutritious and low-calorie foods. Factor 5, the Serves Tasty Food Image, consisted of two items that indicated the importance of one's own and others' opinions regarding the serving of tasty food. It accounted for 8.9% of the variance. Coefficient alpha was used to measure reliability.

The alpha coefficients of the various images were social diet and weight management, .86; self-diet and weight management, .82; parenting and hostess, .76; healthy eating habits, .67; and serves tasty food, .70.

Self-Efficacy

The Self-Efficacy Health Behavior Scale consists of two subscales used to measure respondents' efficacy to engage in diet control and exercise behavior (Sallis, Pinski, Grossman, Patterson, & Nader, 1988). The subscales were developed with subjects varying in age, gender, occupation, and race. Response is on a 7-point Likert-type scale, from *not confident at all* to *very confident*. Coefficient alphas with the African American women were .93 for the 61 items in the diet control subscale and .97 for the 13 items in the exercise subscale. The higher the score, the higher self-efficacy to engage in diet control and exercise behavior.

Sanctions

I measured sanctions for failure to claim the image or to engage in the behavior by using the interview guide question, "What do you think would happen if you were to set a goal to lose a certain amount of weight and were unable to accomplish that goal?" Ethnographic examination of the responses to the question revealed that they were primarily emotional in nature. The women's responses were categorized into two levels of reactions: (neutral and positive = 0, and negative = 1). A *neutral response* was defined as one in which the respondent indicated that nothing would happen as a result of not meeting an expected goal:

> Probably nothing would at times I set the goal at 20 pounds and lost 10. It would not bother me.

A *positive response* indicated that the respondent would examine the situation and propose another plan of action:

> If I didn't meet my goal, then I would be looking at what I was doing because something was incorrect. And even if it was a plateau, then I have to look in terms of maybe I need to increase the exercise part since I don't believe that it is just diet.

A *negative response* usually included an initial emotional reaction, such as depression or frustration and a loss of interest in dieting:

Oh, I would be frustrated, of course, which would mean I would get off the diet, of course.

The assumption was that an expected negative sanction for failure would inhibit a woman's likelihood of engaging in the behavior.

Self-Concept

Self-concept was measured by using the Tennessee Physical Self-Concept Subscale (TSCS) (Roid & Fitts, 1989). It consists of 18 self-descriptive statements to which respondents give one of five responses on a 5-point Likert-type scale, from *completely true* to *completely false*. The TSCS, developed for people of age 12 and older, was originally standardized on a sample of 626 people varying in age, gender, occupation, and race. Alpha coefficient for the scale was .82 in my sample. A higher score indicates a higher level of self-concept.

Stress

Stress was measured by using the Perceived Stress Scale (PSS; Cohen, Kamarck, & Mermelstein, 1983). It is a 14-item scale designed for use with community samples. The PSS includes questions that ask respondents to rate from 0 (*never*) to 4 (*very often*) how often they experienced stress within the last month related to perceived ability and actual ability to cope with various situations. Acceptable internal consistency reliability, test-retest reliability, and concurrent validity have been established for the scale. In this sample, internal consistency reliability using coefficient alpha was .80.

Weight-Relevant Behaviors

The measurement of weight-relevant behaviors consisted of asking questions on the interview guide about three behaviors: diet control, weight management, and exercise. Women's health practices related to diet control included the reduction and elimination of fats, meat, and so on from the diet. The addition of nutrients such as fiber, vitamins, and minerals was also considered a diet control activity. Weight management techniques included aggressive attempts to lose and maintain weight, such as self-imposed or professional weight reduction diets. *Exercise* was defined as an activity that the women participated in at least three times a week and had a minimum duration of 20 minutes.

Ethical Considerations

A signed consent form indicated willingness to participate. Confidentiality was guaranteed, and my telephone number was given to the respondents in case they had questions or wished to request removal of their data from the study.

RESULTS

Body Weight: Actual and Ideal

Body mass index (BMI) ranged from 19 to 40 (mean = 27); 48% of the women had BMIs of greater than 27. *Excess weight* was defined as a BMI of 27.3 or more for women. In addition to their present body weight, the women identified an ideal weight. *Ideal weight* was defined as a body weight at which they would most like to be; 61% of the women had perceptions of ideal weight that were within their height and weight range on the Metropolitan Life tables; and 39% of the women's ideal body weights ranged from 2 to 30 pounds over the suggested weight range for their height. Although the latter groups' ideal weights were over the recommended weight range, they were below the 20% overweight range that has been associated with morbidity and mortality (Van Italie & Lew, 1993). When asked how they determined their ideal weight, over 50% of the women indicated they did so by reflecting on a weight at which they had "looked better," "felt lighter," "felt healthier," and "felt comfortable." The other women determined their ideal weight based on a variety of sources, such as information from health professionals, health club personnel, weight management program staff, and height and weight charts.

Attractiveness of Relevant Images

In Table 8.3, the analysis of the importance of various images to these African American women reveals a hierarchy of importance or attractiveness. The image of a self-dieting and weight-managing woman was the most attractive. It was followed by the image of a woman who serves tasty food, as a woman who has healthy eating habits, the social diet and weight management image, and finally as a woman who is a good parent and hostess.

TABLE 8.3 Ranked Importance Means and Standard Deviations of Selected Images

Images	Mean	Standard Deviation
Self-diet and weight management	3.958	0.703
Serves tasty food	3.000	1.000
Healthy eating habits	2.762	0.975
Social diet and weight management	2.381	0.859
Parenting and hostess	2.271	1.398

Further exploration of images indicated that the women thought a self-diet and weight management image was a more realistic image for them than a social diet and weight management image:

> I didn't lose the weight because of what he said. I lost the weight for myself, what I felt. I have good control. So I try to cut down on what I am eating and increase my exercise.

> Because I feel the information in the Metropolitan Life Height and Weight Tables are not relevant for African American women. It is more important for me to feel healthy. It should be something that I want, instead of something that is dictated to me.

Serving and eating tasty food are very important in the African American culture:

> Every vegetable that I have been taught how to cook, you used smoked meats, like smoked ham hocks, smoked neck bones, smoked pork tails and ox tails. It all had a lot of fat in it but it made the food taste good.

> And the foods we like and the way we like to prepare them probably is the one thing that contributes to us being heavier. And so we might not want to give up the taste. Taste is very important to us.

The majority of the women identified "diet monitoring" as a "keep healthy strategy." Diet monitoring activities consisted of activities that would support the women's stated importance of having a healthy eating habits image:

> Well, I try to eat healthy, more fruits and vegetables. I always try to include the basics for eating more nutritiously.

> I don't eat pork. I don't cook in lard or animal fat. And I avoid certain foods that are known to be high-risk foods in our community.

The importance of serving lots of good food and of being a good parent, components of the good parent and hostess self-image, was supported by the following comments:

> I think our value system is tied up a lot in food. In the grocery store, we buy a lot and pay a lot for food. My friends like to come to my house because they know they will have good food to eat. I like serving good food.

> It is important for me to serve my children nutritious food. It is also important for me to be a good role model for them by choosing the right foods to eat.

Weight Control Behavior

Diet control, weight management, and exercise behavior were highly associated at .01 level of significance. The data indicate that the respondents who were managing their weight were more likely to do so by using a combination of diet control and exercise. Respondents involved in diet control were somewhat more likely to exercise. On the strength of the chi-square statistic, the three variables were combined into a single interval-level variable, weight control. This variable was used in subsequent analyses.

Correlations Among Psychosocial Variables and Weight Control Behavior

Listed in Table 8.4 are the major patterns of influence among the self-presentational model's independent and dependent variables that are correlated at the .01, or .05 level of significance. In relation to the self-presentation model, these relationships indicate that weight control behavior is positively and significantly correlated with higher levels of self-efficacy to diet ($r = .27, p < .01$) and exercise ($r = .52, p < .01$), with embracing the self-diet and weight management image ($r = .53, p < .01$), and embracing the image of someone who has healthy eating habits ($r = .38, p < .05$). Therefore, women who adhered to an internal weight control mechanism, had healthy eating habits, and had high levels of diet and exercise efficacy were more likely to participate in higher levels of weight control behavior.

TABLE 8.4 Psychosocial and Behavioral Variables Correlation Matrix†

	1	2	3	4	5	6	7	8	9	10	11	12
1. Physical self-concept	—	.35*	.22	-.34*	.00	.07	.25	-.31	.10	-.38**	-.52**	.27
2. Diet efficacy		—	.50**	-.26	.31	-.04	.42*	-.18	.09	-.24**	-.17	.27
3. Exercise efficacy			—	.05	.42*	.05	.31	.20	-.13	-.03	-.09	.52**
4. Social diet and weight image				—	.33*	.18	.00	.41	-.04	.19*	-.09	.29
5. Self-diet and weight image					—	.05	.29	.09	-.07	.10	-.12	.53**
6. Parenting and hostess image						—	.06	.31	.00	.05	.06	-.09
7. Healthy eating habits image							—	.06	-.11	-.04	-.18	.38*
8. Serves tasty food image								—	-.04	-.02	-.18	-.06
9. Sanctions									—	-.20	-.19	-.17
10. Stress										—	.26**	.01
11. Body mass index											—	-.35**
12. Weight control												—

NOTES: † $n = 45$.
*$p \leq .05$ (2-tailed); **$p \leq .01$.

The data are supported by the women's statements regarding (a) their adherence to an internal, self-defined standard of weight, as opposed to an external standard:

> I think that a lot of people are weight conscious in the sense that we have been told that for the last few years that we should watch our weight. I think that what the difference is that we are not psychologically bound to the need to be thin. We tend to be able to accept a little more meat on our bones.

> I can remember how I was at 130 pounds. I think that is a good weight for me. It feels and I think it looks good. When I look at the textbook, it says that I should weigh less. I think that would be too small. I feel like the weight tables have not been judged on a variety of women. How can you judge everybody by those standards?

(b) their confidence in their ability to engage in weight control behavior:

> I guess it's pretty much internal, inside of me. I feel like I am going to be the one to do what needs to be done. To continue to lose the weight, I know that I have to be the one to really work on the diet and exercise together. And when I make up my mind to do something, I usually do it. I just know I can.

and (c) their desire to want to eat a healthier diet:

> I try to watch what I eat and how I eat. I try not to eat a lot of fried foods. I don't eat a lot of grease in terms of heavy things. I use the light whipped margarine, and I eat yogurt instead of ice cream.

> The problem with that is I find if I don't eat something for lunch, then I am starving by dinnertime and I eat a whole lot, which is not good. So I try to stock up on fruits and things. So when I am home, I have fruits and things to eat during the day. Another problem is that I get hungry at night and I want to snack. So that's why I have fruits and things to snack on.

In this sample of African American women, self-concept approached significance ($r = .27, p < .10$), perhaps indicating that women with higher levels of physical self-concept are more likely to participate in weight control behavior. Further support for this finding was evidenced in the women's responses to the question "What are some benefits of engaging in diet control, weight management, or exercise?" Women identified physical health and mental and emotional health as significant benefits:

> Well, I want to stay healthy and live longer. My cardiovascular status is better.
>
> You feel better about yourself so then you keep running. You see yourself losing weight, so you feel even better about yourself.
>
> I feel happier, more cheerful, I just feel good. It eliminates stress. I have a sense of well-being.

In spite of these perceived health benefits, women who identified physical attractiveness as a benefit of engaging in weight control behavior were more likely to be involved in higher levels of weight control behavior:

> Well, you look more attractive, you have a tighter body. I think that looking good and feeling good are interfaced, and that figures into your self-esteem.

Additional analysis revealed that women with higher BMIs ($r = -.35, p < .01$) were less likely to participate in weight control behavior and more likely to experience stress ($r = .26, p < .01$).

Women reported that time constraints associated with work and family responsibility and life transitional events such as marriage, pregnancy, and graduate school interfered with their ability to engage in weight control behavior. These events usually resulted in women gaining weight:

> I believe that just being in an office, being confined to a space 8 hours a day, has made me more sedentary and that has affected my gaining weight.
>
> I got married in '87. I became more sedentary. We were eating a lot more steady meals. I wasn't used to it. That's when I gained 30 pounds.

Women were experiencing personal stress, as well as occupational stress. In response to the question "What would you say are the major stressors in your life?" many women responded with:

> Probably my family and my job, pregnancy and work, housekeeping responsibilities, and financial constraints.

In response to a similar question about work site stress, the women identified work overload, supervising others, racism, and sexism:

> We are understaffed. I am responsible for counseling and administrative work. My support staff is not very good, and we have a larger caseload than any other center.

> I am frustrated supervising staff that really aren't dedicated and don't do what they are supposed to do. They are constantly making mistakes. I can't do a lot of things I need to get done because I have to constantly go behind them and correct their mistakes. Some of the people are resentful that I am their supervisor.
>
> I mean our center is very racist. I had to make a job change recently because I had a white male over me who felt that I was incompetent and dumb. And things he would try to run by just wouldn't work. I had to go to the "powers that be" and not make it a personal issue—you know, playing politics. I mean I found it very difficult to stay at a place where somebody was kicking my behind and relating to me like I was a peon. Black women have to be very strong. There are lots of reasons why we have to be; one is to survive in two different cultures.
>
> I do experience some stress as a woman because our chairperson is a male and he does not react well to females. He has this sort of chauvinistic attitude. He feels he has to have the last word, everything. I coordinate the programs for the school. We all had agreed that we would have a program on a certain date. I had cleared it on the calendar and took care of all the procedures. Then I come back to find that he had decided to have it on a different day. He had gone behind my back, took a vote, and we were having a program, that I was sponsoring, on a different day.

Stress interfered with the women's ability to initiate and maintain weight control behavior:

> Yeah, I definitely believe some of the stressors I experience that are job related have an effect upon my weight control—specifically because I will eat, enjoy eating. And find myself eating when I am not hungry. I probably do tend to eat more when I am under stress.

Although the sanctions variable was not significant, the negative direction of the relationship ($r = -.17$) supports the proposition that women who experienced a negative sanction for failure were less likely to participate in weight control behavior.

DISCUSSION

The purpose of this analysis was to report the results of the use of a triangulation methodology, guided by the self-presentational conceptual framework, to explore weight control behavior with middle-income African American women. The model, which was adapted for the purposes of this study, was designed to explain psychosocial factors that influence weight control health practices. Although the application of the model was limited in that the size of the sample was small, the triangulation methodology allowed cross-validation of the findings.

The first of the two propositions of the model that received support was that the expected value of a personal claim to an image (self-diet and weight management image) predicts people's relevant behavior (weight control behavior). This congruence between the qualitative and quantitative measurements confirming the importance of the self-diet and weight management image in weight control behavior is evidenced in several ways. Qualitatively, in the area of self-control/self-discipline, descriptions of past and present self-regulatory behavior designed to reduce and avoid weight problems revealed that this group of African American women were primarily motivated by internal cues to engage in weight control behavior. The self-regulatory behavior, weight control, was usually initiated in response to the desire to be physically attractive and to "feel comfortable in their clothes." Although the most attractive image was the self-diet and weight management image, only 30% of the women were engaged in the full range of relevant behavior (diet control, weight management, exercise) to claim the image. The other women were engaged in various levels of the behavior, thereby claiming various levels of the image.

Quantitatively, analysis of Pearson product-moment correlations among the psychosocial and behavioral variables showed a significant correlation between actual weight control and the self-diet and weight management image. The strength of this correlation further supported the notion that the more attractive it was to be a person who controlled diet and weight, the more likely the participation in the weight control behavior.

As a corollary, the majority of the women did not find a social diet and weight management image very attractive, as evidenced by their expressed lack of concern for others' opinions about body weight and their reluctance to accept height and weight information listed in the Metropolitan Life tables. Instead, they used an internal barometer, "weight at which they felt comfortable," to achieve and maintain body weight. This social image may be relatively inconsistent with a self-diet and weight management image. Accepting the social image would involve accepting the opinions of others and external body size criteria, such as media images and a height-weight table. Although the opinions of others marginally influenced weight control behavior, external body size criteria were consistently rejected by the women.

Images have implications, however, for claims to other images that either overlap with them or are wholly or partially subsumed by them (Schlenker, 1980). A significant relationship was found between the social diet and the self-diet and weight management image (see Table 8.4). As indicated, the latter image was more important to the women in this study. This finding is conceptually congruent with the way people develop images. It would be difficult to construct self-images that are not wholly or partially derived from social images.

People who have been overweight most of their lives have a harder time losing and maintaining weight loss because they have never had the image of a normal-weight individual (Millman, 1977). In this study, 50% of the women who were the most overweight had been overweight as children or adolescents or both. As cited earlier, women with higher self-efficacy to diet and exercise were more likely to engage in relevant weight control behaviors. Therefore, some of the women in this study may not have believed that they had the ability to effect change in weight because they lacked childhood-developed self-images to guide them.

The second proposition supported by the data was in the area of self-efficacy: Women who found the self-diet and weight management image more attractive and had higher levels of diet and exercise efficacy were most likely to engage in weight control behavior.

Self-control and commitment are also important factors that operate in self-efficacy performance judgments and outcome expectations. Analysis of interview data underscored the finding that control of behavior related to weight management and commitment to goals were indeed significant issues for the women. Cultural and social structure, however, may constrain images and the resources for claiming them (Crittenden, 1988). In this study, the women identified cultural factors, such as the value of serving and eating good food and the importance of taste, that influence selected images and, thereby, behavior. These factors may affect motivation to claim an image and self-control to maintain behaviors associated with claiming the image. The results of this study suggest that self-efficacy in combination with self-control and commitment may constitute significant necessary components to sustaining weight control behavior.

A new finding in this study was the indirect effect of stress on weight control behavior. Stress was associated with a higher BMI. Whereas a higher BMI was associated with less weight control behavior, Foreyt et al. (1995) found that fluctuations in body weight were associated with higher stress levels. The women in this study were experiencing stressors in their personal and occupational roles. Middle-class African Americans tend to experience higher levels of stress because of racism (Cose, 1993), and for middle-class African American women, both racism and sexism (hooks, 1993; Walcott-McQuigg, 1995a, 1995b). In this study, stress had a dual effect: It interfered with the women's ability to engage in weight control behavior, and it precipitated an increase in eating behavior.

Contrary to expectations, sanctions for failure to claim the image or to engage in the behavior was not significant. Perhaps increasing the number beyond the single item used would have made this measure more sensitive to variation in response. The majority of the women responded to the question with self-imposed emotional-type sanctions such as frustration, guilt, and depression. External sanctions were not significant concerns for this group of women. Several factors could account for the lack of concern: The high prevalence of overweight in the African American community could account for the lack of perception of external sanctions, and African American women tend to accept a larger body size than Caucasian women (Allan et al., 1993; Kumanyika, Wilson, & Guilford-Davenport, 1993).

Also, weight was not perceived as a barrier to dating, dancing, exercising, and sports. Therefore, if women do not perceive overweight as a problem, sanctions for failure to successfully engage in behavior to decrease or eliminate overweight may be minimal. Powell and Kahn (1995) found that African American men were less likely than Caucasian men to report sanctions for dating larger than ideal-size women. Therefore, African American women's significant relationships may not be affected by body weight issues.

The self-presentation model was chosen to provide a theoretical basis for examining psychosocial factors that influence weight control behavior in a group of African American women. Use of the model guided this study, in which triangulation methodology was used to identify the role of attractiveness of various images, self-efficacy to diet and exercise, the self-concept, stress, and sanctions in weight control behavior. Few studies have examined these factors with African American women. The results of this study support findings from other studies on the role of self- and social images, self-efficacy, self-concept, sanctions, and stress in weight control behavior. Women do not accept the body size parameters in the Metropolitan Life tables, media images, and other external criteria and usually adhere to self-images that dictate weight control efforts (Allan, 1988, 1989; Chrisler, 1993; Clarke, 1989; Thomas & James, 1988).

Self-efficacy judgments have consistently predicted weight control behavior in studies measuring its effect (Bandura, 1986; King et al., 1993; Rossi et al., 1995). And the self-concept has shown much fluctuation, with higher levels linked to successful weight control behavior (Mintz & Betz, 1986). Taken together, these factors underscore the importance of the parental role in fostering a self-concept as a normal-weight individual and in facilitating the development of a self-image that includes diet control, weight management, and exercise behavior in childhood. This self-image, then, will be available to the adult to potentiate self-efficacy in diet control, weight management, and exercise behavior.

Recent research has begun to focus on the processes of socialization and cultural effects of attitudes and values on weight control behavior (Thomas, 1995). Efforts to assist African American women in managing their weight must attend to psychosociocultural influences that shape their self-perceptions of appropriate weight management behavior. Nurses and other health professionals need to incorporate techniques to manage both personal and occupational stress, improve judgments of efficacy to manage weight, and increase levels of self-concept into weight management programs.

Further investigations are needed to determine appropriate nursing interventions to assist African American women in developing appropriate weight control images that are consistent with a healthy life. In addition, models (Kumanyika et al., 1992) and methodologies (Banik, 1993) that account for highly complex phenomena such as psychosocial and cultural factors in health promotion/disease prevention behavior should guide the investigations.

REFERENCES

Allan, J. (1988). Knowing what to weigh: Women's self-care activities related to weight. *Advances in Nursing Science, 11*(1), 47-60.

Allan, J. (1989). Women who successfully manage their weight. *Western Journal of Nursing Research, 11*(6), 657-675.

Allan, J. D., Mayo, K., & Michel, Y. (1993). Body size values of white and black women. *Research in Nursing & Health, 16*(5), 323-333.

Bandura, A. (1986). *Social foundations of thought and action: A social cognitive theory.* Upper Saddle River, NJ: Prentice Hall.

Banik, B. J. (1993). Applying triangulation in nursing research. *Applied Nursing Research, 6*, 47-52.

Burns, N., & Groves, S. K. (1993). *The practice of nursing research: Conduct, critique, and utilization* (2nd ed.). Philadelphia: W. B. Saunders.

Carmines, E. G., & Zeller, R. A. (1979). *Reliability and validity assessment.* Beverly Hills, CA: Sage.

Carr, L. T. (1994). The strengths and weaknesses of quantitative and qualitative research: What method for nursing? *Journal of Advanced Nursing, 20*, 716-721.

Chrisler, J. C. (1993, Spring). Feminist perspectives on weight loss therapy. *Journal of Training and Practice in Professional Psychology, 7*(1), 35-48.

Clarke, P. N. (1989). Body weight: Relationship to conversational distance and self-actualization. *Health Care for Women International, 10*, 43-59.

Cohen, S., Kamarck, T., & Mermelstein, R. (1983). A global measure of perceived stress. *Journal of Health and Social Behavior, 24*, 385-396.

Cope, N., & Hall, H. (1985). The health implications for black women in the U.S.: Implications for health psychology. *Sage, 2*(2), 20-24.

Cose, E. (1993). *The rage of a privileged class.* New York: HarperCollins.

Cowman, S. (1993). Triangulation: A means of reconciliation in nursing research. *Journal of Advanced Nursing, 18*, 788-792.

Crittenden, K. (1988, March). *Causal attribution in sociocultural context: Toward a self-presentational theory of attribution processes.* Presidential address to the Midwest Sociological Society.

Croft, J. B., Strogatz, D. S., James, S. A., Keenan, N. L., Ammerman, A. S., Malarcher, A. M., & Haines, P. S. (1992). Socioeconomic and behavioral correlates of body mass index in black adults: The Pitt County Study. *American Journal of Public Health, 82*, 831-826.

Denizen, N. K. (1989). *The research act* (3rd ed.). New York: McGraw-Hill.

Duffy, M. E. (1987). Methodological triangulation: A vehicle for merging quantitative and qualitative research methods. *Image: Journal of Nursing Scholarship, 19*(3), 130-133.

Flegal, K. M., Harlan, W. R., & Landis, J. R. (1988). Secular trends in body mass index and skinfold thickness with socioeconomic factors in young adult women. *American Journal of Clinical Nutrition, 48*, 535-543.

Foreyt, J. P., Brunner, R. L., Goodrick, G. K., Cutter, G., Brownell, K. D., & St. Joer, S. T. (1995). Psychological correlates of weight fluctuation. *International Journal of Eating Disorders, 17*(3), 263-275.

hooks, B. (1993). *Sisters of the yam: Black women and self-recovery.* Boston: South End.

Kahn, H. S., & Williamson, D. F. (1991). Is race associated with weight change in U.S. adults after adjustment for income, education, and marital factors? *American Journal of Clinical Nutrition, 53*, 1566S-1570S.

King, A. C., Blair, S. N., Bild, D. E., Dishman, R. K., Dubbert, P. M., Marcus, B. H., Oldridge, N. B., Paffenbarger, R. S., Jr., Powell, K. E., & Yeager, K. K. (1993). Determinants of physical activity and interventions in adults. *Medicine and Science in Sports and Exercise, 24*, S221-S236.

Knafl, K. A., Pettengill, M. M., Bevis, M. E., & Kirchoff, K. T. (1988). Blending qualitative and quantitative approaches to instrument development and data collection. *Journal of Professional Nursing, 4*, 30-37.

Kuczmarski, R. S., Flegal, K. M, Campbell, S. M., & Johnson, C. L. (1994). Increasing prevalence of overweight among U.S. adults: The national health and nutrition examination surveys, 1960 to 1991. *Journal of the American Medical Association, 272*, 205-211.

Kumanyika, S. (1993). Special issues regarding obesity in minority populations. *Annals of Internal Medicine, 119*, 650-654.

Kumanyika, S., Morssink, C., & Augurs, T. (1992). Models for dietary weight change in African American women: Identifying cultural components. *Ethnicity & Disease, 2*, 166-175.

Kumanyika, S., Wilson, J. F., & Guilford-Davenport, M. (1993). Weight-related attitudes and behaviors of black women. *Journal of the American Dietetic Association, 93*, 416-422.

Lincoln, Y. S., & Guba, E. G. (1985). *Naturalistic inquiry.* Beverly Hills, CA: Sage.

Metropolitan Life Foundation. (1983). *Height and weight tables.* New York: Metropolitan Life Insurance Company.

Meyer, J., & Stunkard, A. J. (1993). Genetics and human obesity. In A. J. Stunkard & T. A. Wadden (Eds.), *Obesity: Theory and therapy* (2nd ed.). New York: Raven.

Miles, M., & Huberman, A. (1994). *An expanded sourcebook: Qualitative data analysis.* Thousand Oaks, CA: Sage.

Millman, M. (1977). *Such a pretty face: Being fat in America.* New York: Norton.

Mintz, L. B., & Betz, N. E. (1986). Sex differences in the nature, realism, and correlates of body image. *Sex Roles, 15,* 185-195.

Mitchell, E. L. (1986). Multiple triangulation: A methodology for nursing science. *Advances in Nursing Science, 8*(3), 18-26.

Myers, S. T., & Haase, J. E. (1989). Guidelines for integration of quantitative and qualitative approaches. *Nursing Research, 38*(5), 299-301.

National Institutes of Health. (1985). Health implications of obesity (Consensus Development Conference statement). *Annals of Internal Medicine, 103,* 1073-1077.

Norusis, M. J. (1990). *SPSS guide to data analysis for release 4.1.* Chicago: SPSS.

Nunnally, J. (1978). *Psychometric theory.* New York: McGraw-Hill.

Powell, A. D., & Kahn, A. S. (1995). Racial differences in women's desires to be thin. *International Journal of Eating Disorders, 17*(2), 191-195.

Roid, G. H., & Fitts, W. H. (1989). *Tennessee Self-Concept Scale: Revised manual.* Los Angeles: Western Psychological Services.

Rossi, J. S., Rossi, S. R., Velicer, W. F., & Prochaska, J. O. (1995). Motivational readiness to control weight. In D. B. Allison (Ed.), *Methods for the assessment of eating behaviors and weight-related problems.* Thousand Oaks, CA: Sage.

Sallis, J. F., Pinski, R. B., Grossman, R. M., Patterson, T. L., & Nader, P. L. (1988). The development of self-efficacy scales for health-related diet and exercise behaviors. *Health Education Research: Theory & Practice, 3*(3), 283-292.

Schlenker, B. R. (1980). *Impression management: The self-concept, social identity, and interpersonal relations.* Pacific Grove, CA: Brooks/Cole.

Seidel, J. V., Kjolseth, R., & Seymour, E. (1995). *The Ethnograph: A user's guide* (Version 4.0). Littleton, CO: Qualis Research Associates.

Thomas, P. R. (Ed.). (1995). *Weighing the options: Criteria for evaluating weight-management programs.* Washington, DC: National Academy Press.

Thomas, V. G., & James, M. D. (1988). Body image, dieting tendencies, and sex role traits in urban black women. *Sex Roles, 18*(9/10), 523-529.

Van Italie, T. B., & Lew, E. A. (1993). Estimation of the effect of obesity on health and longevity: A perspective for the physician. In A. J. Stunkard & T. A. Wadden (Eds.), *Obesity: Theory and therapy* (2nd ed., pp. 219-230). New York: Raven.

Walcott-McQuigg, J. A. (1992). *Self-presentation and minority women: Exploring psychosocial factors that influence health practices of African American women.* Unpublished doctoral dissertation, University of Illinois, Chicago.

Walcott-McQuigg, J. A. (1995a). The relationship between stress and weight control behavior in African American women. *Journal of the National Medical Association, 87*(6), 427-432.

Walcott-McQuigg, J. A. (1995b). Work site stress: Gender and cultural diversity issues. *AAOHN, 43*(5), 1-6.

Walcott-McQuigg, J. A., Sullivan, J., Dan, A., & Logan, B. (1995). Psychosocial factors influencing weight control behavior in African American women. *Western Journal of Nursing Research, 17*(5), 502-520.

Williamson, D. F., Kahn, H. S., & Byers, T. (1991). The 10-year incidence of obesity and major weight gain in black and white U.S. women aged 30 to 55 years. *American Journal of Clinical Nutrition, 53,* 1515S-1518S.

9

WHERE HAVE ALL THE NICE OLD LADIES GONE?

Researching the Health Information-Seeking Behavior of Older African American Women

CLAUDIA J. GOLLOP

hen Sadie and Bessie Delany gained national public attention around 1990, few people, if any, were less than inspired by not only their rather amazing longevity but also their unconquerable spirit, keen wit, and sharp intelligence. Later, in 1993, when their book *Having Our Say: The Delany Sisters' First 100 Years*, which chronicled their fascinating lives, was published, even more people felt energized by them (Delany, 1993). The book was then adapted for the theater and ultimately found its way to the Broadway stage. The Delany sisters, at 100-plus years of age, had withstood the tests of time and, in return, had tested time itself. To many, they exemplified the positive possibilities of old age as clear-minded, healthy, energetic centenarians. Who would not wish to be so fortunate?

Clearly, people are living longer. Because of changes in lifestyle and advances in medicine and technology, life expectancy has increased greatly during the 20th century. According to demographic projections, more than 100,000 people over the age of 100 will be living in the United States by the year 2000. The percentage of persons over the age of 65 is increasing at an unprecedented rate, and population predictions indicate that, by the year 2020, an unheard of 16.5% of the U.S. population will be 65 years of age or older. According to the 1990 census figures, older adults made up approximately 12.6% of the population, with persons 85 years and over leading as the fastest growing age-group in the country (U.S. Bureau of the Census, 1993). These figures are indeed extraordinary, given the fact that, in 1900, the average life expectancy was approximately 47 years for the general population. At that same time, however, African Americans and other minorities could expect to live an average of 33 years (U.S. Bureau of the Census, 1975).

African American have also benefited from improvements in environmental structures and health care delivery, if in some instances to a lesser degree. Fortunately, the gap has narrowed considerably where life expectancies for African Americans and whites are concerned. Today, the life expectancy for whites is approximately 76 years, whereas for blacks, it is about 72 years.

African American women, however, are at higher risk for morbidity and mortality for such diseases as hypertension, coronary artery disease, and certain types of cancer than the general population. In addition, they often receive health care later and, once admitted, experience longer hospital stays than the average older patient.

This chapter stems from a study that explored the ways older black women receive health information (Gollop, 1993). Historically, this subject has received very little research attention. More must be known about this group and their health information needs, however, if adequate information and the appropriate channels for information dissemination are to be created to serve them. It has been acknowledged in the literature that issues of health may be perceived differently among various racial and ethnic groups (Markides, 1989; Wolinsky et al., 1989). Consequently, further research is needed to determine how best to deliver consumer health information to aging African American women who are in pursuit of protecting and maintaining their health. This point is carried further by Edmonds (1990):

> The health care needs of Black aged women can be better understood if more is known about: (1) their unique characteristics, (2) their own self-perceptions of their health status, (3) factors that account for their health care utilization patterns, and (4) the consequences of their illness behavior. (p. 206)

As such, this work does not fall into the category of narrative research as it may be strictly defined. The stories and insights shared by participants during the time spent with them presented additional results, similar to those often gleaned during some types of qualitative research, such as oral narratives, though not as extensively. I continue this chapter, first, with relevant background of the study, and then with selected outcomes. Next, I present comments of some participants, and finally conclude with some thoughts on the women many of us think we know—the nice little old ladies.

The interest in aging and in the various aspects of the aging process is intensifying. It seems that more books on the subject are being published than ever before (Friedan, 1993; Hayflick, 1994; Manheimer, 1995). This may be attributable, in part, to the fact that the "baby boom" generation is fast approaching older adulthood. With their numbers at roughly 75 million, "boomers" increasingly are a topic of concern regarding the political, social, and economic impact the "age wave" of unknown proportions, expected to be created by them, will have on the country.

Among the major concerns of researchers and policymakers is health care and how to prepare, or rather refashion, the current health care system to serve the multitude of older persons who will begin to emerge within about 15 years. My concern as a researcher was focused on consumer health information as a means of health promotion and disease prevention, which may, in fact, help some older people, particularly older African American women, maintain their own physical well-being and keep others out of the much-talked-about health care maze longer.

At some level, this topic may interest other African American women of all ages. Black women who are members of the baby boom generation and who are facing older womanhood and some of the health issues associated with aging may be especially interested. However, younger women who may find themselves in the role of caregiver for older female relatives, which has been indicated in the literature as a regular occurrence (Chatters, Taylor, & Jackson, 1985), may also wish to give some thought to health preservation issues.

Currently, I hold a particular interest in this topic, but that was not always the case. This chapter is based on my dissertation research. In some ways, I tend to think that the topic chose me, instead of the other way around. As a graduate student assistant, I worked on a project that involved searching for and retrieving information related to black women's health concerns and the social, political, and economic issues related to those concerns. Soon after I began working on this project, it was suggested that some phase of this would make an interesting dissertation topic. Initially, I was somewhat repulsed by and disinterested in the subject as a possible research topic. This, of course, turned out to be a temporary rejection. It didn't take long for me to understand some of the reasons for my fairly strong and visceral reaction to the notion of exploring this topic further. As a 40-something African American woman, I would be forced to possibly face my own future and look at some of those same health concerns that continue to plague many black women each year—hypertension, diabetes, obesity, cardiovascular disease, and cancer—and that, in too many cases, usher in a premature ending to their lives. The fact that I had personally witnessed the deaths of both of my grandmothers as the result of cancer, one of whom had also begun a small battle with hypertension and diabetes years earlier, made the thought of investigating this topic all the more disturbing. The notion of pursuing a research topic that revolved around older African American women and their acquisition of possibly life-saving consumer health information was not simply unnerving and depressing to me in the abstract. In this case, the topic itself had a real face to it—two faces, in fact—that I would have to look into. Would this be too real to maintain any level of objective distance? Would the process be painful? If so, would that create some negative behavior on my part that could alter the research process or its outcome in some way?

As a researcher in training, these may have been the proper queries to pose to myself, but they were mostly unwarranted. Then, I began to think about the subject at length and in depth, and within about a week's time I started to view it very differently and to believe that it would be an important undertaking. I had been a professional librarian, an information specialist, for well over a decade and knew the value of information. In addition, I have always felt very strongly about the availability of and access to information, including health information. It was not long before my interest in the topic grew on several levels, and it seemed to become something of a part of me. In the end, I realized that this was a "new" topic—that, indeed, the subject of the health information-seeking behavior of urban, older, African American women had not been explored in the literature and I was going to be the one to get the ball rolling. I also realized that both of my grandmothers would have been proud of me for doing so.

OVERVIEW OF THE STUDY

The study on which much of this chapter is based explored the ways urban, older, black women acquire health information and some factors that influence those activities. Aside from the age factor, among the other possible determinants, or independent variables, examined were education, self-perceived literacy, mass media use, mobility, and library use. After some synthesizing, four research questions were designed to address the above-stated independent variables: (a) From what sources do older African American women in urban areas seek health information? (b) What factors influence health information-seeking behavior? (c) What role, if any, do the mass media play in the provision of health information? and (e) Does the public library in an urban area have a role to play in the health information-seeking behavior of older black women?

The sample consisted of 45 older African American women living in Pittsburgh, Pennsylvania. At each location, the site coordinator screened potential participants for eligibility regarding age and ability, as well as interest and willingness to participate. For the purposes of this research, *older* refers to persons over the age of 65. All persons agreeing to participate in the study were required to be at least age 65. However, I should note that one participant who was referred to me as being age eligible, when asked, gave her age as 63 even though I was told by the site intermediary that she was actually 65.

Over approximately 5 months, I conducted face-to-face interviews by using a structured interview instrument. The interviews were carried out in three separate neighborhoods in Pittsburgh: Oakland, Homewood, and the Hill District. This was done in an effort to determine whether any appreciable demographic differences existed among the residents of those three areas. In addition to the three communities, the participants were interviewed in three different types of settings: in their homes—an apartment building designed for older adults and people with disabilities (Oakland); in a community-based ambulatory care medical center (Homewood); and in a recreational community center serving primarily African American older adults (Hill District).

It is a well-known fact that face-to-face interviews can be inherently unpredictable. Time is often an issue. Any number of mishaps can wreak havoc with a researcher's schedule. For example, as indicated by the results of the pilot research, I planned to spend approximately 35 to 40 minutes in each interview. During the regular data collection phase, I found that I spent more time than I had anticipated with each participant. In fact, in most cases, interviews ran $1\frac{1}{2}$ to 2 hours long. In this case, however, the "extra" time spent proved to be a positive development. Respondents seemed to relax more and to speak more freely, which allowed them to expand on their answers and allowed me to place their responses into some sort of context.

SELECTED RESULTS

The mean age of the sample was 73.7 years, with participants ranging from 65 to 88 years of age. The mean level of education attained was the 11th grade, with the highest grade completed spanning from the 6th grade to master's degree. Also, a clear majority perceived themselves as being average or above average readers (73.3%). The findings suggest that respondents receive health information from various sources, including their physicians, the mass media, and members of their social networks. The breakdown in order of highest-rated source was television, 86.7%; people (including physicians), 73.3%; magazines, 65.9%; newspapers, 53.7%; books, 35.0%; and radio, 33.3%. In addition, the majority of those interviewed believed that they had a great deal of control over their health.

One objective of the study was to determine whether the public library currently does or could play a part in the acquisition of health information among this group. The results indicate that members of this group (97.8%) have a very positive opinion of the public library and the likelihood it would contain health information they could use, although a much smaller segment used the library regularly (24.4%). Consequently, it may be in the interest of the public library to investigate the role it could play in providing consumer health information to older African American women.

BEYOND THE MYTHS

First some truths. The literature reveals that although black women are at high risk for contracting various illnesses and disabilities, the health status of older black women is further threatened by what is frequently referred to as "triple jeopardy"—that is, the three conditions of being aged, black, and female in the United States. A fourth condition should not be ignored: being poor. According to 1990 census data, 60.5% of black women in this age-group live below the poverty line (U.S. Bureau of the Census, 1991). Poverty can have extremely damaging effects as it relates to the health status of older African Americans. The profound lack of educational and employment opportunities, perpetuated by widespread discriminatory practices in the United States, barred minorities and women from socioeconomic advancement. Thus, many older African American women, whose earning power was usually lower than that of men during their respective years of employment, often live at the poverty line or below in later years. This comes at a time in their lives when it is least affordable because many of them are no longer able to work and often find themselves in need of medical care well beyond their means.

As mentioned earlier, the average age of the participants was approximately 74, with no one being younger than 65. This statistic means that all the women were members of what some demographers call the "Depression generation." They had experienced, at some level, the negative impact of the Great Depression of the 1930s. And as African Americans, during one of the most difficult periods in the nation's history, they had to survive the discriminatory social and political hardships of the day, in addition to the economic ones.

In addition to growing up during the Great Depression, thousands of African American women in this age category were also part of the "great migration" from several of the Southern states. People moved to the large cities of the United States in search of a better way of life in what many hoped would be the "promised land." They were in search of a more socially and politically tolerant environment, as well as more humane employment conditions. It is now known that although many found the living and working environments to be improvements over some of the harsher conditions under which they had lived prior to migrating, they continued to encounter racial prejudice and to hold lower social and economic status than that of the general population.

One might easily conclude that these individuals, whose personal histories reflect such oppressive living conditions, might end up bitter, broken, and spiritless. I found the situation among the participants interviewed to be much to the contrary. The above facts notwithstanding, older African American women also have a reputation for perseverance in the face of adversity.

The face-to-face interviews gave me access to other forms of "data" that provided an added dimension to the research at hand. For example, the ability to observe nonverbal characteristics such as facial expressions, gestures, and other movements can influence the impression the researcher gets. In addition, variations in voice tone, as well as wholly unexpected comments, may be observed and noted during the in-person interview. That aspect of this undertaking helped breathe life into what could have been a rather sterile research experience.

While conducting the interviews, in many of the cases, not only were comments made in addition to the direct answer to the question being posed, but sometimes lengthy "side conversations" or "side chats" took place. Sometimes these unanticipated narratives or side chats were related to the question being asked; at other times, I would be on the receiving end of a question about such things as my family background or my hometown. For example:

Respondent: You aren't from around here, are you?
Me: No, ma'am, I'm not.
Respondent: I thought so. You don't sound like you do. Where are you from?
Me: I am from New York City.
Respondent: New York City! I've been to New York before. I like it there. And you like it here?

But on most occasions, the women I spoke with would talk about themselves, the different aspects of their lives or experiences they had had. I cannot say with any certainty exactly when, during the interview, comments or side chats were more likely to happen. It is very possible that I was unaware of the fact that maybe some questions served as conversational prompts of some kind. I do not believe that any deeply guarded secrets were being revealed. But I did get the feeling that a message was almost always being conveyed to me that these women did not want to be mistaken for simply a cold, hard statistic. They knew they were participating in a research project. Several of them had done so before. But they wanted to ensure somehow that they also were seen as people of substance. There was more to these women than I could see on the surface, and although I cannot be entirely certain about this, in my estimation they seemed to be trying to tell me so through some of those side chats.

These side chats had some distinguishing factors, however. For example, they seemed to occur most readily and tended to last longest when the interview took place in the homes of the respondents. Perhaps the fact that I was on their "turf" and they had some control over the scheduling of the interviews may account for this difference. Nonetheless, a few lengthy side conversations transpired at all locations, even during telephone interviews (five interviews were conducted over the telephone when it was discovered that a prospective interviewee had other time commitments and was unable to complete the interview session).

In one case, when I asked one participant, "How often do you discuss health issues with family and friends?" her response was, "Rarely," and then she said that her family had their own problems. She had family members whom she seemed to care a lot about, but past life events made her feel that no one among them would be able to handle a very important event the way she thought it ought to be handled. She then said that most of them [family] were doing the best they could with their lives but that she really could not depend on them. With that understanding, she had found a sense of security in having made all the arrangements for her own funeral, when the time came. I was struck by this high-energy, feisty, 75-year-old woman who talked about having chosen the undertaker, the coffin, and the grave site. She began to describe the design of her shroud; details I did not record, not only because they were not relative to the interview but also because I was simply stunned by the calm and resolve with which this woman spoke. She had only to select and begin paying for her headstone, something she was going to do shortly. Later during the interview, when we discussed issues around health, she mentioned, in a rather enthusiastic tone, that she participates in an exercise class about three times a week in an attempt to keep her weight and blood pressure under control. She seemed quite focused on living a healthful life. But she was also preparing for the inevitable. I still think of that session with not a little amazement.

When I asked one of the younger women in the sample, a soft-spoken 66-year-old, whether she worked, she said that she did and that she continued to work, not only for the money, which she did need, but also because she "likes to keep busy and get out in the street and do things." She was very interested in health information because she had suffered several life-threatening illnesses herself even though this was not a fact easily drawn from simply looking at her. In addition to hypertension and arthritis, she was a cancer survivor and currently had, at times, severe bouts of asthma, to the point of having portable oxygen canisters delivered to her home regularly. Despite that, she paid particular attention to her appearance. She was almost glamorous, with well-styled auburn hair, makeup applied nearly perfectly, and fingernails manicured. It seemed that she had refused to let life's setbacks defeat her.

When another respondent was asked about the amount of contact and the means of contact (in-person, telephone, other) she had with family members, she responded, "Couple of times a week and mostly by telephone." Then, unexpectedly, she pointed to a small picture on a table and said that it was of her husband. He had passed away several years earlier, but she still missed him greatly. She told me, proudly, that she didn't think many women ever have a husband like hers. He had been much older than she, and they married when she was very young.

Then she added with a sad smile, "He help raise me. He was like a father and a husband to me." This shy, somewhat frail woman seemed determined to bring something of her memory of her late husband to our session, and she seemed to become more at ease when she did so.

During an interview at one of the other sites, I asked an 80-year-old participant about the highest grade she had completed in school. After taking a while to answer the question, she said that she had a master's degree. Then she went on to say that she was educated to become a reading clinician but that the board of education, because of its discriminatory practices, would never place her in such a position. "This is a racist city, or at least it was then," she said. She later returned to school and was certified as a school librarian and was placed in an area high school as the librarian, the position from which she retired. She expressed measurable frustration as a result of those negative experiences. She said, "I have suffered from depression for quite some time, but now I am being treated for it."

Probably the longest interview session took place in the apartment of a very active 82-year-old woman. She was head matron or "church mother" at her church, held an executive position within her sorority, and did volunteer work with various church-related groups. In addition, she taught arts and crafts and even sold some of her creations, such as Christmas ornaments and specialty stuffed dolls. She told me that she left school after the eighth grade to help her mother, who worked as a housekeeper. Most times, she would accompany her mother to work and help out with the cooking and sewing. Then she said, "Do you like dolls?" Before I could answer, she picked up a nearby doll and brought it to my attention. She went on to say that neither she nor any of her siblings ever received toys or dolls for Christmas when she was a child because there was no money for such things. "All I ever wanted was a doll baby," she said. "But I never got one." So, she began to buy them for herself whenever she was able. I told her that I thought the doll was very nice, especially its dress. Then she pointed out a nearly life-size black doll, which was clearly special to her. It was located out of view, so she brought it out to me to see. "This doll is nearly 100 years old," she said. It was a delicate-looking doll outfitted in, to my mind, a beautiful little dress. She seemed to really want to tell this story, so I didn't deter her. She said that she had made the dress the black doll was wearing and that she makes all of her dolls' clothes.

This woman admired the ideal of education and said that she wished she could have gone farther in school. Instead, she had to go to work with her mother. But, at least, she added, "I learned to sew, and that has helped me a lot." Needless to say, I found this participant and her story very intriguing. And although I understand that choosing favorites while conducting research should be avoided, this one has, for some reason, become mine.

An unexpected personal experience of conducting these interviews was that more than half the women expressed a sense of pride on knowing that I was pursuing a doctorate. Some treated me in nearly affectionate ways and repeated over again how nice it was to see a "young" woman like me getting my education at that level. On several occasions, I was invited, even urged, to contact them after the study was over to let them know "how things turned out." Following one interview, the respondent called to say that she was praying for me and wished me well. Another sent me a Christmas card. Thus, it appears that the image of the nice little old lady still stands.

In truth, it is not uncommon to hear terms such as *generous, grandmotherly, kind, caring, sweet, helpful, a great cook,* and *master spoiler of grandchildren* being used in the description of older women. One might ask, Is it really harmful or even unfair to describe members of this population in those ways? Probably not. It should not be assumed, however, that this description implies a cohort of women who are dependent, unaware, or uninformed. The sole mental picture conjured up when people think of women in this age-group should not be one that also overlooks other characteristics, such as those exemplified by the savvy, vigor, and determination of the older African American women interviewed in the study.

Those terms might aptly be used also to describe the 82-year-old doll collector mentioned above. In the process of conducting a follow-up study at the residential site, I was told that this earlier participant no longer resided there. As it also happened, she had found time in her already full schedule to maintain an amorous relationship with a man she had met at church. I remain inspired to report that, within less than a year following the interview, after a brief engagement, the two were married. But not before certain arrangements were made that satisfied some of *her* needs and wishes. For one thing, although they both thought her apartment was too small to accommodate them and the belongings accumulated over two lifetimes, she was not interested in moving into *his* house because, she said, it was too big for her to clean. This issue had, in fact, delayed the wedding for nearly a year. Eventually, he made other arrangements regarding the house, and they settled their mutual space concerns by moving into a larger apartment, which they both approved of, in a new building complex.

In learning that most of these women were interested in health issues so that they could have some control over their lives and their physical well-being, this researcher learned how they not only survived but also thrived between visits to the doctor. For example, one 79-year-old said she read a lot about health because, "You've got to keep up with the times." She then made an interesting observation: "I don't think that doctors were prepared for all these older people living so long. They don't know what to do with them."

Furthermore, although almost no one in this study was without at least one physical complaint or health concern, most women surrendered only as much time to their respective illnesses as was absolutely necessary. A case in point: One 86-year-old who volunteered as a floor monitor at her residence, checking on less active neighbors to see whether they were all right or needed anything, said, "I don't let things conquer me."

These and other observations, some less dramatic than others, placed this research and my perceptions of the lives of these older African American women in perspective. It is true that, over the coming decades, longevity similar to that of the Delany sisters will occur far more frequently and that policymakers and researchers across all disciplines are preparing for the population shift that is destined to create major changes for many of the nation's political and social institutions. For my part, I remain interested in consumer health information research issues as they may relate to older people in general, and more specifically to older African American women, as well as in other segments of the population that may benefit most from the availability of such information but who may be the least likely to be in possession of it.

As mentioned earlier, a structured interview instrument was used in this study, the results of which proved to be informative and very useful. Often, however, those unplanned, uninitiated, and unexpected side chats, not always relative to the study, were most enlightening and are still treasured. They are treasured because they enhanced the entire research experience. The women allowed me a glimpse into their lives, their selves, as they presented me with some thoughtful and thought-provoking responses. Sometimes it was a look at an exceptional characteristic, a skill, or some other part of them that gave me pause. Nice little old ladies? Yes. But they were so much more than the impressions summoned up by the stereotypical images of them. They were each different from the next, but all had character, intelligence, a sense of self, and their own brand of poise—artfully honed quirks and idiosyncrasies that made them who they are.

I remain encouraged by several of the observations made and lessons learned during this work, one of which suggests that it is time to share some of the traditional images of older African American women with other images that speak of women who are still women through and through, simply older. The long-standing descriptions, in my estimation, beg to be reexamined—not necessarily to dismiss the customary, sweeping portrayals of older African American women, but to help all of us realize that some of the nice little old ladies that many people think they know can also be described as fiercely independent, unorthodox, and adventurous, for starters.

REFERENCES

Chatters, L. M., Taylor, R. J., & Jackson, J. S. (1985). Size and composition of the informal helper networks of elderly blacks. *Journal of Gerontology, 40,* 605-614.

Delany, S. (1993). *Having our say: The Delany sisters' first 100 years.* New York: Kodansha America.

Edmonds, M. M. (1990). The health of the black aged female. In Z. Harel, E. A. McKinney, & M. Williams (Eds.), *Black aged: Understanding diversity and service needs* (pp. 205-220). Newbury Park, CA: Sage.

Friedan, B. (1993). *The fountain of age.* New York: Simon & Schuster.

Gollop, C. J. (1993). Health information-seeking behavior of urban, older, African American women. (Doctoral dissertation, University of Pittsburgh, 1993). *Dissertations Abstracts International.*

Hayflick, L. (1994). *How and why we age.* New York: Ballantine.

Manheimer, R. (1995). *Second middle age.* Detroit: Visible Ink.

Markides, K. S. (1989). Aging, gender, race/ethnicity, class, and health: A conceptual overview. In K. S. Markides (Ed.), *Aging and health: Perspectives on gender, race, ethnicity, and class* (pp. 9-21). Newbury Park, CA: Sage.

U.S. Bureau of the Census. (1975). *Historical statistics of the United States: Colonial times to 1970, Part 1.* Washington, DC: Government Printing Office.

U.S. Bureau of the Census. (1991). *Population profile of the United States* (Current Population Reports, Special Studies Series P-23, No. 173). Washington, DC: Government Printing Office.

U.S. Bureau of the Census. (1993). *Current population reports: Population estimates by age, sex, race, and Hispanic origin: 1980-1991* (Series P-25). Washington, DC: Government Printing Office.

Wolinsky, F. D., Aguirre, B. E., Fann, L. J., Keith, V. M., Arnold, C. L., Niederhause, J. C., & Dietrich, K. (1989). Ethnic differences in the demand for physician and hospital utilization among older adults in major American cities: Conspicuous evidence of considerable inequalities. *Milbank Quarterly, 67,* 412-449.

10

AFRICAN AMERICAN WOMEN AND THE EMERGENCE OF SELF-WILL

The Use of Phenomenological Research

ELIZABETH A. PETERSON

INTRODUCTION: BLACK WOMEN AND NARRATIVE RESEARCH

The words of Maya Angelou (1989, p. 2) very clearly describe a quality that has long been considered an attribute of African American women:

> Black women whose ancestors were brought to the United States beginning in 1619 have lived through conditions of cruelties so horrible, so bizarre, the women had to re-invent themselves.
>
> They had to find safety and sanctity inside themselves or they would not have been able to tolerate those tortuous lives. They had to learn to be self-forgiving quickly, for often their exterior exploits were at odds with their interior beliefs. Still they had to survive as wholly and healthily as possible in an infectious and sick climate.

The ability of black women not only to survive conditions of great adversity but also to actually find strength and courage to succeed despite

---

AUTHOR'S NOTE: Quotations from Elizabeth Peterson, *African American Women: A Study of Will and Succes*, 1992, © McFarland & Company, are used with permission.

the adversity was the focus of my research. Being a black woman myself, I had grown up hearing the traditional stereotypes: "Black women are strong." "Black women are the heart and soul of the black community." "If it were not for the faith and the strength of the black woman, we would not have survived as a people." I, like many others, took these generalizations as facts. All the black women I knew were strong, and I soon realized that nothing less was expected of me. I learned at a very young age not to expect the world to be especially kind to me—that as a black female, I would experience the cruelty of racism, prejudice, and discrimination based solely on the color of my skin. Racism was considered a challenge that had to be dealt with by all black people; I was no exception. Like many of my sisters, I accepted the fact that, for me, life would be "no crystal stair" (Hughes, 1959).

The stereotype of the strong-willed black woman has been a double-edged sword. If used as a compliment, it is, in fact, recognizing the resilience, the fortitude of character that many black women seem to possess. But often it has been used to depict a "super" woman who can make it on her own, who does not need the same kind of nurturing and support that other "more feminine" women need. This is not the case, and this perception can be devastating because those who believe it feel no obligation to reach out to those women who are struggling to survive. Therefore, it is important to "search for a deeper understanding of the strong will of black woman, to understand how black women in the past had the courage to confront their conditions and overcome the barriers to their greatness" (Peterson, 1992, p. 2).

USING NARRATIVE RESEARCH

Narrative research makes it possible for the researcher to know an experience in the same way that the subject knows it. Unlike survey research, in which the subject responds only to the questions the researcher thinks are important, the subject in narrative research shares the details he or she thinks are important. To better understand how the experiences of black women influence the development of self-will, one has to be willing to accept the authenticity of their lives as they remember it. The stories that black women tell about themselves can be a rich resource for the researcher. These stories (both factual and fictional) provide little clues that enable the researcher to recognize the essential structures for the development of self-will.

Phenomenological Method

The study of a human phenomenon, such as the will, requires a methodology that enables the researcher to explore the phenomenon as it manifests itself in human consciousness (Peterson, 1992, p. 23).

> Phenomenology is, in the 20th century, mainly the name for a philosophical movement whose primary objective is the direct investigation and description of phenomena as consciously experienced, without theories about their causal explanation and as free as possible from unexplained preconceptions and presuppositions. (Stanage, 1987, p. 43)

Heidegger (1962) wrote that *phenomenology* roughly translates to "let that which shows itself be seen from itself in the very way in which it shows itself" (p. 58). Simply put, it means "to the things themselves!" Therefore, anything in our existence can be scrutinized as it first appears in our consciousness, the way we as humans first experience it. This methodology assumes that all human phenomena have meaning only because we, as humans, feel, experience, and then commit to consciousness the phenomena. Those phenomena then become part of a repertoire of experience. When we encounter the phenomena again, we respond to them on the basis of the feelings the experiences hold for us. "We create meaning in our world not by the things alone, but by our experiences with the things, the object world." By reflecting on our experiences, we can flesh out the processes of awareness that usually remain hidden and "see again" the phenomena as they emerge (Peterson, 1992, p. 24).

Herbert Spiegelberg (1982, pp. 25-26) outlined seven steps, or phases, for phenomenological research:

1. *Investigating particular phenomena.* This step has three operations:
   a. *Intuiting the phenomena.* This involves carefully focusing attention on the phenomena while remaining sensitive to variations in the phenomena that may have been hidden before.
   b. *Analyzing the phenomena.* This involves examining the phenomena in relation to other phenomena (a sorting process) to determine whether what has been intuited so far is actually a true representation of the phenomena.
   c. *Describing the phenomena.* This involves carefully producing specific examples of the phenomena.
2. *Investigating general essences.* From the descriptions of the phenomena in Step 1, particulars are drawn out to be further reflected upon. One might ask, What are the similarities in the examples of the phenomena

that have been produced and reflected upon? Which examples and descriptions can be grouped together?

3. *Apprehending essential relationships.* This step is used to determine what is absolutely essential to the phenomena. This step requires use of the free imaginative variations to separate what is absolutely essential from what is relatively essential of somewhat related, but not essential, to the phenomena.
4. *Watching for modes of appearing.* Here, what appears in consciousness and how it actually appears is explored. An object or concept does not always appear as a whole. Sometimes, as perspectives change, different aspects of the phenomena become visible. Sometimes the phenomena never fully present themselves, but may remain obscured in a fog or haze.
5. *Exploring the constitution of phenomena in consciousness.* This step is used to disclose the typical structure of the phenomena by examining the steps by which they are formed in consciousness. What pattern do they take on as they develop in the person's consciousness?
6. *Suspending belief in existence.* Here is where all presuppositions and beliefs of the observer are "bracketed off." This allows for further intuiting, analysis, and description of the phenomena.
7. *Interpreting the phenomena.* This final step involves the hermeneutic interpretation of the meaning of the phenomena. The goal is to discover meaning that may not be directly discernible.

The seven steps are not fixed. Researchers are free to eliminate some of them. Spiegelberg suggests that all phenomenologists use the first four steps. These steps are reflexive in nature. The researcher intuits the phenomena, analyzes the phenomena, describes the phenomena, brackets off assumptions, and then the cycle repeats.

In the study of self-will, I was particularly interested in the last stage of the phenomenological method. According to Spiegelberg, many phenomenologists do not choose to follow through to this stage. Hermeneutic interpretation, however, is embedded in African American culture. African American storytellers, teachers, and preachers have traditionally relied on their skills of interpretation to communicate complex ideas to their listeners. The ability of a speaker to "break it down" is considered a gift. With this in mind, the purpose of this study was not only to analyze the phenomena as an intellectual exercise but also to put all of the experiences of the women together and create the exemplary strong-willed woman. The woman who emerged from the interpretation would be a woman whom each subject recognized as being herself.

Getting to the point of interpretation is a challenge. Although the steps of phenomenology appear to be simple on paper, they are very complex. In fact, the only way you can learn to do this kind of research is to enter the process. You constantly wonder whether you are doing what you are supposed to do. One thing that helped focus this study was the fact that the objective was not for me to do anything with the data, but rather to let the women be heard. My purpose was to listen to the life stories of my subjects and to note the common threads in all of them. I had to trust my subjects—that the authentic voices of the women were being heard; and they had to trust me as the researcher—that I would report my findings truthfully. One of the real difficulties in doing this type of research is that, often, as an African American woman myself, I felt drawn into these women's lives. So much of their history seemed to parallel my own. I had to be very careful to report what the women said, as opposed to how I felt about what they said or about my own interpretation of a similar experience. For this reason, I used the women's own words, taken directly from the transcripts, to illustrate particular themes.

The Process

For this research, I used two sources of data. The first source was the writings of four African American female writers. Themes of will are prevalent in the works of black female writers. The fictional characters they develop are often composites of all the women they have known (and in the case of Zora Neale Hurston, the characters were often autobiographical). Alice Walker, Toni Morrison, Zora Neale Hurston, and Maya Angelou have provided their readers with characters who exemplify self-will. As I read the writings of these four women, I set aside the fact that, in most cases (except Maya Angelou, whose works are autobiographical), I was reading about a fictional character. I allowed the female characters to come alive and treated their dialogue in much the same way that I would treat an actual interview. Passages of dialogue were lifted out and coded according to the theme they represented.

The second source of data was real-life African American women. These women were not all famous; most of them lived very "normal" lives. The fact that they were normal, however, was what qualified them for this study. Each one had to face tremendous challenges in order to grow up, educate herself, get employment, maintain her family, and so on. None of these women succumbed to these challenges. These women ranged from 25 to 90 years of age and came from various socioeconomic backgrounds. Of the 30 women interviewed, some were college educated, others were not. Many careers were represented as well: one attorney, one nun, five postal workers, two teachers, state employees, and a housewife, to name a few of the many types of careers represented. One woman worked as an activist in the public housing project where she lived. In one instance, I was able to interview four generations in one family: daughter, mother, grandmother, and great-grandmother.

Tape-recorded interviews generally lasted about 90 minutes, but some lasted much longer. Each participant in the study signed a consent form that outlined all the procedures that would be used to preserve anonymity. Before each interview, I asked each of the women whether she objected to being recorded. No one did. I informed them, however, that if at any time they wished to have the tape recorder turned off, I would do so without question. I was asked to turn off the tape recorder several times when the conversation became very emotional. In cases where the subjects' emotions would not enable them to speak, I turned the recorder off without being asked. In addition to tape recording, I took field notes. The notes helped me remember the general mood of the interview. After each interview, I reviewed both the tape and the field notes.

One real dilemma I had was that, after 3 months of information gathering and 30 interviews, I had a tremendous amount of data. In qualitative research, the researcher is supposed to continue the data-gathering process until saturation is reached (Lincoln & Guba, 1985; Merriam, 1988). Put simply, one continues until no new themes emerge. No set number of interviews is required. I had actually gone beyond saturation, but each woman's story was so compelling that I wanted to hear it. To reduce the data, I used only 15 of the 30 interviews in the actual analysis. These 15 were transcribed, coded, and arranged according to theme. The remainder of the data was used for background information. I allowed information from these tapes to inform my analysis, but I did not code the transcripts. "I eliminated all of the interviews from women under 30 years of age. I found that most of these younger women were still very uncertain about themselves and their goals. These interviews were generally much weaker than those who were 30 and older" (Peterson, 1992, p. 3).

The Interview

As a black female, I found that I had easy access to most of my subjects. Even the busiest women took a little time to help "a sister" out. I also found that most of the women were really excited about the research. After one woman and I had sat in her kitchen for about an hour, she suddenly stopped in the middle of her interview and said, "Is this really what you want to know! Girl, I mean I could go on for days if you want to know what brought me this far! I hadn't really thought about it that way, but I am one hell of a strong woman!" To set each woman at her ease, I began each interview by reading the Maya Angelou quote that appears at the beginning of this chapter. I then told the interviewee that she had been recommended to me as a woman who exemplified the characteristic of strength that was being described in the quote. I then told her that I just wanted her to talk freely about her life, the people, and the experiences that had influenced her. This was usually enough to begin the conversation. The most difficult part was staying out of the dialogue while at the same time participating in the conversation. It was very difficult to limit my responses to simple nods of understanding and affirming statements. One way that I resolved this dilemma was to allow time for conversation after the official interview was over. These conversations were very rewarding and helped build trust. After one interview, I went to a street fair with the subject. She had just finished telling me a remarkable story. Some of the graphic details were very personal. The fact that she asked me to go with her to the fair was very gratifying; it put us beyond the formal relationship of researcher and subject. We were just two women enjoying a Sunday afternoon fair. In a few instances, I knew the woman I was interviewing. Trust was already established, and the interview proceeded smoothly.

The Analysis of Data

The phenomenological approach was an appropriate method for the study of the human will. Phenomenology allows the will to be studied as it emerges in the consciousness of individual human beings. In this study, each woman could tell me, without a doubt, the moment when she knew that she "could be bent, but not broken." At this moment, these women became aware of their own self-wills.

After collecting data from the literature and from the interviews, I analyzed the coded transcripts. I first coded the themes that emerged from the literature. Four major themes and four minor themes seemed to dominate the literature of the selected African American authors. For each theme, I was able to refer to specific exemplar quotes.

Major Themes

Theme 1: Mother's Love. The theme of the mother whose undying love was a source of strength appeared in the literature. Sometimes this love seemed almost pathological, as was the case in Toni Morrison's novels *Sula* (1973) and *Beloved* (1974), but it was present just the same. Out of love, the mother was willing to give her life to ensure that her children did not suffer. These women often knew personal sorrow and loss, but their strength helped fortify their loved ones. Zora Neale Hurston, in *Jonah's Gourd Vine* (1934/1990), wrote about Lucy Potts Pearson, whose dying words to her young daughter illustrate her wisdom and her love:

> ... member tuh git all de education you kin. Dat's de onliest way you kin keep out from under people's feet. You always strain tuh be de bell cow, never be de tail uh nothin'. Do de best you kin, honey ... Don't love nobody better'n you do yo'self. Do, you'll be dying befo' you' time is out. (p. 130)

Maya Angelou's mother echoes that sentiment with these words:

> Be the best of anything you get into. If you want to be a whore, it's your life. Be a damn good one. Don't chippy at anything. Anything worth having is worth working for. (Angelou, 1974, p. 24)

Theme 2: The Powerful Vision. Zora Neale Hurston provided much of the material for this theme. Janie Crawford, the main character in Hurston's classic novel *Their Eyes Were Watching God* (1937) is guided by dreams or visions. The novel begins with a passage that reflects on the differences between men and women and the way they dream.

> Ships at a distance have every man's wish on board. For some they come in with the tide.
> For others they sail forever on the horizon, never out of sight, never landing until the
> Watcher turns his eyes away in resignation, his dreams mocked to death by Time. That is the life of men.
> Now, women forget all those things they don't want to remember, and remember everything they don't want to forget. The dream is the truth. Then they act and do things accordingly. (p. 9)

Their Eyes Were Watching God (1937) is Zora Neale Hurston's most autobiographical novel. Many of the characteristics that are attributed to Janie Crawford were, in fact, Hurston's attributes. Later, in her autobiography *Dust Tracks on a Road* (1942), Hurston refers to the visions that she herself has had. These visions she describes as premonitions of events to come. The visions helped prepare her for future tragedy, but they also served as the foundation for her strength. She knew that she would "be in sorrow's kitchen and lick out all de pots" (Hurston, 1934/1990, p. 81), but she also knew that she would "rise from de dead lak Lazarus" (p. 131).

Theme 3: Friendship and Sisterhood. The theme of friendship and the importance of intimacy among women was a powerful one in the literature. This theme proved to be a major theme that emerged in the life histories as well. In the novel *Sula* (1973), Toni Morrison deals very dramatically with the theme of friendship in the lives of Sula Peace and Nel Wright. She illustrates the beauty of a friendship between girls and just as skillfully shows the destruction that can take place when friendship goes awry (Peterson, 1992, p. 47).

As Nel and Sula were growing up together, their friendship was a typical childhood relationship. The girls played together. They liked each other because they seemed to find the other piece of themselves in one another. They "felt the ease and comfort of old friends. Because each had discovered years before that they were neither white nor male and that all freedom and triumph was forbidden to them, they had set about creating something else to be" (Morrison, 1973, p. 52).

Later events that came between the two friends proved to be destructive to them both, but especially for Sula. Sula had some very important ties severed very early in life, and therefore she was left, as Toni Morrison writes, "without a center" (1973, p. 95). Sula vented all her fury on the one she loved most—her friend Nel. The destruction of that friendship was the destruction of her will.

Alice Walker also writes about sisterhood and black women but focuses on friendship as a source of empowerment. *The Color Purple* (Walker, 1982) depicts the evolution of Celie, who begins the novel as the "mule of the earth." Through her very unlikely friendship with Shug, Celie is transformed. In a sense, her will is ignited. The Celie who emerges at the end of the novel is a confident woman. She understands herself and, therefore, can better understand others (Peterson, 1992, p. 52). Her strength is recognized when she is able to reconcile with her husband and recognize that his cruelty toward her is out of his own feelings of weakness and ignorance.

Theme 4: Sacrifice and Survival. Eva Peace, another character in Toni Morrison's novel *Sula* (1973), exemplifies the human need for survival (Peterson, 1992, p. 48). In this novel, the themes of mother love and survival are intertwined. For the family to survive, the love of the mother is tested. How far should a mother have to go to provide for the basic needs of her family? For Eva Peace, the sacrifice of a limb is not too much to ask. After Eva's husband, Boy Boy, leaves her, she is faced with starvation. She leaves her three children with a neighbor. Eighteen months later, she returns "with two crutches, a new black pocketbook, and one leg" (Morrison, 1973, p. 35). The rumor among the townspeople is that Eva laid her leg across a train track in order to collect $10,000 in insurance, enough money to support herself and her family for years to come. Throughout the story, Morrison uses very complex metaphors to illustrate the complexities of human nature. Her characters have the ability to laugh and to cry, to love and to hate, to heal and to destroy, all at the same time.

Minor Themes

Four minor themes were also expressed in the literature. These themes appeared sporadically in the literature but were important enough to the development of the strong female to mention.

Romantic Love. This minor theme is exemplified in the writings of Zora Neale Hurston. This theme is especially found in some of her earliest writing ("The Gilded Six Bits," 1933/1979a), but even in her most famous novel, *Their Eyes Were Watching God* (1937), Janie Crawford's final fulfillment comes when she meets and later falls in love with "Tea Cake" Woods.

Race Pride. Again, this theme was prevalent in Zora Neale Hurston's work. She placed her characters in settings that were very similar to her own roots. Hurston was a very confident and proud woman. Much of her confidence and well-being was a result of her early years growing up in Eatonville, Florida. Eatonville was an all-black town. Zora's father, John Hurston, was the first mayor of the town. Because she grew up in an environment where African Americans were in charge—hardworking and responsible citizens—she never had a sense of inferiority or self-doubt. She did not experience the bitter oppression of racism, which in turn later affected the way she developed the lead characters in her novels. Some of her critics say that she tended to romanticize the South and Southern folkways. Zora's own views were reflected in one of her autobiographical sketches, "I Love to Be Colored Me" (Hurston, 1979b).

Although race pride had a major impact on Zora Neale Hurston's writings, this theme is also found in the writings of the other authors. Toni Morrison very skillfully depicts a black community that is vital and self-sufficient. The community is joined in its effort to make sense out of nonsense, to overcome the pathological destruction of white racism (Morrison, 1974). Sometimes their efforts also seem pathological, but to those whose lives are "haunted" by the memories of a brutal past, the cure fits the disease. Maya Angelou also shares this theme in her autobiographical writings. Angelou also grew up in the South, but unlike Hurston, she understood the cruelty of racial prejudice. In Stamps, Arkansas, black families lived across the pond and down the railroad tracks from whites. She learned to stay within her place, relating to those in her community as people and to whites as "the other" (Angelou, 1969). Despite the restrictions, however, Angelou reveals that she developed an initial sense of well-being by being part of a strong, close-knit family.

Learning From Experience. This third minor, though important, theme was found in Maya Angelou's works. Because Angelou's writings are autobiographical, she is able to chronicle each stage of her development. By doing this, her readers are able to understand how her unique experiences helped shape her character. Learning from experience is a theme that is central to Maya Angelou's works. The fact that she was able to survive and even grow from very traumatic experiences is a testimony to her strength and courage.

A Sense of Destiny. The final minor theme was found primarily in the writings of Zora Neale Hurston. Hurston expressed in several of her autobiographical accounts that she had an overwhelming sense of destiny. She alluded to the "visions" that she periodically experienced. She spent much of her life studying the folk wisdom of black people and even dabbled in the "spirit world" of voodoo, or "hoodoo" as she called it. Zora Neale Hurston studied under the best voodoo priests and priestesses in the United States and Haiti. She believed strongly in her destiny as an anthropologist and a writer, and although her life was never without controversy, she remained true to her beliefs throughout her life.

I then compared the themes from the literature with the themes derived from personal interviews with strong-willed African American women. Four of the themes found in the literature were close matches for the themes found through the interviews. These four themes formed the essential structures of the strong-willed African American woman. These were the themes that I further described in keeping with the phenomenological approach.

Essential Structures of the Strong-Willed African American Woman

The four themes that represent the essential structures in the development of will in African American women are the relationship between mother and daughter, extended sisterly relationships, heightened spiritual awareness, and black community connectedness.

Essential Structure 1: Relationship Between Mother and Daughter. "I am a strong, black woman because I was raised by a strong, black woman." Statements like this one were typical of the interviews conducted for this research. Of the 15 women whose life stories made up the primary data source, 11 emphasized the critical role their mothers had in their upbringing and development. Even more interesting was the fact that, in at least three instances, the father was present in the home and was considered the "head of the household," but still it was the mother who, in their minds, really dominated.

The fact that mothers are so influential in the upbringing of their daughters is not significant in and of itself. Traditionally, in many cultures, women have had primary responsibility for child rearing. What is significant is the fact that the black women interviewed believed that their mothers "made" them what they are today. Often, the tactics used by their mothers seemed particularly harsh, but as these women grew in maturity, each came to understand her mother's wisdom, as in this account:

> I got pregnant with my daughter my senior year of high school, and I was unable to take the track scholarship I had received. So when I graduated, I immediately went into the workforce. I had to get a job. . . . I was really upset with my mother. I wanted to go to college. I felt I had an opportunity and she should take responsibility and raise my child. I was angry with everyone. Now I thank my mother because I feel if she had let me do what

I wanted to do, I wouldn't be the person I am today. Later, when my daughter was thirteen I did go back to school and then Momma was a big help to me. (Peterson, 1992, p. 69)

Black mothers very often passed on heavy responsibilities to their daughters at a very early age. It was not unusual to hear women say they were responsible for cooking all the meals or that they did all the cleaning or cared for younger siblings at the age of 8 or 10. The girls were brought into the fold of women and were taught to model their behavior and activities around them. Often, girls were allowed to be present as the mother talked with sisters or friends. From their mothers, these women learned to be creative as they solved their daily problems. "When my mother wanted something, she found a way. She did not wait around for a man to do for her; she rolled up her sleeves and went to it." These women continued to draw strength and support from their relationship with their mothers on into adulthood. One woman marked her mother's death as "the day she became a woman" because she knew that, from there on out, she was "a woman alone, her rock was gone."

The old adage "Black mothers raise their daughters and love their sons" alludes to the extra responsibilities the black mothers pass on to their daughters. These women expressed that their mothers raised them but loved them too. They believed that the extra responsibility only served to prepare them for a future, a future their mothers knew would not be easy.

Essential Structure 2: Extended Sisterly Relationships. In the novel *Sula* (1973), Toni Morrison skillfully paints the picture of a relationship that goes sour. The friendship between Sula Peace and Nel Wright is a complicated one. The important thing about this friendship, however, is the fact that neither woman could really live without it. When the two women separate, Sula loses the only real relationship she ever had and, as a result, is consumed with evil and literally rots away. Nel suffers as well. She develops a "puff" in the back of her eye that only disappears when her friend, Sula, dies. At the end of the novel, in a very telling quote, Nel exclaims, "We was girls together . . . O Lord Sula" (p. 174). The anguish of this statement sums up her feelings of deep loss.

Alice Walker also writes of the importance of friendship for the African American woman. *The Color Purple* (1982) centers on the relationships of women. The main character, Celie, is helpless and abused until she meets Shug Avery, who is, of all things, her husband's mistress. The two women become friends, and the strength of that friendship enables Celie to grow. In the end, her love for Shug far surpasses any other love she had ever known.

Eight of the women interviewed also spoke of broad friendship/kinship relationships with other women. Several of the women were raised in an environment where their mothers' friends—"aunts"—played a very substantial role in their upbringing.

> When I was fifteen years old, my mother and I fell out. I don't even remember what it was all about now. But I was mad. So I decided that I'd get even and run away. I pack up my bag and went over to my godmother's house. She was so glad to see me. She told me to come right on in. We had a ball! I let her cook for me and she cooked all my favorite food. She even sent her husband out for the things they didn't have on hand (laughter).
>
> I stayed there for a few days, then I started getting worried when nobody from home called for me or came by. What didn't they miss me? What kind of parents did I have? I didn't know that she (the godmother) had called mother almost as soon as I got there and told her I was safe, so don't worry. I went home I think, that weekend. Mother acted like nothing happened. I don't think I ran away anymore after that. (Peterson, 1992, p. 76)

These women thought these relationships took much of the stress of child rearing off their mothers, and later they developed similar networks of their own. They have come to rely on their own friends to serve as "aunts" for their children and express sympathy for black women who are out there "struggling alone." These women easily relate to the problems that many black women face because of race and gender. For this reason, they are willing to help out a "sister." This understanding was very helpful during this research. In two instances, I was only able to get interviews with two of my informants because they realized I was, like them, a "sister" trying to make it.

Essential Structure 3: Heightened Spiritual Awareness. "God ain't a he or a she, but a It" (Walker, 1982, p. 202). In this passage, Celie and Shug discuss the nature of God. Celie was raised to be afraid of a God who resembled an old white man and sat in the clouds and handed down punishments. God was especially sure, she thought, to punish her, a poor, ugly black child. Shug, however, came to love a God who lived in everyone and everything. All that was good came from God, and evil and sin were matters of interpretation. For Shug, God was the spirit of life, and by sharing her God with Celie, she was able to empower her.

This same notion of God as the spirit of life was common in the women I interviewed. All the women had been raised "in the church," and although three admitted they now have no true church commitments, they still considered themselves spiritual people. For these women, God is a natural part of life.

> I early decided that I wanted to serve God, don't ask me where that came from, I would say the spirit, but now when I think about it, I had gone to Catholic school and I like the nuns, they were friendly, they related to me. I was a good student in school so they allowed me to get to know them more as people.
> ... So I went off to the convent ... [and] during those years of hardship, I was still growing in grace with the Lord. In the prayers we said everyday, I certainly felt accepted by the Lord, affirmed by the Lord, and affirmed in terms that what I was doing was what the Lord wanted me to do. So even though all of this craziness was going on around me at all levels, there was a communion going on; and I was hearing the Scriptures and hearing the Psalms. I would say that is the secret of my "success," my belief and faith and my active relationship with the Lord. (Peterson, 1992, p. 81)

The church is seen by those still active in church as more of a faith community. The church is a binding place where people come together to share their faith and fellowship with one another.

> My mother always kept us in church and I loved going to church because that is where you get your spiritual guidance, your spiritual healing. (Peterson, 1992, p. 80)

Another woman had this to say about the significance of the black church experience:

> I don't like going to church and staying three and four hours, but you gonna find me like you find the majority of the Black population in church on Sunday. Because that is our one source. The one thing we have in common is that we know what the Lord can do for us. I don't care how far you stray away, you always come back to the Lord. (Peterson, 1992, p. 104)

For these women, their faith in God has given them a sense of peace and strength, and as they look back on their lives, they express a deep compassion for those who have not known God in the very personal way that they have come to know Him. This is where traditional organized religion often falls short and the spirit takes over.

> Now that I'm grown, I've come to grips with God. I go to church. I realize that it wasn't because of God that I suffered so much as a child. God wasn't punishing me. It took a long time to realize that. I was abused because I had a father who had problems and a mother whose religion got in the way. It wasn't God, but religious faith that was the problem. (Peterson, 1992, p. 105)

Faith is one thing that unites African Americans with their African roots. This seems ironic: Forced Christianity was one mechanism that white landowners used to strip the Africans of all vestiges of their native land. Lincoln (1984) explains the spiritual base of African American faith that stems from the "religious universe" that was the root of the African experience. The slaves, stripped of their native religions, were still able to relate to the idea of God as a Supreme Being. So, "the act that was meant to take away the African people's last link with home and ensure their subjugation was the act that was eventually to set them free" (Peterson, 1992, p. 79). This spiritual base enabled black people to come together to share in their faith and to heal their wounds.

Essential Structure 4: Black Community Connectedness. Very closely related to the experience of spirituality and the relationship to the church is the relationship with the black community. The church, in general, has long been a focal point of community activity. This relationship was part of the experience of these strong women. One woman spoke of how her parents stressed community and church involvement when she was a child. She was told over and over again that her life was not hers to keep selfishly, but that she was to share her life with others. "Growing up in Alabama, in the shadow of Tuskegee, you know, we were really into self help as a community. It was kind of a motto in my family."

Close relationships and extended families have been and continue to be the mainstay of a strong black community. African American psychologist Joseph White (1984) suggests that community mindedness is part of the "survival equipment of African American people" (p. 33). More recently, Molefi Asante (1988) writes that the notion of expanded community is part and parcel of an Afrocentric worldview.

In the literature selected for this study, each of the authors places her central characters within communities that help shape and define their personalities. Zora Neale Hurston's writings always reflect the positive experience that she had as a girl growing up in the South but in a community where blacks had autonomy. Her female characters do not question their blackness or feel inferior because of it. Black folkways and traditions are celebrated within a community that has made its own rules, free from white authority.

Toni Morrison, Alice Walker, and Maya Angelou also place their characters within the framework of a broader community. Each female exists within a complex network of family and friends who are sometimes closer than family. Their networks, however, also include neighbors, church members, and other people whose only relationship is that they also share the black experience.

The African American woman has played a vital role in the black community. During slavery, black men and women worked side by side as equals. A spirit of cooperation developed between men and women, boys and girls. Everyone understood that they all had to work together to survive. After slavery was finally abolished, the need to survive still forced most black females to labor outside their homes while at the same time they struggled to hold their families intact. In one interview, a woman described her experience of raising five children after her husband left her:

> Sometimes I would be so tired.... Lord! I don't know how I made it. All I could do was pray. I worked, and the people at work supported me. They all knew how it was, some of them was going through the same thing themselves. I had to rely on my oldest child a lot. She did pretty good most of the times (pause) and the neighbors. They always kept an eye out.

At the time of the interview, this woman was raising her grandson. She had gained custody of the child after he was born addicted to crack cocaine. The pain that she had suffered was evident, but she still continued to work hard to support her family.

Using Phenomenology to Describe the Strong-Willed African American Woman

Upon analysis of the data, the essential structures described above were apparent. The interviews provided rich material that could be used in writing a thick description for each of the essential structures. The next step was to follow through the hermeneutical process and propose a definition of the strong-willed black woman (Peterson, 1992, pp. 88-90). The challenge was to provide a definition that was broad enough to allow for the unique personalities and experiences of the women whom I interviewed, yet at the time captured the common thread that intertwined all their stories. By using two key informants, I was able to "keep honest" as I completed this task. These women read my work and my interpretations based on the data. They helped clarify and focus my interpretations. I knew that I had it right when one of my readers, who lived in California at that time, called me one morning. She said that she was able to call me so early because she had been up all night reading and that, at one point, she "was so upset that she had to put it down because she was crying her eyes out." At first, I was concerned until she went on to say that it was because she thought it "hit so close to home" for her as a black female. This was exactly what I wanted to do—hit close to home.

The use of oral narratives in phenomenological research is and continues to be a rewarding process for me. It has helped me as a researcher better understand myself and other women like me. In the final analysis, I picture the strong-willed African American woman as being like a magnet: She draws people into herself and, by so doing, increases her own capacity and strength.

REFERENCES

Angelou, M. (1969). *I know why the caged bird sings*. New York: Random House.
Angelou, M. (1974). *Gather together in my name*. New York: Bantam.
Angelou, M. (1989). Introduction. In B. Lanker, *I dream a world*. New York: Stewart, Tabori, & Chang.
Asante, M. (1988). *Afrocentricity*. Trenton, NJ: African World Press.
Heidegger, M. (1962). *Being and time*. New York: Harper & Row.
Hughes, L. (1959). Mother to son. In *Selected poems of Langston Hughes* (p. 187). New York: Vintage.
Hurston, Z. N. (1937). *Their eyes were watching God*. Philadelphia: J. B. Lippincott.
Hurston, Z. N. (1942). *Dust tracks on a road* (2nd ed., R. E. Hemenway, Ed.). Urbana: University of Illinois Press.
Hurston, Z. N. (1979a). The gilded six bits. In A. Walker (Ed.), *I love myself when I am laughing and then again when I am looking mean and impressive* (pp. 208-218). New York: Feminist Press. (Original work published 1933)
Hurston, Z. N. (1979b). I love to be colored me. In A. Walker (Ed.), *I love myself when I'm laughing and then again when I'm looking mean and impressive* (pp. 152-155). New York: Feminist Press.
Hurston, Z. N. (1990). *Jonah's gourd vine*. New York: Harper & Row. (Original work published 1934)
Lincoln, C. E. (1984). *Race, religion, and the continuing American dilemma*. New York: Hill & Wang.
Lincoln, Y., & Guba, E. (1985). *Naturalistic inquiry*. Beverly Hills, CA: Sage.
Merriam, S. (1988). *Case study research in education: A qualitative approach*. Newbury Park, CA: Sage.
Morrison, T. (1973). *Sula*. New York: New American Library.
Morrison, T. (1974). *Beloved*. New York: Knopf.

Peterson, E. (1992). *African American women: A study of will and success.* Jefferson, NC: McFarland.

Spiegelberg, H. (1982). *The phenomenological movement* (3rd ed.). The Hague, The Netherlands: Martinus Nijhoff.

Stanage, S. (1987). *Adult education and phenomenological research.* Malabar, FL: Krieger.

Walker, A. (Ed.). (1979). *I love myself when I am laughing and then again when I am looking mean and impressive.* New York: Feminist Press.

Walker, A. (1982). *The color purple.* New York: Pocket Books.

White, J. (1984). *The psychology of blacks: An Afro-American perspective.* Upper Saddle River, NJ: Prentice Hall.

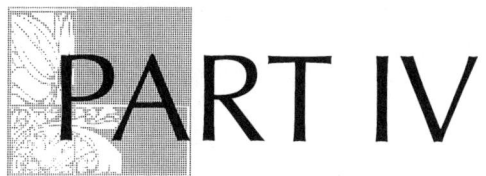

PART IV

Research Processes
Negotiating Institutions

11

RECONSTRUCTING THE HISTORY OF MUSICIANS' PROTECTIVE UNION LOCAL 274 THROUGH ORAL NARRATIVE METHOD

DIANE D. TURNER

he history of Musicians' Protective Union Local 274, American Federation of Musicians, is important because black musicians have often been studied, but seldom as workers. Labor historians have generally ignored the experiences of black musicians as urban professionals, their roles in the American labor movement, and the emergence, development, and maintenance of more than 50 black musicians' unions in the American Federation of Musicians. Proper use of oral narrative research was an invaluable methodology during my research.[1] The history of Union Local 274 would have remained obscure without it.

The reconstruction of Local 274 through oral narrative research represents African American musicians' organized efforts at the grassroots levels: to participate in the American labor movement, to cope with the complexities of urban life, to resist white cultural domination, to eradicate racism in U.S. society, and to improve their economic conditions in the music industry.

Beginning with an analysis and brief history of my research on Local 274 through the interpretation of interviews,[2] I describe in this chapter the essential role of the oral narrative method in the process of reconstructing the union's history. I provide an account of each step used to reconstruct the history of Local 274, including my personal discovery of the union. I conclude the chapter with evidence that supports the benefits of the oral narrative, as a method, to document a segment of 20th-century African American urban, cultural, and labor history.

MY ANALYSIS OF LOCAL 274

I analyzed Local 274 as a social phenomenon rooted in the consciousness and collective behavior of a group of black urban professionals: African American musicians. My research documents how black musicians affectively determined their own destinies, regardless of racism, sexism, and segregation, by maintaining cohesive groups. My approach provides an accurate view of black musicians' struggles and activities in the labor movement and examines them during a period in Philadelphia when most black workers were not participating in organized labor. My research also examines dual unionism in organized labor and the effects of civil rights legislation and union mandates dealing with separate black organizations in the music industry. The history of Local 274 begins to widen the research on separate black musicians' unions and their role in the American labor movement. It lays the basis for further study of the implications and outcome of civil rights legislation and the subsequent union mandates to adhere to federal laws. It provides a labor history from the bottom up, focusing on rank-and-file black musicians' collective responses, as urban white-collar professionals, to local issues, national issues, and union leadership. Last, it provides the basis for further study of African American musicians as urban professionals.

A BRIEF HISTORY OF LOCAL 274

Musicians' Protective Union Local 274, American Federation of Musicians, was chartered on January 2, 1935, after black musicians were denied membership in white Local 77. The chartering of Local 274 established dual unionism in Philadelphia. From its emergence in 1935 to its demise in 1971, Local 274 maintained a conflictive status as a "separate, colored" musicians' union. It did not, however, view itself as such. Its primary function was to service the interests of its membership. Although it was made up predominately of black jazz musicians, it served all musicians regardless of race.

The institutionalization of Local 274 provided a vehicle for black musicians to break down the barriers that were socially constructed to deny them opportunities. Black unionized musicians also fueled the creation of an important institution that identified with African American culture, had pride in it, and promoted black musical forms. Its strength and autonomy as a musicians' union was grounded in the self-expressions of its predominately black jazz membership. Rich African American music traditions were perpetuated in the union, fostering musicians like Dizzy Gillespie,[3] John Coltrane, Byard Lancaster, Benny Golson, Mickey Roker, Clara Ward, Archie Shepp, Jimmy Oliver, and Bootsie Barnes.[4] Black and white musicians were able to find a common ground through the creation and articulation of various genres of African American music promoted and preserved in black union halls. In the process, some progressive white musicians were advocates of equality for black musicians as they struggled against racial discrimination in the American labor movement.

Dual Unionism and the 1960s

Dual unionism, an accepted practice in the American Federation of Musicians from the chartering of Chicago's black Local 208 in 1902, came under attack during the 1960s. With the passage of the Civil Rights Act of 1964, the American Federation of Musicians was targeted as one of the most segregated labor unions in the United States. The American Federation of Musicians' International Executive Board responded to the charge of segregation by issuing a directive prohibiting dual unionism based on race. The International Board initiated a program to merge all black and white unions existing in the same jurisdiction. The merger program began on a voluntary basis, but after problems arose during and after amalgamation took place, many black unions preferred to keep their autonomy. This meant keeping control of their assets, electing their own officials who represented black musicians' issues and concerns as a special interest group, promoting social and cultural cohesion, and maintaining traditional jobs.

Local 274 staunchly refused to merge with white Local 77 and rejected all merger proposals, becoming the last independent black union within the ranks of the American Federation of Musicians. As a consequence of Local 274's rejection of the American Federation of Musicians' mandate to civil rights legislation, its charter was canceled in 1971. The expulsion of Local 274 from the ranks of the American Federation of Musicians in 1971 marked the end of many decades of dual unionism based on race and, more important, black autonomy in the music industry.

SOUNDS OF THE CITY PROJECT

I discovered Local 274 while employed as the oral history coordinator at the Afro-American Historical and Cultural Museum in Philadelphia, Pennsylvania. I was involved in the preliminary research phase of an exhibition entitled "Sounds of the City," which depicted the contributions of African Americans to musical traditions in Philadelphia. Beginning with an introductory gallery of the African roots of black music, the exhibition focused on 20th-century musical genres, including gospel, classical, blues, rhythm and blues, and jazz from the 1920s to 1970.

During the planning stage of the exhibition, consultants were hired from various black musical fields to provide background information and to compile data on the rich black musical traditions in Philadelphia. Their preliminary research uncovered popular personalities who performed African American music, favorite songs, performance venues, and personal notes of interest that could be used to guarantee the success and uniqueness of the exhibition. They discovered, however, a lack of secondary and primary source materials, which resulted in a dearth of available information and materials from the 1920s through the 1940s. In general, there was a lack of comprehensive written sources on all aspects of Philadelphia's black culture in the 20th century.[5] As a consequence, the researched information contained large historical gaps.

I was recruited to fill in the historical gaps within a given time frame. It was my responsibility to locate information in the form of individuals to interview, documents, photographs, memorabilia, and artifacts related to the period 1920 through 1940. I relied on oral narrative research to accomplish my goals.

Methodology

Oral narrative research was a major component in my search for information about African American music in Philadelphia from the 1920s through 1940. My initial strategy was to begin with the names of personalities involved in black music documented by consultants, find out whether they were alive and residing in Philadelphia, and attempt to contact them. Through additional library research, I expanded the list of important musical personalities who resided in Philadelphia. Once a substantial list of names was compiled, I attempted to locate individuals, contact them by telephone, and arrange interviews.

Designing a Questionnaire and Release Form

A key phase in oral narrative research is the actual research design. Designing a release form, which gives you permission to use information in taped interviews, is one of the first steps to be completed. Several designs can be used (Kyvig, 1982). Next, developing a working list of questions for informants to answer is essential to the success of any project. Standardized questions provide a means to contrast and compare informants' answers during the interpretive phase. My development of a questionnaire went through several phases, which included background research, decisions about subject categories, inclusion of historical themes, and a consciousness of race, class, and gender issues in formulating questions. The development of my questionnaire included a first draft for my initial use, a second draft distributed to other individuals involved with the project for critique and feedback, and then a final working copy. Questions moved in chronological sequence, beginning with earliest recollections to present. I was also careful to phrase questions so that they did not produce yes and no answers, but rather descriptive narrative. This form became an important factor during the actual interviews. The more descriptive the answer, the more data to interpret and analyze.

As an African American and woman historian, this phase reflected not only my formal training but also my personal sensitivity to potential gender, race, and class issues in Philadelphia's music community. Questions were constructed to address topics (e.g., issues of race and race relations) in the music industry; to document familial and educational backgrounds of black musicians; to identify differences among black musicians and the various social classes within the larger African American community; to identify black female musicians, female members of Local 274, the instruments black women played, and their experiences; and to interview black women musicians.

Gender-sensitive questions were designed to reflect the real-life experiences of black women in music. For example, interviews with piano

Photo 11.1. Philadelphia Piano Ensemble with Trudy Pitts (*3rd row, 3rd from left*), early 1950s. (Photograph by John W. Mosely; Charles L. Blockson, Afro-American Collection, Temple University.)

and organ players Trudy Pitts (in July 1994) and Shirley Scott (in October 1994) provided great insight about two black women who began careers in music at very early ages. Both came from musical backgrounds and were influenced by mothers. Both began formal lessons at 6 years of age. Both were born in Philadelphia. Both are still actively involved in teaching, composing, recording, and performing jazz.

Doing my homework (background research on each personality) prior to interviews was key to accomplishing a good session. I conducted preliminary research to find out as much as I could about the musical personalities to be interviewed. In the case of Trudy Pitts, I located a group photograph (see Photo 11.1) in the Charles L. Blockson Afro-American Collection at Temple University, taken during the 1950s when she was a member of the Philadelphia Piano Ensemble before she crossed over into jazz. The ensemble consisted of seven pianos and 14 women pianists. Two women performed on each piano, and they all played at one time. Prior to viewing the photograph, Ms. Pitts made no mention of her membership and experiences in the group. Through use of the photograph, I enabled her to recall another segment of her career in music.

Research Processes: Negotiating Institutions 183

Trudy Pitts, who teaches at the University of Arts in Philadelphia, was born in South Philadelphia and started her musical training as an aspiring concert pianist. She attended Philadelphia Musical Academy and Juilliard School of Music in New York. She spoke very candidly about her career, which started with her aspirations to become a concert pianist and her decision to shift her creativity to jazz performance and improvisation. I asked her about her personal experiences pursuing a career in music as an African American and a women. She had the following to say:

> Being a female and being an African American person, I saw obstacles present early on just by being in the world of music—in that world of music—symphony and classical world. By talking to my peers, by going to concerts, by doing research, by reading. Just by using my ears and eyes and conversation. I saw that the task that I was trying to accomplish was really not going to happen for me at the time that I needed it, which was in the part of my life where I was fresh out of college and still striving to perfect my performance—because that goes on for a lifetime. That striving never does stop. But at the part of your life when you want to get involved in being a professional concert pianist, I saw that the time was not right and it was not going to materialize for me. So rather than being a diehard, and staying in that venue, and subjecting myself to the disappointments and the insults and all of the other things that black people must endure in order to not only be an artist but to be a human being with values and morals, I kind of veered my musical works into another direction, and thereby came the school teaching . . . the church work . . . training choirs, accompanying classical and opera singers, accompanying dance people . . . and anywhere that I could get an in is where you would find me in terms of the music. As long as it was music, I felt that I had to keep striving until I found my own water level which I finally found when I entered the world of jazz.

During the interview, I asked Trudy about her transition from classical to jazz. She explained:

> I found through listening to it, sitting down and just dibbling and dabbling with it on the piano, I had an affinity for chord structure. I found that I could hear what they were doing and kind of get into it without too many problems. . . . I found out that with my classical background and the knowledge of the piano and the knowledge of the whole piano and all the keys thereof that I didn't have a problem with laying down chord change. Now, improvisation—that's a whole other thing that goes on for the rest of your life. Trying to do that and I feel that I'm very busy trying to improvise today. It never stops. The freedom that it offers you is overwhelming, and it never stops.

I also asked Ms. Pitts about her parents' reaction to her decision to cross over and play jazz. This is where knowledge of class issues inside the African American community proved important. She explained:

> It broke my mother's and father's hearts to see me going off into bars playing music after I had strove so hard to develop what they called "a higher form of playing." But, we know today that jazz is the highest form of music in the world in its creativity and its freedom. But, there was a different mind-set in those days.

Ms. Pitts's answer confirmed the dynamics of class that operate among black people, especially related to black music.

Another prominent musician, Shirley Scott, is an assistant professor in the Fine Arts Department at Cheyney University (Cheyney, Pennsylvania). I asked her some very pointed questions related to gender. She responded in a forthright manner:

> One should not be judged on gender. One should be judged on what one can produce and how well.

I asked Ms. Scott how she felt about critics of jazz, who are predominately white males. She spoke about critics and their role in the setbacks of black women in music:

> Any kind of critic, if they're criticizing, they're critiquing music. They are usually people who wanted to be musicians and could not make it, and so they talk about what somebody else is doing or not doing and not having the faintest idea of what it's like to do it because they can't do it.... I don't pay attention, really, to critics because I think that I'm intelligent enough to make a decision for myself as to what's good or what I like and what I don't like. I don't have to have somebody else to listen to it to make up my mind.... One of the finest musicians, I think, that ever graced this planet was Mary Lou William, and you don't hear nearly as much about her as you should. Another is Melba Liston. They're known not only for their playing but for their ability to create the music and to arrange the music.

I posed many questions related to black women in music, and she offered her view in terms of revising black music history—in particular, jazz history—to include the contributions and roles of women:

> We as women have to do that. We know what's going on with us. We have to toot our own horn. They say that the squeaky wheel gets the oil. We have to make noises. We have to do it ourselves. And maybe you can't

expect somebody else to do it. We know it's wrong. It's not fair. So then if we know that, then we know that some steps should be taken to right this wrong, and women, I think, are the best people to do it.

Again, I cannot overemphasize the importance of my awareness of gender, race, and class issues in producing the types of answers that touched on aspects of black men's and women's experiences in music, which are often neglected.

Prior to the actual interviews, I sent informants the list of questions to examine. This was helpful to interviewees, as many informants were senior citizens, who ranged in age from 60 to 93. Reviewing the questions in advance of the actual interview gave them time to think about their answers and the opportunity to recall certain events, activities, and information.

First Impressions

Initial contact with potential interviewees was usually made through a telephone call. The introductory telephone call was a crucial step in my research. I found that "first impressions" were lasting ones, and my strategy was to be careful not to be "pushy" during the initial telephone call, but to establish a good rapport with informant. At the same time, I attempted to stress the importance of interviewing them at their earliest convenience because of a limited time frame to accomplish my goals. I introduced myself and identified the institution I represented and how I got their names, stating any contacts they personally knew who referred me to them. I then explained the purpose of the call, gave them some information about the forthcoming exhibition, and stressed their importance as a source of information for the success of my project.

Depending on their initial response, I asked their permission to conduct an interview. In some instances, I had to make several telephone calls before I asked for an interview. This process is where intuition and patience paid off. If they sounded enthusiastic about the project, I arranged an interview the next day or within a few days. If they were hesitant about talking to me or had any misgivings about the project, I asked them whether I could send them some additional information about the project. After a few days, I called them to confirm that they received the information in the mail and asked them whether they had a chance to read it and whether they had any questions. In some instances, a formal letter legitimated the project. If the potential informant was still hesitant about being interviewed, I got his or her permission to call back in a few days. In the interim, I sent a brief letter thanking the persons for their time and expressed my pleasure at speaking with them on the telephone and reiterated their importance as a resource for the success of my project.

A few individuals did not think they had any information and were not enthused about talking to a stranger. With these people, I had to be very patient while at the same time convince them of their pivotal role. I sent them additional correspondence and calendars of museum activities and events. Also, I called them once a week just to ask how they were doing and to confirm that they received additional correspondence. I kept a daily journal that included a telephone log, record of correspondence sent to individuals, and important notes on progress, along with my impressions of each informant. Although this approach was time-consuming, I found that it was the most effective way to accomplish my objectives and to establish good rapport and get informants to agree to interviews.

Establishing Creditability

The narratives of black musicians became an essential resource for reconstructing the history of African American musicians in Philadelphia's labor movement. To maximize data on my research, it was crucial to get full cooperation from Philadelphia's black musician community. This meant I had to earn the respect of the community. I achieved this through hard work, honesty, and dedication. I made myself visible in the music community by attending live performances. I also held workshops where black musicians were able to articulate their issues and concerns about the music profession. I fulfilled all commitments made to the musicians' community. When interviews were scheduled in the homes of informants, I was always on time. During sessions, I was very careful not to impose my personal views to influence answers. I was very sensitive to maintaining integrity through the interview process, particularly when it came to very controversial or confidential information. When asked to turn off the tape recorder, I obliged my informants and took notes with their permission. This camaraderie allowed a relationship of mutual trust to develop.

Through these activities, I was able to establish creditability. I was viewed as an "insider," as opposed to an "outsider," which gave me access to information and individuals that I would not have been given as an outsider. I was recognized as a sincere and dedicated researcher with integrity, who was not only committed to reconstructing an accurate history of black musicians' experiences in Philadelphia but also involved as an active member of the jazz community. Thus, I received the Philadelphia musical community's full cooperation.

Location of Interview

Another important step in the oral narrative research was the actual location where interviews were conducted. I attempted to accommodate the informants by getting them involved in decision making. For example, I asked the informant to select a place where he or she would be most comfortable. In some instances, the initial interview was conducted at the museum.[6]

Some interviews were arranged but then were canceled by the interviewees. I found that a good strategy was to call the informant a day prior to the interview as a reminder. Still, other informants, who were too polite just to say no to my request for an interview, scheduled and then canceled at the last minute, hoping I would give up on them. During these instances, I thanked them for calling to cancel and politely arranged another interview until the interview actually took place. Later, the same informants admitted that they were giving me a hard time and that I didn't give up, and we would laugh about it. This phase required flexibility, patience, and persistence.

Once we had the opportunity to talk in person during the initial interview, second interviews were often conducted at informants' homes. Access to their homes literally opened the doors to their personal collections, which proved invaluable. I discovered a number of primary source materials related to Philadelphia's 20th-century black culture maintained in individuals' homes. Personal collections were dispersed throughout the city, housed in nontraditional repositories, remaining some of the best-kept secrets in Philadelphia. They were not housed, for the most part, in libraries, archives, historical societies, or museums. Thus, I found oral narrative research an essential phase in locating photographs dating to the early 1920s through the 1940s,[7] documents like some of the official records of Musicians' Protective Union Local 274,[8] artifacts such as Lee Morgan's trumpet,[9] and memorabilia like the *Annual Spring Concert Program* of the black Philadelphia Concert Orchestra, dated 1912.[10]

Access to informants' homes also required travel in the field. Flexibility was crucial because some interviews were conducted on weekends. To complete some interviews, I literally had to put everything else in my life on hold. For example, one morning after a concert in Philadelphia,

Photo 11.2. Author interviewing McCoy Tyner at Four Seasons Hotel, May 1995. (Photograph by Pedro J. Matos; used with permission.)

I got the opportunity to interview the world-renowned jazz pianist and composer McCoy Tyner. I had corresponded with him about a month prior to the concert to ask his permission to interview him. I also attended his fabulous performance and waited approximately 1 hour after the concert to confirm the interview for the following day and to find out the actual site of interview. I was able to confirm that the interview would take place but that Mr. Tyner had not checked into a hotel. This meant that he couldn't give me his actual location. I had to wait for a telephone call after he checked into a hotel, which meant that I had to stay close to a telephone until I heard from him. I did not live in Pennsylvania at that time and had traveled to Philadelphia to interview Mr. Tyner. I spent the night at the home of my brother, who does not have the call waiting feature on his telephone. I waited on pins and needles for the call. Mr. Tyner did call, and my brother was very happy when he was able to use his telephone again. More important, I had an excellent interview with McCoy Tyner (Photo 11.2). Once again, patience and flexibility were crucial.

Use of Written Sources and Other Forms of Documentation

In conjunction with oral research narrative, I used written sources and other forms of documentation at libraries, archives, special collections, museum collections, and other repositories. This search included the survey of local and regional newspapers—in particular, the *Philadelphia Tribune,* an African American newspaper founded in the city in 1884. Other local newspapers included the *Philadelphia Daily News, Philadelphia Bulletin,* and *Philadelphia Inquirer.* Regional newspapers included other black newspapers such as the *Pittsburgh Courier* and *The Afro-American.* At the national level, *The New York Times* was surveyed. Music journals included *International Musician, Variety,* and *Billboard.* Archival documents from Philadelphia repositories such as the Charles L. Blockson Afro-American Collection at Temple University and national repositories such as the National Archives, where the NAACP files are housed, and the AFL-CIO and American Federation of Musicians records and journals. Use of written sources and other forms of documentation that included photographs allowed me to distinguish fact from fiction by being able to substantiate the accuracy of the narratives and to confirm facts with supporting evidence.

Interview Techniques

I began each interview with a casual conversation so that interviewees had the opportunity to loosen up and relax. Once I thought that this was accomplished, I then asked them whether they were ready to begin the taped interview. I found that it was important to get informants' consent to turn on the tape recorder; this tactic gave them a sense of control, which enabled them to relax.

I began each taped interview session by stating my name, the date, place of interview, and the person to be interviewed. During the initial interview, I asked informants to state their full names, dates of birth, where they were born, and to give a brief biographical sketch of their careers. I then moved to questions related to their familial background, such as the names of their parents, their occupations, and their reasons for migrating to Philadelphia. I continued with their earliest recollections of their neighborhoods and the influence of music in their early lives. The questions proceeded in chronological sequence from early years to the present. An important interview technique was to listen carefully to the narrative and to make sure I did not speak until the informant was done talking. It is better not to signify during an interview because there is high probability of disrupting the continuity of answers. I also memorized questions on the questionnaire that I developed so that questions and answers would flow in a conversational manner. This technique helped interviewees relax and give very descriptive and candid answers because they thought they were having a conversation with me, as opposed to answering a set of formal questions.

Immediately following each session, I listened to the tape to critique my technique and to take notes on any additional information or questions that were not covered on tape for the next session. During this process, I indexed each tape by using the counter on the tape recorder to identify key subjects discussed. This indexing enabled me in accessing data before typing transcriptions.

Discovery of Local 274

I met now-deceased Franklin E. Walker while conducting interviews for the museum project. Mr. Walker, a 71-year-old bassist, gave me my first history lesson about Local 274. He was a charter member of the union in 1935. Mr. Walker was born in Spotsylvania County, Virginia, on January 18, 1907. He migrated to Philadelphia with his mother and three sisters in 1914 so that the family would be closer to his father, who was employed in the Navy. The Walkers arrived in Philadelphia and took up residence in the northern section of the city. Franklin E. Walker began his music career in grammar school, singing in a boy's choir. He started his professional music career singing and playing the ukelele. He formed a singing group called Franklin Walker and the Dixie Serenades and played bass fiddle (F. E. Walker, personal interview, November 11, 1986). Mr. Walker spoke about Local 274 and why it was organized. He told me,

> We didn't have a black union at that time, and if a musician wanted to play, we had to get what was known as a "traveling card" out of Newark, New Jersey.... Local 77 did not want a black union, and they did not admit blacks to their local. But Kerngood, the national secretary, said if we got 100 musicians together that the federation would give us a charter.

His statement stimulated my curiosity, and I wanted to learn more about the union. Walker stated, "Local 274 was started by organized groups. They took them first because that would be the majority. Doc Hyder, he had a 14-piece big band." Several questions came to mind: Was he talking about a black musicians' union? Was he speaking about the existence of segregation in Philadelphia's labor movement? Why didn't Local 77 admit black musicians into its membership? Was the federation he spoke of the American Federation of Musicians? Why was Local 274 organized?

My second history lesson on Local 274 came from James Euclid Adams, a saxophonist and the last president of Local 274. Mr. Adams became my main informant. He was born in Nashville, Tennessee, on September 7, 1911. He became interested in music during high school after hearing bands like Earl Hines, Duke Ellington, Cab Calloway, and Chick Webb broadcast on the radio. Mr. Adams wanted to become a musician, but his father, a country schoolteacher, thought that "playing music was a waste of time, and being very religious . . that musicians, especially jazz musicians, were disciples of the devil" (J. E. Adams, personal interview, April 17, 1987, and April 4, 1992). Adams attended Tennessee State College, majoring in fine arts and art education, where he was instilled with the value of black self-reliance. Throughout his college career, he played saxophone, which occurred after his father's death. His 10-piece band arrived by car in Philadelphia in 1937 by way of Cape May, New Jersey. Mr. Adams joined the union in 1938, got involved in union activities, and was eventually elected president of Local 274. He served as president for several terms, including the period of the union's expulsion from the American Federation of Musicians for refusing to merge with former white Local 77. Mr. Adams thought that Local 274 had a right to remain autonomous and proclaimed that the black musicians' union had integrated prior to the focus on desegregation and that "Martin Luther King has never said for any black to give up what he's got to go somewhere else. What he has said is open up your rolls to everybody who wants to come in" (J. E. Adams, personal interview, July 1988). His position reflected the sentiment of the majority of black locals in the American Federation of Musicians prior to their demise with the death of Local 274 in 1971. Mr. Adams concluded, "We wanted to keep what we had! It was our house! We built it! Sweat, tears, and blood!" (J. E. Adams, personal interview, July 1988).

BENEFITS OF ORAL NARRATIVE RESEARCH

The process involved in the oral narrative was rewarding, but at the same time very time-consuming—for example, arranging interviews, writing follow-up correspondence, actually perfecting interview techniques, and indexing and transcribing the taped interviews. Any serious scholar can seek funding, however, and if not available, invest his or her personal funds. I invested my personal funds in a decent tape recorder and transcribing machine because of the long-range benefits of such an investment. Although I spent many hours involved in various phases of the oral narrative process, the benefits outweighed the time factor. Some of the benefits are described below.

Building Bridges to the Past and Present

Oral narrative research provided me with a vehicle to honor elders and to celebrate their contributions while they were still living. Many black elders, who are keepers of African American history, do not get the recognition they deserve because our larger society does not place an emphasis on their importance. Oral history interviews gave me the opportunity to document these people's experiences, to show my appreciation of their struggles, and to learn some very important life survival skills from firsthand accounts. It was also good therapy for the seniors and reinforced my sense of black pride.

Documenting and Recapturing History

I was afforded the opportunity not only to document black musicians' experiences but, more important, also to salvage their history. For example, several of my informants—Franklin E. Walker, Harry "Skeets" Marsh, and Dan Jones—have since passed, but a record of their career histories in the music profession remains in the form of taped interviews, reproductions of documents, and photographs. I made the conscious decision to invest in a radio-quality tape recorder, and the sound of the taped interviews was of high quality. In the future, I have an option to air their experiences through a radio documentary. More important, their experiences are included in a manuscript being prepared for publication.

Through the oral narrative, I recovered many important documents and was given permission to reproduce photographs and valuable documents, which provided some visual record of the past and also affirmed the histories of black musicians. Documents included court transcripts, records of Local 274, programs of special events, membership applications, and financial reports. (The initial long hours spent surveying newspapers did not produce the wealth of news clippings in the possession of individual musicians.) I was then able to go back to library microfilm and focus on periods of importance in the history of the union.

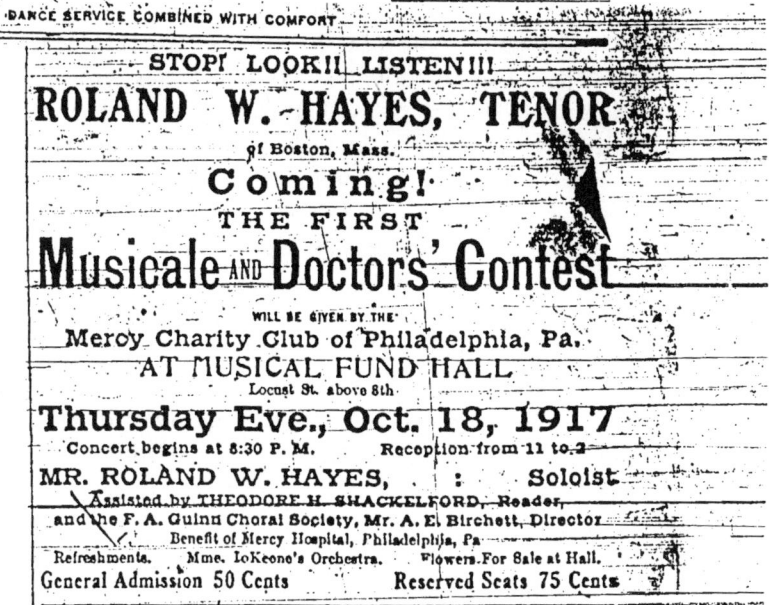

Figure 11.1. Advertisement from the *Philadelphia Tribune*, 1918. Note "Mme. Io Keene's Orchestra" near the bottom of the ad.

The Women of Local 274

I was introduced to black women who participated in Philadelphia's labor movement, such as Trudy Pitts and Shirley Scott, through their membership in Local 274. Other former members of Local 274 included Nina Simone, who applied as Eunice Waymon; pianist Beryl Booker, who played with Slam Stewart and formed an all-female jazz trio during the 1950s; singer Helen Page; saxophonist Myrtle Young, who played in the International Sweethearts of Rhythm; singer and cocktail drummer Ruth Mobley; drummer Doris A. Gibson; violin and viola player Vivian E. Pitts; bassist Erma Jean "Luella Venesa" Jones; and gospel singers and pianists Clara Ward and her sister, Willarene "Willa Ward" Moultrie. My research also uncovered black women who were musicians prior to the formation of Local 274, such as Madam Io Keene (see Figure 11.1) and Gertrude Taylor, a former member of Local 591.[11]

Activism in the Jazz Community of Philadelphia

Through my oral narrative research, I became actively involved in the jazz community of Philadelphia. I became a founding member of the Jazz People's Collective, which held a series of workshops to improve the status of jazz. I also got involved with the social wing of Local 274, the Philadelphia Clef Club of the Performing Arts. Through my research, I acquired a certain level of knowledge and experience regarding black musicians in Philadelphia and started receiving correspondence and telephone calls inviting me to participate in jazz-related projects. I was commissioned by the National Jazz Service Organization to draft the organization's program plan, which included an archival component. This responsibility proved to be an important inclusion because records were found in the basement and were not discarded; instead, they were viewed as important records. They included some records of Local 274, which I was given access to for my research. I was recruited by the board of directors to participate as a volunteer in the capacity of proposal and grant writer, fund-raiser, and waitress. Because of my involvement, I was given an honorary "A" Membership in the organization. I accepted it with great pride because A Memberships were available only to musicians; as a person who fell in the category of scholar, not musician, I was deeply moved by their gesture. The organization was recently granted a $2.5 million grant from the William Penn Foundation for construction of a new building on the Avenue of the Arts in Philadelphia. Also, I am currently involved in a project titled "Philadelphia Women in Jazz" and in a manuscript on the history of jazz in Philadelphia.

I worked in the capacity of archivist at the Charles L. Blockson Afro-American Collection during a phase of my research. Mr. Blockson received funding to install African American state historical markers in Philadelphia, and he encouraged me to submit a proposal for Musicians' Protective Union Local 274, American Federation of Musicians. The Pennsylvania Historical and Museum Commission approved my proposal for the installation of a marker, which has been placed at Local 274's old headquarters at 912 S. Broad Street.

Personal Benefits

The process of oral narrative also has benefits at the personal level. As a jazz aficionada, I got the opportunity to hear a lot of great jazz, which motivated me in my research. I acquired a new set of friends in the jazz community of Philadelphia, including "my significant other." I also consumed many delicious meals at the homes of my informants, who turned out to be my newfound friends. The friendship and hospitality extended to me were especially important during the days as a doctoral candidate in history. Because I was living on a shoestring budget and feeling very stressed at points, these people literally provided me with the necessary fuel to analyze and interpret my data.

Through the interaction with black women in Philadelphia's jazz community, I found a support group. Through the documentation of black women's life experiences in music, I am inspired to continue to pursue important research in 20th-century African American history in a profession that is still dominated by white males. I also encouraged and challenged African Americans and other people of color to join me in not only documenting the black experience in American history but also other fields of higher education at the university level. This is an ongoing process of active recruitment.

CONCLUSION

I approached my topic as an organic intellectual. I am a scholar, an active member of the jazz community, and a jazz aficionada. During my research, I became an active participant in the cultural production of jazz and influential in Philadelphia's jazz community. I continue to support jazz, to document the experiences of black musicians, and to participate in workshops and projects to improve the status of jazz. I have also designed two university-level courses—History of Black Music and History of Black Women in Music—that give students the opportunity to examine black cultural production from the historical vantage point of black musicians, their struggles in organized labor, and how a record of the rich history of the black experience has been documented in African American music.

NOTES

1. I would encourage a course or workshop in oral narrative research prior to conducting any interviews or work in the field. It is important to acquire a certain level of expertise to establish creditability with interviewees. See Frisch (1990), Portelli (1991), and Grele (1991). Journals on the topic include *Oral History Review* and *International Journal of Oral History*.

2. My oral narrative research included interviews with black musicians (predominantly jazz musicians who made up the majority of Local 274's membership), former club owners, and jazz patrons.

3. Gillespie started his professional career in the Frank Fairfax Orchestra. Fairfax was a key figure in the organizing effort that resulted in the chartering of Local 274. His

orchestra was also an institution for many musicians who went on to become prominent in jazz, such as Dizzy Gillespie.

4. The list of prominent black musicians who were former members of Local 274 is extensive. Former members include Bill Cosby; Bill Doggett; Doc Bagby; Kenny Barron; Cal Massey; bassists Nelson Boyd and Spanky DeBrest; tenor saxophonists Lynn Hope and Jimmy Heath; alto saxophonist Louis Jordan; drummers James DePreist, Butch Ballard, Lex Humphries, and Philly Joe Jones; and trombonist Al Grey, to name a few.

5. The lack of available information for this period had nothing to do with the competency of the research consultants, but rather a need to document African American contributions to music in Philadelphia for the 19th and 20th centuries.

6. As my oral narrative research became more extensive, I also used spaces at Temple University, where I conducted interviews.

7. A valuable collection of photographs is the Charles L. Blockson Afro-American Collection at Temple University. Photographs found in the possession of interviewees included those of live performances of musicians at dances, social affairs, fund-raisers, teas, bars, and nightclubs.

8. From James E. Adams's personal collection and the Philadelphia Clef Club of the Performing Arts.

9. From James Morgan's personal collection.

10. From Dr. Russell Minton's personal papers. In 1900, the Philadelphia Orchestra, which excluded black membership, was founded. Subsequently, Edward Gilbert Anderson founded a black orchestra company, the Philadelphia Concert Orchestra, in 1905, incorporated in 1908.

11. Local 591 was the black subsidiary of white Local 77, organized in 1915 to protect black musicians. See *Philadelphia Tribune* (1916), Philadelphia Colored Directory Company (1923), and Taylor (1990).

REFERENCES

Frisch, M. (1990). *A shared authority: Essays in the craft and meaning of oral and public history.* New York: SUNY Press.
Grele, R. (1991). *Envelopes of sound: The art of oral history.* New York: Praeger.
Kyvig, D. (1982). *A nearby history.* Nashville, TN: American Association for the Study of Life and History.
Philadelphia Colored Directory Company. (1923). *Philadelphia colored directory.* Philadelphia: Author.
Philadelphia Tribune. (1916, June 13).
Portelli, A. (1991). *The death of Luigi Trastulli and other stories: Form and meaning in oral history.* New York: SUNY Press.
Taylor, F. J. (1990). Black musicians in the *Philadelphia Tribune,* 1912-1920. *Black Perspective in Music, 18,* 1-2.

12

METHODOLOGICAL CONSIDERATIONS IN FIELD RESEARCH

Six Case Studies

PATRICIA GREEN-POWELL

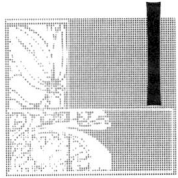In this chapter, I discuss technique and methodological orientations to field research and the implications of these for decisions affecting setting, recording modes, participant observation, data analysis, and ethical considerations. The principal field research method discussed is naturalistic observation.

To fully comprehend the research setting, a plethora of questions must be addressed, including the following: (a) What environmental factors contribute to the career advancement of black women in educational administration? (b) What are the perceived barriers to black women's progress toward the principalship? (c) What are the perceived facilitators to black women's progress toward the principalship? and (d) What role, if any, do mentors play in helping black women obtain

---

AUTHOR'S NOTE: The pseudonyms chosen for the six case study profiles in this chapter are Ida B. Wells, Billie Holiday, Harriet Tubman, Sojourner Truth, Madam C. J. Walker, and Mary McLeod-Bethune. The nationally recognized work of these six historically prominent women was not intended, however, to parallel the work and accomplishments of the women included in this study.

positions in educational administration? An understanding of the setting is dependent on the way research questions are defined and on the precision and relevance of the language used to frame them.

Recording observations, impressions, and interactions may be accomplished through multiple modes. Among these are tape recordings, field notes, and daily journaling. The tape recorder seems most appropriate when the purpose of the study is to explore complex issues in considerable depth with a limited number of respondents. It is important, however, for the researcher to support tape recordings of conversations and events with mental and written notations of impressions conveyed through nonverbal cues, passive behaviors, and nonevents.

The daily journal is recommended as a means of recording personal experiences and the researcher's reflections on those experiences. Journaling helps the researcher in developing a capacity for introspection and reflectivity and an enhanced cognizance of personal attitudes and emotions felt during the course of the research.

As a participant-observer, the researcher interacts with participants, both observing and partaking of their activities. He or she conducts informal interviews with them and others who are involved in the social environment under study and, through these involvements, reconstructs their reality.

The interview is the best method for capturing the feelings, attitudes, and perceptions of the participants under study. The advantage of the interview as a research tool is that it is possible for the researcher to talk directly with his or her subjects and to investigate their thinking firsthand. The format of the interview may vary. In standardized open-ended interviews, the interviewer must ask participants the same questions in the same sequence to reduce interviewer effect and bias. Standardizing questions, however, can constrain and limit the natural flow and relevancy of the response. In contrast, in the informal conversational interview, the questions emerge from the immediate context and are asked in the natural course of events.

Data analysis requires the researcher to capture the complexity of reality and to make convincing sense of it. One method of data analysis, *grounded theory*, entails the systematic and intensive analysis of data, often sentence by sentence or phrase by phrase, from the field notes, interviews, and other documents. In the technique of *constant comparison*, the hallmark of grounded theory analysis, data are extensively collected and coded by means of induction, deduction, and verification to produce a well-constructed theory.

Ethical procedures involve obtaining permission from the agency or organization, securing informed consent, preserving the anonymity of the participants, and securing the field notes and tape recordings. Ethical considerations also figure prominently in practices pertaining to trust building, maintaining confidentiality, and reporting results.

The methodological considerations introduced here are discussed in the context of six case studies conducted with black female principals in Florida. The facilitators and barriers affecting their progress toward the principalship provide fertile ground for explaining the methodological intricacies of field research.

I became interested in qualitative research design and the oral narrative research method simply by chance while developing the research topic for my doctoral dissertation. In the course of my graduate study, I enrolled in several research method classes in which qualitative research design and the oral narrative method were discussed at great length by various professors. Once I began to read through several published dissertations that used the qualitative and oral narrative research designs and I gained experience through a research class practicum, I knew without a doubt that I wanted to conduct qualitative research.

While working as coordinator of academic programs in the College of Education at Florida State University, I interacted with many elementary- and secondary-level school principals in the southern counties of the state. In several of those districts, I noticed the absence of black female principals. I have, for a number of years, been particularly interested in issues related to women in education. For days and months, I asked myself several questions concerning the lack of black female representation in principalship positions, including, What barriers exist? and How salient is each barrier for preventing women, particularly black women, from entering school administration? By the same token, a few schools did have black principals, so I wanted to know how they got there. Historical record has shown that women have always been second choice in the selection of school leaders. This record was accurately reflected in the various counties I visited. I wanted to determine the reasons for this situation and to explore further. Hence, the doctoral research project had a framework.

METHODOLOGY

Obtaining Permissions

As stated earlier, ethical considerations are vital to conducting research. Informed consent, which implies that the subjects have a choice about whether to participate, was secured prior to data collection.

Permission from the participating school districts was obtained immediately. I encountered no difficulty, primarily because I had developed a professional working relationship with the superintendents over the years while coordinating student-teacher placements for teacher-education students. Each school superintendent agreed to allow me to conduct the study in his district.

When I approached the research participants, each wanted to be assured of anonymity. To preserve their privacy, I assigned a pseudonym to each subject and informant and omitted the names of individual schools. Information collected about the participants was kept confidential. Field notes and tape recordings were securely protected. I maintained the data, and no one else was allowed access to it.

One of the most intriguing experiences for me involved the assignment of pseudonyms to the six female subjects. These women, each of whom was employed in a visible role in the public school system, agreed to participate in the study only if anonymity and confidentiality were assured. Once I described my plan for using pseudonyms, they were convinced that they wanted to participate.

Because the research suggested that women and minorities are dramatically underrepresented in education administration, I suspected that these six women had revealing stories to tell about how they had acquired their respective positions and that they had succeeded only with some difficulty. After much deliberation, I decided to use the names of six black women whose names were familiar and who had made significant contributions to history. These women were also heroines in their own time.

Handling Personal Bias

I recognized the biases that I held in terms of affirmative action and equal opportunity practices, mentoring, and the career mobility of black women. Because my earlier employment had focused heavily on hiring practices and procedures and on career mobility, I took this background into account when making my observations and interpretations. It was my goal to represent the realities of what was observed as descriptively and accurately as possible while constantly monitoring for biases brought to the study.

I kept a daily journal in which I recorded "personal" experiences during the course of the study. This journal fostered introspection and generally helped me become more cognizant of my own attitudes and feelings so that I could remain alert to any personal biases that might have tainted the process.

Selecting the Site and Sampling Processes

Two public school districts in Florida were the targeted geographic locations for the study. These districts were selected because of their high percentage of black female principals. In one county, 25% of principals, or 4 out of 16 total, were black females (according to a Florida Department of Education representative interviewed in 1992). In the other county, 13.5% of principals, or 5 out of 37 total, were black females (according to information obtained in a 1992 interview at the Equal Employment Opportunity Commission).

In addition, having grown up in one of the counties, I knew many of the administrators, principals, and teachers who participated in the study. I had also worked with administrators and principals in one of the counties in various educational endeavors, such as coordinating student teaching, planning inservice training, and promoting staff-development activities. This familiarity proved to be an advantage in gaining access to participants. I was careful, however, to guard against the biases toward which such familiarity might predispose me as I collected and analyzed data and formed bonds of trust with the participants.

Using Purposeful Sampling

Merriam (1988) states that two types of sampling are used in research: probability and nonprobability. Because generalization from a statistical perspective is not the goal of qualitative case study research, nonprobability sampling is the method I used in this study. Nonprobabilistic sampling is termed "purposeful sampling," according to Patton (1980, p. 100).

The population of interest for this study was a group of principals who fit the selected criteria of race (black), gender (female), and employment (public school principals). The participant selection process involved the following steps:

1. Identify black female principals of the district.
2. Contact all black female principals and introduce them to the study for the purpose of determining their interest in participation.
3. Schedule an interview with each.

During the interview, I discussed the parameters of the study with each principal to determine the willingness and ability of each to participate. Participation required that the principal be willing to interact with me in interview settings. The final sample consisted of six black females.

Choosing the Research Design

Qualitative research design was the method I chose for gathering data. This type of design is ideal when the researcher is interested in seeking insight, discovery, and interpretation, rather than testing hypotheses. In my research, the phenomena of facilitators and barriers to the progress of the six black women toward the principalship were investigated for the purpose of gaining insight and making discoveries about the means by which these six women gained entry into the principalship.

Qualitative designs are naturalistic in that the researcher does not attempt to manipulate the research setting. The research setting is a naturally occurring event, program, community relationship, or interaction that has no predetermined course established by and for the researcher.

The point of using qualitative methods is that an understanding of naturally occurring phenomena requires that they be observed in their naturally occurring states (Patton, 1980). The qualitative design in this study sought to "capture" what the female principals had to say in their own words in their "natural setting." Bogdan and Biklen (1982) identified five features of qualitative research: (a) It is concerned with the context of the data gathering (the natural setting is the direct source of the data collected), (b) it serves primarily as descriptive research, (c) it is concerned with the research process, not merely with the outcomes or products, (d) theory emerges as the data are being gathered and grouped, and (e) it is concerned with participant meanings and perceptions. These features were the foundation of this research study.

Adopting a Research Instrument

The primary research instrument adopted for this study was the researcher acting as participant-observer. The role of the researcher as data collection instrument was guided by the following suggestions for collecting case study data:

1. The researcher should be able to ask appropriate questions and to interpret the answers.
2. The researcher should be a good "listener" and not be trapped by his or her own ideologies or preconceptions.
3. The researcher should be adaptive and flexible, so that newly encountered situations can be viewed as opportunities, not threats.
4. The researcher must have a firm grasp of the issues being studied, whether within a theoretical or policy orientation and even if in an exploratory mode. Such a grasp reduces to manageable proportions the relevant events and information to be sought.

5. The researcher should be unbiased by preconceived notions, including those derived from theory. The researcher should also be sensitive and responsive to contradictory evidence. (Yin, 1989, p. 63)

As participant-observer, I had the option of using several research methods simultaneously. In this study, data collection methods included document analysis, the interview, and direct observation.

Using Multiple Sources of Evidence

Case studies using multiple sources of evidence are rated more highly in terms of overall quality than those relying on a single source of information (Yin, Bateman, & Moore, 1983). Evidence for this case study was obtained from four sources: the researcher as participant-observer, document analysis, interviews, and direct observation.

Researcher as Participant-Observer

Using the participant-observer strategy, the researcher seeks to interact with the participants, observing and engaging in their activities with them and others who are involved in the social environment under study and, through these involvements, to reconstruct their reality.

Document Analysis

Document analysis in qualitative inquiry makes use of excerpts, quotations, or entire passages from organizational, clinical, or program records; memoranda and correspondence; official publications and reports; personal diaries; and open-ended written responses to questionnaires and surveys (Patton, 1980). Documents provide valuable information because of what the researcher learns directly by reading them. They can also provide the stimulus for questions that can be pursued only through direct observation and interviewing.

The documents analyzed included district affirmative action policies, practices, procedures, and plans, as well as human resource management development (HRMD) plans.

The Interview

The interview was the method most effective in capturing the feelings, attitudes, and perceptions of the black female principals under study. It may be noted that only in the study of human beings is it possible for the scientist (researcher) to talk with his or her subjects and investigate directly their thinking processes.

There are, according to Patton (1980), three basic types of interviews: (a) the *informal, conversational interview,* characterized by no set format of questions; (b) the *general interview,* in which the researcher has a predetermined set of questions to be explored with each participant; and (c) the *standardized, open-ended interview* that is "a set of questions carefully worded and arranged with the intention of taking each respondent through the same sequence and asking each participant the same questions with essentially the same words" (Patton, 1980, p. 198).

This study employed both the informal, conversational interview and the standardized, open-ended interview in gathering data. (See Appendix A at the end of this chapter for the orienting questions used during open-ended interviews with participants.)

Through the interview process, I gained from the research participants their significant memories of the past and plans for the future. And because I was interested in capturing deep and sensitive feelings, as well as the reasons for their feelings and perceptions, opinions, and attitudes, the informal, conversational interview and the open-ended interview provided the most effective methods of inquiry.

During the informal, conversational interview, the questions emerged from the immediate context and were asked in the natural course of a conversational exchange. During the open-ended interview, participants were asked the same questions in the same order. This technique served to reduce interviewer effects and bias; however, the use of standardized questions also, to some extent, constrained the process and limited the naturalness and relevancy of the response.

Direct Observation

Direct observation (with the researcher acting as an outside, nonparticipating observer) occurred at the school sites. Observations ranged from formal to casual data collection activities. I observed faculty meetings conducted by the six principals at the school sites, as well as the regular daily routine of each principal during workdays. Further, I observed and gathered data about the physical environment, which is often an important factor in what happens within the environment.

Maintaining Rigor

Guba and Lincoln (1981) offer alternative terms in describing the criteria for maintaining rigor in qualitative research. Instead of the terms *internal validity, external validity,* and *reliability,* as traditionally used in educational research, Guba's study posited the terms *credibility* for internal validity, *fittingness* for external validity, and *auditability* for reliability. These sets of terms hold essentially the same meaning in discussions of whether a study is true, applicable, and consistent.

Internal Validity/Credibility

The *credibility* (Guba, 1981), or internal validity, of an explanatory case study is based on establishing a causal relationship whereby certain conditions are shown to lead to other conditions, as distinguished from a spurious relationship (Yin, 1989).

The criterion of credibility involves the question of how well the findings of the study match reality. One assumption in a qualitative case study is that humans make or perceive multiple realities.

In this study, the role of the researcher in ensuring credibility was to match (a) the participants' perceptions of reality in regard to the facilitators and barriers of progress toward the principalship with (b) perceptions indicated in the review of literature. Using triangulation, reviewing with participants the data and the researcher's interpretation of the data, observing over an extended time, and involving the participants in some aspects of the study—all these practices helped ensure credibility.

External Validity/Fittingness

The criterion of *fittingness* involves the question of whether the findings of the study can be applied to another situation (Merriam, 1988)—that is, how generalizable are the results of the study? The primary aim of a qualitative case study like this one, however, is to gain an in-depth understanding of a particular phenomenon or specific phenomena, rather than to generalize or state what is generally true across populations.

For the purposes of a qualitative case study, Cronbach (1975) and Patton (1980) proposed that "working hypotheses" replace the objective of generalizability in social science research. These working hypotheses, according to Patton (1980), "provide perspective rather than truth, empirical assessment of a local decision-maker's theories and context-bound information rather than generalizations" (p. 283).

Nevertheless, in an effort to meet the criterion of fittingness, or external validity, the following were included in the research design:

- Extensive descriptions of the time, place, context, county, community, and culture of each school and principal were presented.

- Lengthy and intrusive data collection occurred for 6 months.
- Participant language was used whenever possible in the final report to validate conclusions.
- A multiple case study approach with ethnographic data-gathering techniques and a grounded theory analysis was used.

Reliability/Auditability

The criterion of *auditability* involves the question, How consistent or dependable are the results of the study, given the data obtained? "Rather than demanding that outsiders get the same results, one wishes outsiders to concur that, given the data collected, the results make sense—they are consistent and dependable" (Merriam, 1988, p. 173). To aid the researcher in achieving results that are auditable or dependable, the following guidelines have been suggested:

- The investigator should explain the assumptions and theory behind the study, his or her position vis-à-vis the group being studied, the group being studied, the basis for selecting informants and a description of them, and the social context in which data were collected (Goetz & LeCompte, 1984).
- Especially when multiple methods of data collection and analysis are used, triangulation strengthens reliability, as well as internal validity (Merriam, 1988).
- The researcher should describe in detail how data were collected, how categories were derived, and how decisions were made throughout the inquiry. These methods should be presented in such detail "that other researchers could use the original report as an operating manual by which to replicate the study" (Goetz & LeCompte, 1984, p. 216).

Using Recording Modes

Data were collected primarily through tape-recorded interviews. Tape recordings were needed to ensure the accurate and complete transcription of responses to the open-ended interview questions. The study depended on the accuracy and completeness of the record of what each principal said and how she said it. The tape recorder allowed for the fullest and most in-depth exploration of complex issues without loss or misrepresentation.

I actually looked forward to listening to the interviews after each session. I was particularly amused when one of the principals said to me, "Now turn the recorder off. I don't want this ever repeated or ever entered into your research. This statement may come back to haunt me." Another said, "Now what I am about to say does not need to ever be repeated, so turn off the machine. You and I may both go jail or get arrested."

Prior to each taped interview session, I checked all recording equipment. I did not want to risk tape recorder failure. I also traveled with a second recorder in my car, just in case I encountered problems with the first one.

The tape-recorded data were later transcribed, along with observer comments. Field notes were also taken so that nonverbal cues could be recorded and observer reflections made. In addition, I maintained a daily journal (see Appendix B at the end of this chapter for a journal sample). All transcripts, field notes, and observer comments were dated and kept on file for verification and audit purposes.

Performing Data Analysis

Data analysis requires the researcher to capture the complexity of reality (phenomena) and to make convincing sense of it (Strauss, 1989). According to Strauss (1989), this process requires that, first, the researcher be guided by the participants' interpretations, the researcher's own interpretations of the participants' response, and the analysis of the data collected during the study. Second, the grounded theories generated by this type of study, which are the final products of data analysis, must involve combinations of many concepts and linkages among those concepts. Third, the researcher must closely attend to and examine data in detail to discover the complexity of what is contained in and what is suggested beyond the data collected. This study used what Strauss describes as a grounded theory of analysis. *Grounded theory* is "a detailed grounding ... by systematically and intensively analyzing data, often sentence by sentence or phrase by phrase, of the field notes, interviews, or other documents; and ... by constant comparison, data are extensively collected and coded, using the operations of induction, deduction and verification, thus, producing a well constructed theory" (p. 22).

I used induction, deduction, and verification to explore and analyze the data. *Induction* (reaching a general conclusion by observing particular instances) refers to the process that leads to the discovery of a hypothesis. According to Strauss (1989), the insights, hunches, or generative questions that constitute the inquiry come from the researcher's experience with the phenomenon studied.

Deduction (reaching a conclusion about particulars by reasoning from general/universal premises) requires not only the ability to think logically but also experience in thinking about the particular kinds of data under investigation. My research experience enabled me to think effectively and propositionally, to make comparisons that furthered the line of deduction.

Verification (the process of establishing accuracy) involves the researcher's knowledge of the sites, events, actions, actors, procedures, and techniques. My knowledge was the result of personal and professional experience.

The concept-indicator model was used to direct the conceptual coding of a set of empirical indicators (the actual data), the data being such things as behavioral actions and events, observed or described in documents and in the words of the participants (Strauss, 1989). This model is based on the constant comparison of indicator to indicator, which requires that the researcher examine comparatively behavioral actions/ events and then "code" them by naming them as a class of events/ behavioral actions; each class named then becomes a coded category. The process of constantly comparing indicator with indicator enables the researcher to find similarities, differences, and consistencies among the indicators.

Themes were generated from the data and an ongoing analysis as this study discovered the perceptions that black women principals have regarding the facilitators and barriers to their attainment of principalships. The goal of this study was to gain insight into the experiences and environmental factors that contributed to career mobility, rather than to confirm or refute a particular theory of how these women gained their positions.

Writing the Case Study Report

Focusing the Report

This case study report focuses on analytic abstractions for the purpose of presenting a theory on the perceptions that black female principals have regarding the facilitators and barriers to their attainment of principalships. The presentation represents a commingling of theory and data.

In this study, the three major types of focus—thesis, theme, and topic—as outlined by Bogdan and Biklen (1982) were blended together; that is, the descriptions offered by the principals regarding facilitators and barriers to principalships give insights into present theories on methods for obtaining access to principalships and into the experiences that contribute to career advancement.

The use of a *thesis focus* assisted me in using the data to communicate how these principals gained access to principalships. Central to this study was the presentation of the major themes or "overarching concepts or theoretical formulations that emerged from the data analysis" (Merriam, 1988, p. 190).

In the *themes focus*, the themes of the study were used as frames, or "basic structural units," to illustrate the insights that these principals offered about the procedures and processes by which they entered the profession. These themes were "brought to a level of abstraction that made [the study] generally more applicable rather than an isolated concern" (Merriam, 1988 p. 191).

Further, this study had a *topic focus*. By describing the principals' perceptions of facilitators and barriers, the study provides insights about how access to positions of school principals may be gained. In addition, the role of social context was clearly depicted. This depiction provides critical information that contributes to the linking of theory and practice, with the knowledge of the "consumer" as a participant in the learning process.

Planning for Trustworthiness

To achieve valid and reliable results in this type of research study, I used a process of continuous, informal testing of information, called *member checks*. Lincoln and Guba (1985) assert that the use of this process ensures truth, value, or credibility. The investigator conducts member checks by (a) soliciting reactions and responses to his or her reconstruction of what has been said or otherwise found out and to the constructions offered by other respondents or sources and (2) employing a terminal, formal test of the final case report with a representative sample of stakeholders.

A pilot study was conducted to test my proficiency in interviewing techniques. This exercise led to improvements in several areas of the interview process and thus to more productive interviews.

The pilot participant, who was not a study participant, was asked the same questions as the study participants. The purpose of the pilot study was to clarify the questions that were to be asked of the study's participants and to ascertain the feasibility of the questions and the length of time required for the interview. General comments and critiques were also requested from the pilot participant. Feedback from the pilot respondent was incorporated into the final interview guide.

The Six Case Studies

Case Study of "Billie Holiday"

Billie has been a secondary school principal for 12 years. Before her appointment to the secondary principalship, Billie was an assistant principal for 9 years at a secondary school in the county where she is currently a principal. Billie was a classroom teacher for 5 years, 3 of which were in another county school district in Florida. She holds a bachelor of science degree, a master of education degree, and a doctor of philosophy degree in administration and supervision. She is married and has one child.

Billie is a member of several professional organizations, including the Florida Association of Secondary School Principals and the National Association of Secondary School Principals. She is a member of a national black female sorority.

Case Study of "Ida B. Wells"

Ida has been an elementary school principal for 5 years. Before her appointment to the elementary principalship, Ida was an assistant principal for 4 years at an elementary school in the county where she is currently a principal. Ida worked as a classroom teacher for 6 years. She holds a bachelor of arts degree, a master of science degree, and an educational specialist degree. She is divorced and has two children. Ida is a member of the Phi Delta Kappa honor society.

Case Study of "Harriet Tubman"

Harriet has been a secondary school principal for 4 years. Before her appointment to the secondary principalship, Harriet was a curriculum assistant for 12 years at the high school where she is currently principal. Harriet was an English and Spanish teacher at this same school for 15 years. She holds a bachelor's degree and a master of education degree. She is married and has no children.

Harriet has held many civic and political positions in the school district and community, as well as in her church, including commissioner of county public libraries and volunteer coordinator of the county school system. She is a member of several professional organizations, including the Florida Association of Secondary School Principals and the National Association of Secondary School Principals. She is also a member of a national black female sorority.

Case Study of "Sojourner Truth"

Sojourner has been an elementary school principal for 3 years. Before her appointment to the elementary principalship, Sojourner was a curriculum assistant for 9 years at three different schools in the country. Sojourner was a classroom teacher for 10 years. She holds a bachelor of science degree and a master of education degree in administration and supervision, as well as a master of education degree in elementary education. She is married and has one child.

Sojourner is a member of several professional organizations, including the Florida Association of School Administrators and the Florida Association of Elementary School Principals. She is a member of a national black female sorority.

Case Study of "Madame C. J. Walker"

C. J. has been an elementary school principal for 5 years. Before her appointment to the elementary principalship, C. J. was an assistant principal at an elementary school for 3 years. C. J. was also a classroom teacher for 12 years. She holds a bachelor of science degree and a master of education degree. She is married and has two children.

C. J. is a member of several civic and community organizations, including the Capital Area Progressive Women. She is a member of the Florida Association of School Administrators and the Florida Association of Elementary School Principals. In addition, she is a member of a national black female sorority.

Case Study of "Mary McLeod-Bethune"

Mary has been an elementary principal for 4 years. Before her appointment to the elementary principalship, Mary worked as an assistant principal for 2 years. Mary was also a classroom teacher for 23 years (17 of which were in another county). She holds a bachelor of science degree and a master of education degree. She is married and has one child.

Mary is a member of the Florida Association of Elementary School Principals. She is a member of Phi Delta Kappa honor society and of Delta Kappa Gamma and is also a member of a national black female sorority.

Performing Data Analysis

By the end of the field research and data collection process, I could literally fill my home office with paper, notebooks, documents from the district offices, memos written by the principals, and a variety of other printed information that I knew would be important to me as I attempted to "make meaning" of this roomful of information. I was somewhat nervous and overwhelmed by the task ahead of me. I had learned early in research classes that data analysis was both time-consuming and tedious, so I approached the process with mixed emotions. On the one hand, I was eager to get the information in some workable order and to find out exactly what the interview and field notes would reveal about the six principals; on the other hand, I also knew that I had a monumental task of analyzing the data in a meaningful way.

"Data analysis is the process of systematically searching and arranging the structured interview transcripts, field notes, and other material . . . to increase . . . understanding of them" (Bogdan & Biklen, 1982, p. 145). Actually, data analysis is an ongoing process that begins early in the data collection.

A grounded theory approach (Strauss, 1989) was used for data analysis. My task was to generate theory from holistic data. The coding paradigm developed by Strauss was used to code the data. Strauss explains the paradigm as a "reminder to code data for relevance to whatever phenomena are referenced by a given category, for the following: conditions, interactions among actors, strategies and tactics, and consequences" (pp. 27-28).

Initially, I generated categories, themes, and patterns in accordance with recurring phrases or key statements. I tested the emergent themes against the data and searched for alternative explanations of the data.

During the analysis of the data, I also used the "cut-up-and-put-in-folders" approach (Bogdan & Biklen, 1982, p. 166). Multiple copies of the raw data were made. The first copy was used for coding. The second copy was cut according to the codes and marked to identify where it came from in the original set. Manila folders were labeled with the categories. The units of data were then cut and put into the appropriate folders and were examined further for possible assertion.

The data are arranged in a format that presents the themes that emerged from conversations with the principals. Below, I present one example of these emergent themes in the form of a gerund phrase. I also discuss one example of an assertion constituting grounded theory within the framework of the emergent themes.

Theme 1: Recognizing Leadership Qualities

The principals cited the hard work, commitment, competence, and confidence they displayed in their previous positions (as teachers and assistant principals) as facilitators to obtaining their principalships. Each woman was articulate in pointing out the accomplishments and achievements that she believed played significant roles in her appointment to a principalship.

During the interviews, these principals often mentioned that their leadership qualities had been recognized and encouraged by others. They also reported that they would either volunteer for or be assigned to special projects or tasks at the schools where they were employed. They perceived working with special projects or tasks as ways of becoming involved in decision-making and administrative-level duties and as opportunities to work closely with the principal and to gain experience.

Assertion 1. These principals see themselves as having moved ahead because of their own hard work and where they were in their own lives and because their abilities were recognized and encouraged by others.

Mary: Upon coming to this county, I had a wealthy background in leadership skills. This was mainly because my principal in another county school system afforded me many opportunities to take over leadership positions. In this particular county, there were no assistant principals at the elementary school level, and therefore someone had to be in charge when the principal was away. I guess the principal at the school recognized the qualities in me and bestowed the responsibilities on me.

Billie: It was just coincidence that I got the job of principal. I was in the right place at the right time. The principal at the school discovered that I had a master's degree in education. I began to work closely with the assistant principal, and she trained me to be the curriculum assistant. At midterm, I took over as assistant principal. I was assistant principal for 9 years, and when a principalship position became available, I had the administrative experience and I was encouraged.

Ida: When I was teaching, I thoroughly enjoyed it and really wanted to be a teacher for a lifelong career. But I was divorced in 1983, so that necessitated me improving my financial status at home because I did have two children to raise. So the financial responsibility of raising two children alone was a great impetus for me rising into the principalship.

Sojourner: About 10 years ago, I was fortunate enough to be selected as curriculum assistant at a middle school, leaving the elementary school and going to a middle school. I got an opportunity to get lots of administrative experiences. So, I think, after having worked as a curriculum assistant and being given all of the responsibilities and duties of a principal, I was really ready to advance to become a principal.

Harriet: Basically, I feel that, through my effort in being very conscientious about seeking the principalship, I had people to always listen to my ideas, and they sort of bought into the sharing of accomplishments and goals that I had in mind. Then, in 1979, I realized that, well, this is the chance for me. I served as curriculum assistant, and my husband saw great potential also in me, and he kept encouraging me to venture into the principalship.

C. J.: Basically, I started as a teacher in this county. I taught for 11 years and moved into an assistant principal job. There were others around me who had confidence in me and pushed me to apply for a principalship.

Forming Conclusions

The findings of this type of study are derived from the qualitative data and cannot be generalized beyond the bounded group of six black female principals. Conclusions apply, therefore, solely to the group investigated in this particular study.

Because the purpose of the qualitative research design and oral narrative method used in this study was to render a true picture of each participant's "story" and her accomplishments through "thick description," it was easy to make recommendations and draw conclusions from the large amount of material and documentation that was gathered and analyzed. In addition, case study research is valuable for increasing insight and an understanding of how experiences become meaningful to those involved.

The verbatim translation of the interviews and the member checks that I conducted with each of the participants allowed me to ensure the accuracy of the final information selected for inclusion in the study.

STRENGTHS OF ORAL NARRATIVE RESEARCH FOR EXPANDING AND TRANSFORMING KNOWLEDGE ABOUT BLACK WOMEN

As a result of having completed the oral narrative research design, I feel a special bond with each of the six black women who agreed to participate in the study. I spent approximately 6 to 7 months interacting with and observing them. The content and context in which the information was shared, the interviews, field notes, and documentation reviews captured so much about them—their personalities, moods, families, environments, and professionalism.

As a researcher, I will always treasure the research time that was spent with each, the knowledge and insight gained about black women in public school administration, and their stories of how they got there. In view of the page limitation for this chapter, I cite only a few of the important ideals that I learned from the black women through the qualitative research design that I conducted.

The principalship is probably the single most powerful force for improving school effectiveness and for achieving excellence in education. It is critical, therefore, to select principals who are qualified and competent to guide staff, students, and the community. If given the opportunity, women and members of minority groups can make positive contributions to public school administration.

Despite the bleak picture for women and minorities in educational administration, some have made it. The six black women in this study viewed themselves as having successful experiences in their positions. These women were strong advocates of "moving through the ranks," beginning as teachers and then serving as assistant principals before moving to the positions of principals. These women were ambivalent in addressing the roles that mentors had played in helping them obtain their positions. They saw themselves basically as "self-made" and hardworking. They believed that mentoring was important but not essential. They discussed the support of mentors in ways that did not detract from their own accomplishments.

The impact of racism and sexism was not discussed in detail during the taped interview sessions. These women did, however, report that racism and sexism were barriers to their progress toward the principalship. On several occasions during the taped interview sessions, when the conversations began to center on discrimination and racism, several of the principals requested that I turn off the recorder because they did not want the information included in the research study.

The relationship between family and career has been seen as a difficult one for women. Women who work and are family members must face conflicting expectations and needs. The expectations are based on traditional values regarding a woman's place. In addition, the logistics involved in coordinating family and professional life are sometimes difficult or awkward to manage. The women in this study appeared to have achieved a good balance between family life and career life. They appeared confident that although they were engaged in activities at school, things were running smoothly at home because spouses or other family members were assisting.

The black female principals in this study viewed themselves as having experienced success and satisfaction in their positions. They appeared confident in their ability to lead and in their administrative competence and commitment.

Many educators have held the belief that black principals are capable of supervising only schools with a large concentration of black and other minority students. Five of the six women principals in this study were principals of schools that had large concentrations of minority students from low socioeconomic backgrounds.

SUGGESTIONS FOR APPROACHES TO TEACHING METHODOLOGY

Qualitative research and the oral narrative research methods as used in this study would be useful to university faculty, students, state and local policymakers and school administrators, and teachers. The results of the findings in this study give clear discussion of how black female appointments to the principalship were made through the use of objective principal selection procedures (used in Florida public school districts).

In addition, this research could serve as a guide to develop techniques and methodological orientations to conducting field research, as well as foster an understanding of how field research can be used to understand a particular problem or unique situation in great depth—specifically, how qualitative research methods can be used in understanding naturally occurring phenomena in their naturally occurring state. Evidence for this research was from four sources—participant-observation, document analysis, interviews, and direct observation. All of these research sources of evidence could be used as valuable teaching methodologies to fully understand the usefulness of qualitative research design.

REFERENCES

Bogdan, R. C., & Biklen, S. K. (1982). *Qualitative research for education.* Needham Heights, MA: Allyn & Bacon.
Cronbach, L. J. (1975). Beyond the two disciplines of scientific psychology. *American Psychologist, 30,* 116-127.

Goetz, J. P., & LeCompte, M. D. (1984). *Ethnography and qualitative design in educational research*. San Diego: Academic Press.

Guba, E. G. (1981). Criteria for assessing the trustworthiness of naturalistic inquiries. *Educational Communication and Technology Journal, 29*, 75-92.

Guba, E. G., & Lincoln, Y. S. (1981). *Effective evaluation*. San Francisco: Jossey-Bass.

Lincoln, Y. S., & Guba, E. G. (1985). *Naturalistic inquiry*. Beverly Hills, CA: Sage.

Merriam, S. B. (1988). *Case study research in education: A qualitative approach*. San Francisco: Jossey-Bass.

Patton, M. Q. (1980). *Qualitative evaluation methods*. Beverly Hills, CA: Sage.

Strauss, A. L. (1989). *Qualitative analysis for social scientists*. Cambridge, UK: Cambridge University Press.

Yin, R. K. (1989). *Case study research: Designs and methods*. Newbury Park, CA: Sage.

Yin, R. K., Bateman, P. G., & Moore, G. B. (1983). *Case studies and organizational innovation: Strengthening the connection*. Washington, DC: Cosmos Corporation.

Appendix A

Interview Guide: Questions for Participants

Although a vita of each principal will be requested prior to the interview, the questions in Part I of this guide are designed to elicit information about the participants' professional and personal characteristics—information that will provide a composite profile of each female principal. Part II of this guide is designed to collect information regarding the participants' views of the factors or strategies that helped them in gaining access to the principalship. Part III is designed to collect information regarding the participants' perceptions of the facilitators and barriers to gaining access to the principalship. The questions in Part IV are designed to collect information regarding the participants' predictions of what the future will hold for aspiring females and the participants' advice to women aspiring to gain access to principalships and even higher administrative positions. Also, included in Part V is a question designed to elicit information from participants regarding their retrospective view of the career decisions each had made. This guide is not all-inclusive of the questions that will eventually be raised.

PART I

Tell me the story of how you obtained the principalship.

What impact, if any, have personal responsibilities had on your career decisions and advancement?

What work experiences led to the acquisition of your present position?

How do you balance job-related administrative duties and home management?

PART II

What specific factors or strategies do you believe helped you attain a principalship?

When did you decide that you would pursue a principalship?

At what point in your career did someone encourage you to seek the position of principalship?

Did/Do you have a mentor?

If so, describe the mentoring experience.

If no mentoring experience, describe supportive roles others have played in your career development.

PART III

What particular changes in the district's principal selection process have you seen since you became principal?

What are the most significant problems or barriers you have personally experienced as a black female principal?

What encouragement/discouragement did you experience from within your school system when you began pursuing a principalship?

What barriers do you believe women still have to overcome before an "open door" policy is established by the majority of public school systems?

What characteristics of employment/professional environment within the district school system served as facilitators to your acquiring the principalship?

What personal and professional characteristics, skills, and abilities do you perceive served as facilitators to your acquiring the principalship?

PART IV

What specific factors or sources do you believe have been supportive of black female principals after they have attained principalship?

In your opinion, what factors will be most helpful for females aspiring to gain access to the principalship?

What advice regarding professional preparation would you give to other black females aspiring to gain access to the principalship?

PART V

- What do you believe the future job opportunities for principalship will be like for aspiring black female principals?
- What specific advice would you give to women aspiring to gain access to principalships and even higher levels of administrative positions?
- Knowing what you know now, if you had a chance to make changes in your career, would you choose the principalship again? Why?

Appendix B

Sample of Daily Journal

I arrived at "Elementary B" school site around 6:45 a.m. I was still somewhat sleepy and actually tired from listening to the taped interviews from all the previous site visits. As I sat in my car waiting until the 7:00 a.m. scheduled hour, I reflected on the neighborhood I had driven through to get to the school. The houses ranged from small wooden "A-frames" to beautiful two-story brick traditionals with two-car garages.

When I drove on to the particular street where the school was located, I noticed about 6-8 older-looking black men around a large fire that was built in a large barrel. These men were passing a bottle and laughing and talking. A little farther down the street, near the school site, I saw an attractive black woman retrieving her daily newspaper from the newspaper box. She smiled and waved good morning, and I returned the smile and waved good morning. As I exited my car and walked toward the school, I thought how early the principal had arrived. I knocked on the locked door, as instructed previously by the principal, and she used her key to unlock the door from the inside. She laughed and said how prompt I was. She held a large cup of coffee from a local McDonald's and told me that she had just finished a sausage biscuit. We conducted the interview in her lovely decorated office. This is my third scheduled interview with her, and she seemed a little more relaxed.

It was during this interview that she instructed me to shut off the tape because she was about to tell me something she did not want to be written or repeated. But she wanted me to know this information so that I could better understand how some of the white and black male teachers feel about her being their principal.

As soon as she instructed me to shut off the recorder, I did. I did not offer any opinion when she finished her statement. I simply asked if I could start the recorder again, and she smiled and replied yes.

The interview was interrupted twice—once when a teacher who arrived early asked for her mail, and again when a parent called to schedule an appointment. The interview lasted about 30 minutes. I gathered my personal belongings, and she turned to her computer to type out the morning announcements.

Walking down the quiet corridor, I thought how old the school building must be. The floors and walls were in need of repair. There were wall pictures of work done by the students, announcements on the bulletin board, and a portion of the wall had a painted mural of a small school (little red schoolhouse). But I can truly say that the building was clean.

My next appointment with this principal is next Thursday afternoon at 3:30. I want to observe a faculty meeting.

13

SOCIAL CONFORMITY AND SOCIAL RESISTANCE

Women's Perspectives on "Women's Place"

KIM MARIE VAZ

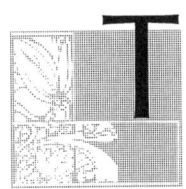he cover photograph of the black sociologist Ira Reid and his interviewees gracing the 1940 edition of his book *In a Minor Key: Negro Youth in Story and Fact* has always fascinated me. I use the cover photograph to launch a discussion on "received knowledge" with students who enroll in a course I teach entitled Research Issues on Women of Color (Vaz, 1992). In the photograph (see Photo 13.1), Reid sits on a porch, with a notebook outstretched, conducting an interview with a "Negro" woman. The interviewee sits on a low stool and simultaneously prepares food while responding to interview questions. She is flanked by numerous children. Conspicuously absent are her adult male peers—husband, father, brother, uncles, and neighbors. The only males in the photograph are very young boys and Reid, whose position relative to the women and the children is artificially elevated with the help of a step stool. My search in the book for an explanation of the title *In a Minor Key* was unsuccessful, but the implication for a "one-down" or subordinate status for black people is being conveyed no matter what spin the title is given. Whether because of age or race, the restricted "musicality" of the "Negro" life wins out as the ruling connotation. What are we to conclude from the book's title and the picture?

Photo 13.1. Cover photograph from Ira Reid's *In a Minor Key: Negro Youth in Story and Fact* (1940 edition).

What fate awaits Negro girls and boys? Implied in word and image is that Negro boys can look forward to their disappearance unless they somehow magically transform themselves into "outsiders within" (Collins, 1986) particular Negro communities as exemplified by Reid. And Negro girls have only to expect as their lot the burdens and joys of producing and reproducing large families. Whose angle of vision is being promoted here—that of the *Life Magazine* photographer who "captured" Reid "capturing" the "reality" of Negro youth, or of the American Youth Commission, which authorized and published but did not necessarily endorse Reid's research? Does this snapshot convey the premise of Reid's interpretation of his research findings? Is it at all useful to analyze a cover photograph and title? After all, should we judge a book by its cover; an author and organization by their book?

Received knowledge in academia is the taken-for-granted categories and interpretations that have been produced (through empirical research, philosophical speculation, and/or poetic channeling) by a community of experts, predominantly white men, who engage in a process of validating each other's knowledge claims (Collins, 1990). A fundamental epistemological assumption in this tradition is that what one "sees" (through the "collection of data") is free from one's judgments about what has been observed. Until very recently, the received knowledge about racial inequality, like integration, was decidedly skewed. The problem of status inequality between blacks and whites was interpreted primarily in the light of the impact of racism on black people; that racism had consequences for white people affecting every aspect of their daily lives was totally obscured from view. That part of socialization for becoming a white person involved psychological conditioning for the denial of his or her privileged (not necessarily monied) status was, for the white male-dominated academic establishment, neither fodder for empirical research nor an invitation to theoretical speculation. "Race" was something only black people had, and "attached" to race was a position of disadvantage that could be investigated and quantified.

Although Reid was not white, he was selected by the commission for his sociological expertise to discover for them "what it means to be born a member of America's largest minority." Reid provided a daunting catalog of social, legal, and economic practices that perpetuated the caste-like position of African Americans in the 1930s; yet, his interpretations articulate the received knowledge of liberal discourse on the issue of racial inequality. I have come to understand the premise of this discourse to mean that although discrimination exists and creates black "pathology," individual whites in white communities are not necessarily culpable. There is the admittance of foul play by various entities and society as a whole, but all within the purview of a more fundamental white innocence. An alternative view, indeed that one does exist, wherein the behavioral choices of black people are consequent to the "pathological" practices that whites use to create and maintain a separate white identity for individual white people and "whiteness" as an "American" character was, of course, not entertained. The "pathological" black family, with its "dominant" or "matriarchal" mother working overtime to eke out a life for her large brood and an absent, noncontributing black husband/father, is a cornerstone of this view. Reid saw black families as largely "chaotic," black neighborhoods as "slums," and the black community plagued by the "criminal" element. There were variations in black families, he allowed, but the "bulk of Negro youth" lived under these conditions. "Negro youth emerge from a home environment filled with problems both social and cultural. Their families, in the main, do not have long, unbroken set of rules and sanctions to keep them intact which characterizes some of the older white populations" (Reid, 1940, p. 25). Reid attributed the conditions of black family and community life as stemming from an early period of having been in bondage and also to municipal neglect, real estate covenants, and lack of sanitary regulation enforcement, all of which were perpetuated by the government, landlords, and the community at large. Reid ultimately blamed poverty for the problems of the black community: "Negroes have been victimized because of their low plane of living and little economic independence. They have appeared servile because they have been oppressed; they have been oppressed because they are poor" (p. 110).

The new discourse on the social construction of whiteness interrupts and challenges the received theoretical formulations about the persistence of racial inequality. Ruth Frankenberg (1993) has described the social geography of whiteness that allows white people to acknowledge racial oppression as it shapes the economic lives of black people but that blinds them to their own race privilege. Thus, whites can see their lives as "racially neutral—nonracialized, nonpolitical" (p. 49). Frankenberg's cartography locates each site where race and racism shape the lives of white people: residential segregation, the projected "fear" of black people; verbal assertions of white superiority, African American and Latino women's invisibility as domestic workers in white families, and so on. These patterns emerge from a "system of material relations" (p. 70) and are linked to a set of ideas about race: who has it and what happens to those who have it. Peggy McIntosh (1995) goes so far as to list 46 special assets that she has access to, not because of merit, but because of white skin privilege. Lifting the blinders off white denial of privilege affords an opportunity to witness the racial dance steps of the United States. In Reid's received knowledge approach, white people are the measuring rod. How well black people "measure up" to these standards is then an indication of black health and well-being, or absence of pathology. Nevertheless, for all his inclusion of the discriminatory practices meted out to black people in his era, discrimination in the final analysis was seen as damaging to black people because it prevented them from reaching white standards. In view of the challenge to white liberal discourse by critical race theorists, I would add to Reid's concluding statement that white people have been victimizers because of their decision to promote their ways as representing a "higher" plane of living. They have been victimizers because their economic dependence on black people has been rigorously denied. They have appeared dominant because so many have been oppressors; they have oppressed because they have chosen not to share.

Feminist oral narrative research, for me, consists of the most important of all human endeavors—the listening to and telling of women's stories—and this is a suspicious activity in the domain of received knowledge. I find useful Bettina Aptheker's (1989) ideas about the importance of stories for discovering women's standpoints. She notes that women's stories point to the knowledge claims of women—that is, what phenomenon from a woman's perspective should be taught or necessitates further study. And women's stories contain the answers to some of our dilemmas. When we are in need of assistance, we remember a story because the help we need is contained within it. Through the story process, we invent meaning, preserve cultural identity, and give and receive emotional support; and we learn that women are not always victimized and curtailed by circumstances but that many have, in June Jordan's words, "made a way out of no way." Feminist oral history, in line with feminist teaching, provides both understanding and opposition to the social inequalities that women face. Through collecting these stories, these treasures, women's personal visions for a life free from multiple dominations are given voice. As collectors of these treasures, feminist/womanist researchers can disseminate the story of how life is for women under patriarchy and delineate how oppression need not be continued. We map the route away from oppressive practices and toward more scenic, more enjoyable, more peaceful, not necessarily more efficient, alternatives.

ORAL NARRATIVE RESEARCH

My introduction to oral narrative research came by surprise when I was in Nigeria, conducting dissertation research using a standard quantitative approach on marital conflict resolution among cross-cultural couples (specifically, foreign wives of Yoruba men). The dissertation I proposed and the one I ultimately completed were not one and the same. Once in the "field," I was repeatedly advised to simply "let people talk." Thus, my qualitative research skills developed through self-instruction. Many of the interview questions that guided my initial data collection efforts after I switched from a structured, deductive, quantitative methodology to an open-ended, inductive, qualitative approach addressed how foreign women became adjusted to life in Nigeria. These questions were directly linked to my learning to live there and were methodologically significant because they led to comparisons of how different women managed; that is, some women drew boundaries between themselves and the culture, and others did not. In addition, I naively assumed that all wives were attempting to assimilate. What became immediately apparent was that not all women were interested in integrating deeply. This faulty assumption led to the identification of four levels of cultural adaptation among these wives. Furthermore, not all women had experience with the same cultural traditions. For example, some women were living in polygynous homes and others were living in monogamous ones. From this observation, I came to see that each woman was coping with a different tradition selected by her husband from a limited number of cultural components (e.g., polygyny, religion). This observation ultimately led to the notion that although husbands "changed" in different ways, the consequences for the majority of wives were the same. The men's changes led to a process in which foreign wives learned to manage their own covert disapproval of the shifting marital role structure.

My first field experience took place between May 1988 and January 1989 in Ile-Ife, Osun State, Nigeria. Approximately 28 mixed couples resided in Ile-Ife during that time. Only 3 of those couples did not live on the university campus. As I was introduced to the couples in the mixed marriages, I kept a log that included everything I both heard and observed about them. Over the course of the field experience, I chatted with wives in the market or at the supermarket located on campus. I visited with wives at their places of work. I ran errands for some wives and ate dinner with others. I socialized with the women and their families by calling on them at home. Many wives visited my home as well. My daughter became friendly with several of the couples' children, and she attended their birthday parties. When I arrived in Nigeria, I intended to interview African American and Caribbean women married to Nigerian citizens. At the main study site, Ile-Ife, 10 couples met the criteria. Before deciding to switch to a qualitative methodology, I broadened my sample to include any woman who was a citizen of a country other than Nigeria. I did so because I found out that both the local people and those who became participants in the study thought there was no difference between being a white or black foreign wife. Many pointed to the impressive cultural immersion of white foreign wives. And in the beginning, white women were more willing to share their experiences with me than were African American women. Subjects consented to interviews but were reluctant to give written permission to be quoted. After attempting to draw up an agreement that few were willing to sign, I abandoned that project. All interviews were conducted in English. I tape-recorded interviews where possible. Only two wives refused the recorded interview. In general, husbands were resistant to probing questions. Their reasons for refusing interviews included lack of time to answer interview questions and that they had nothing to add to what their wives told me. Of those who agreed to an interview, only four were receptive to a second interview. Nine of the husbands were very affable. I developed satisfying, friendly relationships with their families, and we often met for social visits. Only one husband displayed concern that I might stir up discontent among the wives. He asked me directly whether I had told any wife that she should leave. Two wives did not want me to talk to their husbands. Both were afraid of the consequences of having disclosed family secrets to an outsider.

The first set of interview questions that I developed were of the *grand tour* variety (Spradley, 1979). Such questions ask subjects to tell the interviewer everything that is important about a particular lifestyle. Interviews with informants were never structured. Each informant had a particular issue he or she wanted to address or was especially knowledgable about. Interviews with expatriate wives concerned their contact with the culture and their adjustment. Expatriate wives served as a comparison group with respect to assimilation and contact with Yoruba culture. Interviews with the offspring of foreign wives also were unstructured. I asked this group to tell me how their lives differed from those of their peers with two Nigerian parents. I also asked them to assess their mothers' adjustment. Some of the wives suggested that interviews be conducted in a group; in that way, each woman could think of additional experiences through their dialogue. A local branch of Nigerwives, Nigeria (the foreign wives' association) organized a meeting on my behalf to discuss some of the pertinent issues in their lives. They thought I had been ignoring too many of their crucial concerns. At that point, I was searching for an alternative methodology that would allow the study's analysis to develop from what respondents thought were the most important problems they faced. A colleague introduced me to the grounded theory approach, which became this study's final methodology.

After a month of grand tour questions, I focused on (a) levels of acculturation and ethnic identity, (b) perception of and compliance with local customs, (c) adjustment to life in Nigeria, (d) interaction with Yoruba people, and (e) quality of the marital relationship. I developed a semistructured questionnaire based on these four areas.

Glaser and Strauss (1967) developed the *constant comparative method*, in which categories emerge as behaviors and events are contrasted. Those behaviors and events having an underlying uniformity form a category. Such categories serve to explain how the problem of those being investigated is resolved. The sequence of events in data analysis begins immediately after some data have been collected. The aim is to identify relationships between the emerging categories. *Memoing* is a process of keeping a separate record of ideas, hypotheses, and observations. The record is written at a higher level of abstraction than line-by-line analysis. Memoing and coding generate new questions that are answered by gathering additional data or by reexamining old data. Information is collected on a category until no new relationships or dimensions can be found, and the category is then considered saturated. The analyst then moves on to additional categories, constantly comparing data to ferret out dimensions and relationships.

The first type of coding is called *open coding*. It is a line-by-line analysis that generates a host of questions about words and phrases of each line. A demonstration of the data analysis approach can be found in Table 13.1.

A memo that followed from the above line-by-line coding can be found in Table 13.2.

The second type of coding is *axial coding*. Data are coded around one category at a time. The dimensions of the category are listed, and hypotheses concerning relationships, consequences, conditions, interactions, and strategies are formulated and given preliminary answers. At this point, analysts engage in *theoretical sampling*, in which new data are collected and coded on the basis of the need to answer the questions that their hypotheses pose. Theoretical sampling guides data collection by directing analysts to individuals, groups, or events that will yield further dimensions of the categories and that will explain their relationships to other categories. The core category emerges from open and axial coding. The core category is identified by its attributes; that is, the core category occurs frequently in the data and relates to many categories. The core category is like the main theme of the story that is unfolding from the data analysis. During the third and final type of coding, *selective coding*, data are analyzed and collected only around the core category.

In the grounded theory approach, data are collected and analyzed on an ongoing basis. The first analysis I attempted was a search for general and recurring themes. Through the line-by-line analysis as a coding technique, three categories emerged: (a) women's perceived

(text continued on p. 233)

TABLE 13.1 Core Category Development: An Example of Line-by-Line Analysis

The core category in this study, "wives' covert conflict management," emerged using the line-by-line open coding data analysis technique.

Example 1

Interview Data	Line-by-Line Analysis
A Nigerian husband doesn't abandon you, but he doesn't support you the way he would abroad. He has his own friends, and women are expected to interact with women and make your own life. In Europe, the man wants to live like a European. When he returns, the pressures of the culture get him. When it comes to having to choose between buying shoes and clothes for himself and maintaining a wife, he takes care of himself. My husband did not want to take his dear money to Kingsway, which was a big place where everybody bought imported goods. He decided that I was going to learn to eat Nigerian food.	: Turning point or critical : juncture in: : : (a) the couple's social life : : : : : : : (b) their economic : expenditures : : : : Husband decides to "train" : wife to live according to : local customs.
What he didn't bargain for was that I was to become so Nigerian.	: Wife perceives his action as : an attempt to control her. : Critical turning point for : wife.
He wanted to manipulate me to suit himself. He wanted to save money. He didn't bargain on my following Nigerian thought processes. I followed it to its logical conclusions, which was to become a Yoruba woman. If he wanted to treat me as a European woman, I would be European, but if he wanted to treat me like a Yoruba, I would be a Yoruba woman. When you begin to think like a Yoruba woman ... (shifts sentence structure) A Yoruba woman says myself, my children, and my business, not necessarily in that order. Her husband is only important when she is still young and thinks that she can change him. It is the day she wakes up and decides that this man is never going to change. This happens to foreign marriages and Nigerian marriages, but in Nigeria, you wake up a lot earlier.	: Wife sees husband's action : as social control. : Wife's reaction to : perceived domination : is the use of a direct : strategy or ploy to : counter husband's attempt : to change her. : She will control her : own change. : Wife is transforming her : thinking from her primary : socialization to meet the : demands of the : environment. : : : Implies the wife's decision : gains momentum rapidly. : :

continued

TABLE 13.1 Continued

Example 1	
Interview Data	Line-by-Line Analysis
What you have to do is to make a choice. You say, "I hate this country, I hate this group of people, I hate this rotten way of life, I will never change. It's like a prison sentence. One day it will be all over and I will go home." Or, you wake up and say, I'm not going to be on the losing side. I'm not going to end up shapeless and unhappy, I am going to do what Yoruba women do when they are faced with the same things.	: Wife's critical turning point. : : : Referred to in other : interviews as "toughing : it out." : Critical turning point for : wife—development of a : response style. : :

Example 2	
Interview Data	Line-by-Line Analysis
For those women who leave, deep down, they don't feel they really belong here. They just go. The sky is the limit as to what you can do. It depends on the goals you set for yourself. You have to believe that there is some input you can make in society and in your family. Anyone who knows that you are not a Nigerian, they are waiting for the day to come when you pack your bags and go. They are waiting for that day. "How much can she take?" When you go, they are not surprised because you never really belonged here. That's what the bottom line is with Nigerians. Other Nigerians who have been born here know that this is their Nigeria. Where are they going to run to? In making it your home, you have to do a lot of self-sacrificing. In a way, you can say that you are in a prison. You do feel trapped. No matter how bad things get, you are expected to endure. The extended family expects it. The wife is supposed to keep her head above water. She is not supposed to let the pressure get to her. She has to be strong enough to cope with things. She has to look at life as a whole. She cannot be selfish. She has to look out for the family. The family means something. She just has to be strong and stick it out. That is part of the special role of the mother. For those who stay, after a point in time, you realize that, by going along with it,	: Consequence of social : alienation. : To avoid social isolation, : a foreign wife must be : able to make herself : useful. : Social alienation is very : strong among women who : leave or have trouble : adapting to the culture. : Foreign wives are expected : to have difficulty. : : : : Consequence of social : alienation: : feelings of imprisonment, : entrapment, sacrifice. : Part of the self-sacrifice. : Speaks to the difficulty : of becoming part of the : extended family for those : having difficulty : adjusting. : : : : : This is a view that the : role is immutable. : Getting locked into a : particular way of looking

TABLE 13.1 Continued

you are giving strength to the commitment that you've made. There will be a reward at the end. You may not live to see it. There is a strength in it. It is part of your role. You learn to get the feel of what you are doing.	: at one's situation. : : Commitment is the pathway : to becoming locked in : to a perspective. :
Anyway, it is easier to go along with it than to start all over again. If my relationship started to go bad, I wonder what I would do. I do not want to go back to my home country and become a single parent. Life would be difficult there. In Nigeria, I have a nanny who washes the clothes and prepares the meals. No matter how hard it is here, life is still wholesome.	: Points to fear responses : identified by foreign : wives in the areas of : (a) single parenting, : : : (b) improved economic : status,
The pressures abroad had not reached Nigeria. Nigerian men, who are up to the task, take care of their responsibility at home. Once the man takes care of that, you learn to overlook the extended family responsibility. There are times in which you have to do a favor for a mother-in-law and you have to overlook the fact of it not being your responsibility. You think, I'm too good to do that. You close your eyes to things and try to adapt to another place.	: : and (c) finding suitable : partner. : Type of response to : undesirable state of : affairs—closing one's : eyes. : : :
I do not know if I could find a man to marry who would not mistreat my children. Nigerian men value their children. If the wife decides to go, he wants to make sure his children stay. That is why Nigerians marry.	: Part of the fear. : : An expression of the : idea that the children : belong to the men.

sacrifices and responsibilities, (b) depths and limits of integrating into Yoruba society, and (c) women's responses to the variety of pressures they felt. I began to ask questions about the conditions, strategies, and consequences of coping with these pressures that had destructive consequences (e.g., withdrawal, cynicism). This questioning led to a more focused analysis of the specific situations that women were coping with (e.g., an unfaithful husband, finding breathing room from the extended family). By continuing the line-by-line analysis, other themes emerged: (a) a husband being the determiner of what the wife will cope with, (b) the limited number of cultural components that husbands selected, and (c) the difference between women who were obviously unhappy and those who were not. I began to recode interviews with key study participants and informants around in vivo codes such as "hard lives,"

TABLE 13.2 Memo Aim: Identification of Response Styles

I have been told repeatedly now that the husband is not the best facilitator or cultural mediator. Why? He is seen as the source of the problem. A foreign wife learns how to handle her position by watching the behavior of others. This begins a process of cultural integration and can be thought of as doing "cultural integration work." I have identified four strategies used by women who have gone deep into the culture. First, friends are made with Yoruba women and their advice is sought. Second, the husband's distancing strategies are accepted. (Wives have spoken of husbands' strategies to formalize their relationships—e.g., sleeping in separate rooms or calling the husband "sir.") Third, women maintain separate financial accounts. Fourth, these women are cordial with the local traditional authorities, bowing to greet them in accordance with tradition while also believing that foreign wives must support each other. The reason for their continued support of foreign wives is that the outside world does not understand their particular problems. Those who chose a remarkable degree of integration appear to fit the society. Notice that it is a choice, one that stems from a decision to do the cultural work; but it is a choice made from the women's feelings of being tough and being able to survive anywhere. This raises the issue of response style and associated behaviors. Compare this with other foreign wives who described the role of the wife as awkward. For them, the way things are supposed to be done feels awkward. *Awkward* implies a feeling that the role is difficult, hard to handle, inconvenient, uncomfortable, trying. It makes them feel unskilled and embarrassed. Instead of interpreting the behavior of successful Yoruba women as ways to get ahead in society, they use their primary socialization to interpret the local women's behavior. I often heard this category of foreign wives refer to the successful Yoruba women as aggressive and rude. They find their "ostentatiousness" distasteful. Although they do understand the basis of the successful Yoruba women's behavior as stemming from the disadvantages of blocked opportunity structure, they preferred to consider them "unladylike." The integration process that foreign wives undergo stems from a decision between sticking to one's primary socialization or rising to the environmental demands. When a woman trains herself to live in the society, she is doing active cultural work. By the time a woman finishes this cultural work, she has redefined her emotional and affection needs from her husband. She holds on to her marriage, but not to her idea of the companionable marriage. By all outside accounts, she is maintaining a happy home. More important, she has secured herself emotionally and financially, and her primary identity, that of wife, is left intact. Three attributes distinguish those who are "tough" from those who "tough it out": (a) after the husband's change, the wife's decision to integrate or do the cultural work; (b) the wife's redefinition of her emotional and affection needs; and (c) the wife's standing on firm financial, social, and emotional ground (the wife decides she must be the source of her own security).

"thick skin," "tropicalizing," "changes in the husband," and "toughing it out."

A second line of analysis emerged, based on concerns raised by the informants. One such concern was related to the declining economy and its impact on the women's morale. I asked couples to describe the facilities not available now and the hope that was held in the 1960s and 1970s that improvements in the local infrastructures would spread. I asked for examples of what they were or were not able to do now that they could do 5 years ago. The deteriorating physical environment was the context within which the women were operating. The goal was to understand how the women's coping strategies were related to the country's sudden economic devastation, to their changing relationships with their husbands, and to Yoruba culture in general.

Another question arose as a by-product: To what extent did the men use the culture to their advantage, or to what extent did they believe in it? The structure existed, but the manner in which a husband could use it was up to him. I then developed a grand tour questionnaire for husbands. To integrate these diverse themes, a key concept was needed that accounted for the majority of the data; I called this concept "covert conflict management." On the basis of assumptions that I made going into the field, I expected to find couples who had worked out the major sociocultural differences between them. What I found was a great deal of smoldering resentment on the part of the wives. Much of that resentment was generated by the changes their husbands had undergone on returning to Nigeria. Husbands decided to conform to certain customs and adjusted their behavior accordingly. In response to their husbands' changes, wives attempted to bring their overt behavior in line with their husbands' decisions. Where these involved major issues (e.g., polygyny, religion), wives continued to covertly disagree with their husbands. The tensions produced in a marriage when husbands decide to conform to aspects of the culture require that wives bring their behavior in line with the change and that they somehow manage their own covert disapproval. Through line-by-line analysis, the core category—covert conflict management—emerged. Selective coding around the core category led to the discovery that wives manage their covert disapproval of certain issues by adopting one of two categories of response styles. Their response styles are characteristic ways of managing the stimulus of husband change.

Women adopt response styles on the basis of whether they see environmental events as controllable. The Category 1 response style, or "being tough," reflects the overall attitude of mastery over the environment and has two attributes: (a) deliberately setting out to learn and use the Yoruba wife role to develop a satisfying life and (b) modifying one's psychological requirements for a husband's affections and attention. Women adopting the Category 1 response style commanded respect and authority from their extended family and the wider community because they were able to prove their usefulness beyond the nuclear unit. These women consciously adapted to the culture, often learning the language and attaining a high rank in their husbands' families. A minority of this category of women embraced the culture on its deepest level, expressing this through their involvement in traditional religion. The Category 2 response style, or "toughing it out," had three attributes: (a) closing one's eyes and ignoring the undesirable surroundings and other unpleasant environmental events; (b) feeling that one must conform to a prescribed role, rather than amend that role to fit personal needs; and (c) fearing changes in the status quo. It is a response style of pretending to live out a prison sentence that is to be completed when the children are adults. In toughing it out, women attempt to fulfill aspects of the role of Yoruba women without understanding how to use that role to their advantage. They retain emotional dependency on their husbands that is unevenly reciprocated. These women conclude that they must stay in their marriages not only because of their commitment but also because they are able to continue in their role as wives. Starting over again in their own countries or living in Nigeria without their husbands is unthinkable. Only "tough" women can do that. Women who tough it out fear single parenting, fear not being able to find jobs in their home countries, and dread the thought of having to find someone to marry again.

The Category 2 response style reflects the overall attitude of fatalism and includes an attempt to minimize cross-cultural contact. Women adopting the Category 2 response style interpret their marital commitment as fixed, fear the thought of separation from their husbands, and decide to endure their family lives irrespective of whether the role of wife is good for them personally. Such women display a chilling cynicism, a disturbing withdrawal, or escapism through religion. This group of women seldom reach a high level of authority in their husbands' families. Those women who decide to tough it out neither resist the culture nor go out of their way to learn about it. A fraction of this category of women rigidly hold on to their values even though they recognize their inefficiency in the Nigerian setting. In toughing it out, women pay the emotional price in bitterness or withdrawal. The inability to learn to become self-reliant left this category of women feeling alienated and powerless, both in their marital relationship and in the community at large. Nevertheless, adopting either category of response style allows foreign wives to achieve the goal of family stability. The striking difference between the two groups rests in the efficacy of their approaches for enhancing their personal development and long-term emotional and financial security. In the rare instances in which husbands remained "unchanged" from their days abroad, these response styles were unnecessary.

Being tough and toughing it out are two ways to manage the covert conflict arising from the changes in the husbands and marital relationships. An additional tactic related to the core category is "staying sane" techniques. Staying sane techniques were used by all women to maintain morale and to raise their energy level to accomplish routine tasks. Techniques for staying sane were activities that reconnected a foreign wife with the values and lifestyle of her own country. Staying sane techniques offered momentary escapes from the unfamiliar and sometimes objectionable modes of existence. These techniques were basic (e.g., traveling home regularly) and often food related. For example, affluent women shared imported items (e.g., candy bars, cheese, coffee) with the less affluent. Staying sane techniques were used by all women irrespective of their response style.

Analyzing the interviews and observational data collected in this study through the hypothesis-generating approach of grounded theory led to intensive line-by-line coding and memoing. The analysis gave rise to a core category, covert conflict management, with two response styles. The task of foreign wives was to regain some amount of control over their interpersonal lives once they were confronted with the changes in their husbands and changes in their marital relationships. Changes in husbands were seen as inevitable, given the pressures of the culture. In an effort to maintain their marriages, wives changed themselves. Foreign wives most frequently resorted to strategies that were covert. They could continue to make emotional investments in their relationship and suffer because of its low and erratic rate of return. Such women grew bitter, withdrew from society, or turned to religious dogma to justify staying in their marriages. They conformed to their husbands' definition of the culture, not because they understood it as a strategy, but because it was easier than maintaining their own values. Or, foreign wives would distance themselves emotionally from their husbands and go all out to learn to live in the community. Those who had undertaken the cultural work seemed to be saying, "By conforming to the culture, the culture itself would set them free." They decided that their husbands would not change to suit them and saw that their husbands demanded that they adhere to Yoruba customs in some limited ways. In response, these women carried their personal changes to a "logical conclusion."

LIFE HERSTORY RESEARCH

My next research project drew on life herstory research methods (Vaz, 1995). The broad distinctions among life histories, biographies, and autobiographies concern the relationship between the narrator/subject

Photo 13.2. Kim Vaz and Nike Davies at a Fulani compound in Osogbo, Nigeria, reviewing transcripts from previous interviews, June 1994. (Photograph by Deborah Plant; used with permission.)

of the research and the researcher. In an *autobiography*, a person reconstructs her life to present her own viewpoint on how significant life events and forces have determined or shaped her challenges and achievements. In a *biography*, the biographer often does not rely on the direct input of the person he or she studies. Biographers describe, analyze, and theorize about the lives of individuals by using a variety of sources in addition to any primary documents the subjects may have produced. The final product of *life history* research is the result of dialogues between a narrator and a researcher. Each brings to the project differing agendas, worldviews, and dimensions of social power. Carrying out life history research involves participant-observation, in-depth interviewing, and a review of the literature on the "core themes" that the researcher and narrator define as their foci.

I interviewed Yoruba women artists—Oyenike Davies (see Photo 13.2) and Muniratu Bello—as well as their former co-wives. It would considerably reduce the workload of the researcher if one could just turn on the recorder and the narrator's life would then just flow out, but that does not happen.

The life herstory interview guide becomes a most important tool for constructing the story. I developed the interview guide by drawing on a variety of sources in women's and transcultural studies (particularly Belenky, Clinchy, Goldberg, & Tarule, 1986; Darrow & Palmquist, 1977; and Shostak, 1981). The life herstory interview guide consists of questions that span the entire range of women's lives. See Table 13.3 for the life history interview guide I used in this study.

I followed David Mandelbaum's (1973) suggestions of analyzing these interviews around "turnings," "adaptations," and "dimensions." *Turning points* mark the major transitions of life when individuals assume new roles, ascribed or self-chosen. They lead to new social interactions and modifications in the self-concept. I organized Nike's life herstory around several turning points, beginning with the impact of her mother's death when Nike was a child and the gnawing poverty that plagued her family thereafter. Next, I highlighted her decision to defy her father's plans to an arranged marriage and her "escape" to a traveling theater group, and so on. Using Mandelbaum's idea of *adaptations*, or the identification of the significant opportunities and obstacles the individual encountered at various points in life and the discovery of how the person adapted her behavior (or did not) to navigate the situation, what changes were made, and what behaviors were maintained, I was able to draw a picture of Nike's strategies for negotiating patriarchal rule that she faced at home, in the theater group, in her marriages, and in the competitive, male-dominated world of Yoruba contemporary art. To understand the social and cultural *dimensions* of Nike's and Muni's lives, I extensively reviewed the literature pertaining to Yoruba art, theater, cosmology, farming, marriage traditions, and transformations.

Life herstory research methods are my preferred research tools, and I have since used these strategies in two more studies. I admired the recovery process and transcendence of physical limitations achieved by my childhood friend and next-door neighbor in New Orleans, Louisiana—Nelita Manego—who, owing to a gunshot wound inflicted by her husband (before he shot and killed himself), sustained a complete spinal cord injury and is now a paraplegic. I wanted to learn how a woman recovers from such profound loss, and thus I asked whether I could record her life herstory.

In conducting background research to carry out the interviews, I immersed myself in the literature on the adjustment process for spinal cord-injured individuals and other themes I believed would be relevant to understanding her current life—widowhood, domestic violence, skin color and hair texture politics among blacks in New Orleans, black masculinity, and ideas about standards of the perfect and beautiful body. Before I began working on Nelita's life herstory, I had just

(text continued on page 245)

240   COLLECTING TREASURES

TABLE 13.3 Life Herstory Interview Guide

I. Childhood and Adolescence
   A. Microeconomic conditions in the town or village where you grew up:
      1. What were the primary job activities of those persons in your immediate community? How did these jobs relate to others in the community, in the towns or villages, in different states, African countries, overseas?
      2. How much money did people make in your community? How much do they use to support relatives and children? What people did your family support, and why did they support them? How much went for food, rent, clothing, transportation, education, personal hygiene, etc.? What was done with extra income? What happened when there was not enough income?
      3. How did most people end up with the jobs they had?
      4. Were these temporary jobs? Did they hold more than one job?
      5. What skills were required for different categories of jobs? How did individuals acquire these skills? Which jobs were more prestigious?
      6. What were the working hours for most people?
      7. What were the primary agricultural activities in the area? What crops were raised? Were certain crops raised because of climate, soil, political, labor, equipment, price, irrigation, or other reasons? What animals were raised, and what were they used for (e.g., food, work animals)?
      8. How much time was actually spent planting, harvesting, and doing similar direct work in the fields? Was there an off-season? Were farmers idle during long periods of time? What did they do at such times? How was the work divided among family members, extended family, and the community? Were the agricultural products used mostly by the family or marketed?
      9. How much land did the individual or family use? Did s/he or they own it? What were the conditions of ownership? How was land acquired, and how was it passed on?
      10. What factories of any kind or size were in the area? What did they produce? Where did they sell their goods? Where did they acquire the materials they needed? Who owned the factory, and when was it built? How many people did it employ? What were their wages, skills, and working conditions? Were there any union activities in the area?
      11. What were the primary service activities in the area (e.g., health, education, transportation, finance, civil service, communications)? How large were these, and how efficient were the services provided by the government or private groups?
      12. Where did people purchase the goods they did not make themselves? Describe a typical experience at the market. Who sold at the market? What was sold? Where did they get the goods? How often were the big markets? How did you get there? What would you wear?
      13. How were the words *employment* and *unemployment* used? What are some proverbs associated with the word *work*? Was there unemployment?
      14. Was anyone trained at the secondary and college level in your area? How were these people different from the majority of people? What kinds of jobs did they have, where did they live, and whom did they socialize with? Were they called special names?
      15. How did people save money? How did they accumulate wealth?
      16. How did taking care of the elderly and/or having a large number of children increase or decrease the likelihood of acquiring wealth? Was this system good or bad?

TABLE 13.3 Continued

B. Micro-Level Questions
   1. What kind of person was considered a good worker, a bad worker?
   2. How did the community react toward those who don't work, can't work, or won't work?
   3. Toward what ends were the people working? Were they trying to get ahead or just live?
   4. How did religious beliefs affect farming practices?
   5. Were people concerned with acquiring foreign luxury items? If so, which items, and how did they go about getting them?
   6. Did prices on goods differ in the village and in the town?
   7. What kinds of work cooperatives existed in your town or village?
   8. What kinds of things were thrown away? What was not thrown away? Why?
   9. Were there any major construction activities or development projects going on in your area? How did they affect daily life? Was anyone from the community involved?
   10. How and where did you get water? Did you have electricity?
   11. How did people get foreign exchange? Were they concerned about it?
   12. Were there any food-assistance programs in the area?
   13. Were there any foreigners in your area? How did they affect the economy of the area?
   14. When was television, radio, telephone introduced in your community?
C. Local Political Structure
   1. What was the form of the local government? How did they come to power? Were these paid positions? Was the local political scene dominated by one family or group? Was local government corrupt?
   2. Who were the individuals that had power? From what class, ethnic group, or religion did they come?
   3. Were the people dissatisfied with their local government? What were the values the local government tried to promote?
   4. What was the political mythology of the ruling group?
   5. Did the rulers ever make demands on the local people for money, obedience, etc.?
   6. Were the local people taxed? How were those taxes collected?
   7. To what extent did the village people feel the presence of the government, and in what ways (e.g., through taxes, agricultural extension services, military, police, government bureaucrats from outside the area, government regulation on prices)?
   8. How much power did village leaders really have, and how much of their function was purely ceremonial?
   9. Were people more interested in local, national, or international affairs?
   10. Were people reluctant to talk politics? Where did people discuss politics? Did women participate in these discussions? Were any topics taboo?
   11. How did independence affect the people in your community?
   12. How did the Biafran war affect your community?
   13. How did the oil boom affect your community?
   14. If agricultural workers or other occupational groups felt exploited in your community, how did they respond?
   15. Did the local people feel inferior to the whites who were present? How did they show their feelings?

(continued)

TABLE 13.3 Continued

- D. Social Structure
    1. Who were the important people in your community? How did they get to be important (occupation, education, ability or skill, land ownership)? What did these people own? Where did they live? Who did they socialize with? How did they dress? Was it possible to have a high income and low status or a low income and high status? Did high-status people have political influence? How were high-status people linked to the rest of the people?
    2. Who were the wealthy women in the community? How were they treated? What were their occupations? What did they own? What positions did they hold? How did they influence local politics? Were they married? Did they ever become female husbands?
    3. How did the poor in your community live? Where did they live, and in what type of physical structures? Did their children attend school? How was their general health? How were they viewed in the community?
    4. What kinds of associations (formal and informal) existed (e.g., Islamic, social welfare organizations)? Which were more influential, prestigious, and most common? Who were members of these groups? Did rivalries exist among them? What were the functions of these organizations?
    5. What were the important leisure time activities for adults and children?
    6. What were the sizes of the households? What was a good wife; a good husband; and a good child? How frequent was divorce? Why did divorce occur? How were the servants treated? What was their relationship to the people they worked for? Were people receptive to birth control information?
    7. What were the general greetings, table manners, and expressions of deference and respect in the community?
    8. Whom did people go to for advice or help with different questions (e.g., religion, politics, problems over money or emotions)?
    9. What roles existed for people with handicaps?
- E. Religion
    1. What were the major religions? Were there any foreign missionaries in the community? How did they make their presence felt? What traditional practices were observed?
    2. Were there any sacred places in your community? Who could enter and use the facilities? What were some of the offerings made? What were the particular dress associated with each group?
- F. Music, Art, and Architecture
    1. Describe the popular music of the time. Who was producing it? What instruments were used? Did it compete with traditional music? Did people still play traditional music? Where did they do it? What instruments were used?
    2. Describe the traditional art forms in your community.
    3. How were buildings made? What materials were used? Who built them?
    4. Who were the artists and musicians? Where these more likely to be men or women? What was their social status? What were the important positions or leadership roles? What was the relationship between the musician and the artist? How were they trained? Did they come from a particular class? Whom was their work intended for, and for what purposes? Was this a distinct group from craftspeople? If yes, repeat questions for craftspeople.
- G. Food
    1. What were the most important foods in the diet? How was food prepared? Who prepared it? What did the daily meals consist of, and at what time where they taken? Where there any food taboos? What table manners were followed? How were guests treated?

TABLE 13.3 Continued

- H. Family History
    1. *Problems:* Did you or anyone else in your family experience alcoholism, drug abuse, fighting, major disability or physical illness, gambling, indebtedness, poor reputation, prostitution, physical abuse, frequent arguments, incest, physical abuse, rape, prison, stealing, poverty, mental illness, death of an important person, or loss of a child? Describe the events and consequences of any such occurrences.
    2. *Life in the Compound:* Describe the relationship among the women in the compound, the men, and the children. What kind of hierarchy existed? What were the rules followed? Who lived with whom? Describe the physical layout of your compound. What was the major source of income for compound members? Describe the religious traditions followed. What festivals were observed? What was your role, and what were the other roles? What happened when someone disobeyed the rules? How were people rewarded or recognized for good things they did or that happened to them? What happened when someone was born? When they died? What initiation ceremonies were followed? Were girls circumcised? What happened when a new wife came into the compound? What is the history of the lineage? Are there any rivalries? What titles does your clan own, and what properties? Describe your family cloth. What is its origin? When it is worn? What are the praise songs of your family?
- I. Personal Development
    1. *Informal Training:* What were you taught about being a woman and about the appropriate behavior of a man? Did you believe this was the correct way to be? Did you expect to go into polygyny or monogamy? Did it matter? What skills were you taught? When you wanted to know something, whom did you go to? Whom did you recognize as authorities? How did you know or decide they were the authorities? When was the first time you ever disagreed over your aspirations for life? How many children did you want to have? How did you develop an interest in art and local theater? What was the community's thoughts on these new art forms?
    2. *Formal Education—Semisubjective Factors:* What schools did you go to? How far did you go, and why? Did you participate in special programs? Who paid for your education? Who were the teachers? Did you wear uniforms? What courses did you take? Did you always have the necessary supplies? How many students were in the classroom? How were students rewarded and punished? Did you receive agricultural training in the schools? Describe the facilities (e.g., classrooms, equipment). How were the teachers trained? What language was used? Did the schools try to promote positive orientations toward physical labor, or did they attempt to teach specific skills that may by used to make the economy more modern? Were you taught to value individual achievement or group achievement through cooperation? Which traditional values did it reinforce, and which "modern" ones? Which books did you use? Describe some of the pictures in the books. Were girls encouraged to go to secondary school and university? What are your classmates doing now? Did the school best serve the needs of the middle and upper classes, or the needs of all the people? What standards were used to judge students' abilities? What cultural settings, norms, and values were projected by the teaching materials?
    3. *Formal Education—Subjective Factors:* What has stayed with you from your primary school experiences? Who were the good and bad teachers, the good and bad programs? What was helpful about your primary school experience? What didn't the school provide that is important to you? What would you like to learn now? What is the best way to learn it? Looking back over your whole life,

(continued)

TABLE 13.3 Continued

      can you tell me about a really powerful learning experience that you've had, in or out of school?
II. Growing Into Womanhood
  A. Married Life
    1. *Joining Their Husband's Compound:* Describe the events leading you to your joining the artists. Where did you live? Whom did you live with? Describe the people you met, the things you learned. How were expatriates involved in your life? Was money a problem? What kind of work did you do?
    2. *Being a Wife and Mother:* Describe the events leading up to becoming his wife. How did life compare to being a junior wife, then a senior wife? Describe the relationships between the co-wives. What rules did you follow? Describe the problems of your family life. What were the events surrounding a woman's first birth, the death of her child, her own illness, the illness of a child? What happened when a new wife came into the compound? Did you ever have an outside lover, and how was that managed? How did you earn money? What were the joys of being a co-wife, the pains? What kinds of maternal responsibilities did you have? What did you do when a child was ill? What was your daily life like as a mother? What did you provide for your children? What health care facilities were available? Did you use them? What diseases and illnesses were common? Was there a dependence on traditional medicine? What healers were consulted? What cures suggested? Were they effective?
    3. *Life in the Compound:* Did you or anyone else in your marital compound experience alcoholism, drug abuse, fighting, major disability or physical illness, gambling, indebtedness, poor reputation, prostitution, physical abuse, frequent arguments, incest, physical abuse, rape, prison, stealing, poverty, mental illness, death of an important person? Describe the events and consequences of any such occurrences. Describe the relationship among the women in the compound, the men, the children. Who lived in the compound? What kind of hierarchy existed? What were the rules followed? Who lived with whom? Describe the physical layout of your compound. What was the major source of income for compound members? Describe the religious traditions followed. What festivals were observed? What was your role, and what were the other roles? What happened when someone disobeyed the rules? How were people rewarded or recognized for good things they did or that happened to them? What happened when someone was born? When they died? What initiation ceremonies were followed? What is the history of the lineage? What titles did your new clan own, and what properties? Describe your family cloth. What is its origin? When was it worn? What were the praise songs of your family?
    4. *Becoming an Artist:* What new techniques were you learning? How were you developing as an artist? Was that important to you? How did you differ from a traditional craftswoman? Who were the artists and musicians? Where these more likely to be men or women? What was their social status? What were the important positions or leadership roles? What was the relationship between the musician and the artist? How were they trained? Did they come from a particular class? Whom was their work intended for, and for what purposes? Was this a group distinct from craftspeople?
III. Beyond Married Life
  A. Background
    1. What stands out for you in your life over the past few years? What kinds of things have been important?

TABLE 13.3 Continued

   B. Self-Description
      1. How would you describe yourself to yourself? Is the way you see yourself now different from the way you saw yourself in the past? What has led to the changes? Have there been other turning points?
   C. Gender
      1. What does being woman mean to you? Do you think there are any important differences between men and women? Have you always thought this way? What has led to the change in your view?
   D. Looking Back Over Your Life
      1. What relationships have been really important to you? Why? How would you describe those relationships? How have these relationships been changing, and what has been making them change? Have you had a relationship with someone who helped shape the person you have become? Discuss each of your children. How have they been important to you in helping you become the person you are? Where do you see yourself going in the next 5 years? Who will be the most important people in your life?

SOURCES: Adapted from Belenky, Clinchy, Goldberg, & Tarule (1986); Darrow & Palmquist (1977); and Shostak (1981).

completed the narratives of Oyenike and Muniratu, whose shared characteristics, in addition to having been the wives of abusive husbands, included defiance of their fathers in the wake of their arranged marriage ceremonies. Throughout the narratives of these women are vivid descriptions of momentary defeats in the face of male rule and little (and sometimes majestic) triumphs over these oppressive forces. Both women's behaviors and attitudes were organized around the goal of outwitting patriarchal figures to achieve their self-defined goals. As Nelita began to tell me her story, I was initially listening for her critique of male rule, no matter how implicit, in her narrative. As our work moved forward, it became clear to me that she interpreted her life from the vantage point of the importance of adhering to social norms. After spending so much of my time teaching about and researching black women's resistance to gender and racial constriction, here was an opportunity for me to dissect the social conventions of the community where I grew from girl to woman and to examine a woman's desire to conform to those norms. What did these norms lead a woman to expect, to hope for, and to almost give her life for? Because I had always found many social conventions problematic and resistance to them necessary for my own psychospiritual survival, conducting research for Nelita's narrative meant viewing life from the angle of a woman whose behaviors, attitudes, and aspirations were organized around conformity to the very norms I saw as restrictive. To understand the privileges and problems encountered by women who are "at home" in conventional society, I had to begin formally charting the social forces that led women to question themselves when they did not meet the social standards rather than the institutions to which they had pledged their allegiance. The price extracted from such women was the denial of their own reality. They did not acknowledge that they saw what they saw and felt what they felt when their lives began to deviate from the ideal. The cost of their conformity was the suppression of the self.

The third and most recent project in which I incorporated life herstory research methods was a study of the strategies that African American women use to "rebuild" the self after it has suffered the vicissitudes inflicted by racial and sexual oppression. I conducted in-depth interviews with four African American women who have consciously chosen to challenge the limitations of cultural scripts. I searched for women who understand their lives as a "journey." I selected the following as examples of women who are peeling back the layers of imposed identities: Phyllis McEwen, a womanist poet; Sallyann Grant, an advocate for the hearing impaired who is living through her family's rejection of her lesbian identity; Osunbunmi Olafemi, the cofounder of Oyotunji Village in Sheldon, South Carolina (a deliberately created African village consisting of African American permanent residents, circa 1970 to the present); and Latifa Akram, a woman who embraced Islam through the Nation of Islam more than 20 years ago and today follows the path of Sunni Islam. Although these women have walked varying roads in the determination to cope with a society that has alienated them, they have, through the course of journeys, arrived at a sturdy sense of self. They are not at all consumed with seeking societal approval. They function with clarity and vitality, and although they are autonomous, they care about and are involved with their communities.

DISSEMINATION OF RESEARCH FINDINGS

I report my research findings in standard ways—that is, through academic publishing—but I also create ways to inform a general audience about analyzing events from the perspective of black womanism/feminism. I coproduced a videotape that memorializes four women brutally murdered in Tampa in the early 1990s. That tape is entitled *Spirit Murder: Stopping the Violent Deaths of Black Women* to convey the ideas that black women's lives are undervalued by the community at large and that there was something everyone could do to correct the situation

(Vaz, Filippo, Thomas, & Plant, 1993). The project "Choreographing Life's Journey" is an interactive multimedia presentation available on CD-ROM for IBM compatibles with a 486 processor, MPEG board, and quad-speed CD player. The presentation consists of full-motion video, slides, text, and narration providing the context of each woman's life. The patriarchal order is in our heads, in the air we breathe, in the food we eat, in the people we see and touch. I encourage my students to become as creative as possible to influence their audience by using as many sensory modalities as are possible.

PEDAGOGICAL SUGGESTIONS

Before my students begin their own life history research projects, I have them read and complete oral book reports of published research. Pertinent books for this project include the following:

Essed, P. (1990). *Everyday racism: Reports from women in two cultures*. Alameda, CA: Hunter House.
Etter-Lewis, G. (1993). *My soul is my own: Oral narratives of African American women in the professions*. New York: Routledge.
Ladner, J. (1993). *Tomorrow's tomorrow*. New York: Anchor.
Mirza, H. (1992). *Young, black, and female*. London: Routledge.
Richie, B. (1996). *Compelled to crime: The gender entrapment of battered black women*. New York: Routledge.
Rollins, J. (1985). *Between women: Domestics and their employers*. Philadelphia: Temple University.
Scott, K. (1991). *The habit of surviving: Black women's strategies for life*. New Brunswick, NJ: Rutgers University Press.

A second activity that I use, and one that is very effective for developing students' interviewing skills, is photo analysis (Akeret, 1991). Students bring in a few photographs of family and friends and place the photographs on a long table. Then each student selects a photograph that is not her or his own and that is of an unfamiliar person/people. Each student responds to questions about how she or he feels about the photograph. Then the student is asked to describe any disturbances in personal feelings when viewing it and to provide a descriptive phrase for it. Next, the student is asked to assess the photograph for evidence of love, "domination," and so on. Finally, the student discusses how she or he would interact with the person/people in the photograph. For students personally, this exercise generates discussion around issues of living in a raced and gendered environment. For example, a white student brought in a photograph of camp counselors with whom she had worked over the summer. The pictured group rather resembled a cheerleading squad, and in the middle was a lone black woman. A black student reviewed the picture and provided a rather shallow, safe interpretation (akin to the idea that everybody appeared to be having a great time). I asked what she thought about the single black woman in the photograph, and much feeling came forth regarding what life is like for her in a predominately white setting. The student's reaction was similar to a habit described by Kesho Scott (1991)—that to survive in white settings, black women often suppress or try to ignore their instincts, impressions, and experiences to offer responses more acceptable to white establishments. Not being able to offer and be one's true self certainly adversely affects the productivity and potential creative contributions that black women can make. For the white student whose picture it was, listening to the other student's real sentiments forced her to confront, for the first time, the idea that black people have different experiences in white settings than white people do. Even though the white student has relatives that are biracial, it never occurred to her to think of what life may have been like for her black colleague. The camp was an important experience for the white student because many of the counselors identified as lesbian, and it forced her, for the first time, to confront her own homophobia. I asked students to use this technique with the women they were going to interview to discover the women's family and personal myths, changes in family and personal relationships over time, and dreams thwarted and those fulfilled.

Oral narrative research, whether at home or abroad, leads to powerful transformative experiences for researchers. It can extend and broaden our identities; it can refashion our hopes and dreams, our very ideas about what is possible. Ultimately, it is a research methodology that is profoundly personal. As we challenge ourselves to extend the boundary of the self, we are prepared to challenge academia to do the same.

REFERENCES

Akeret, R. (1991). *Family tales, family wisdom*. New York: Henry Holt.
Aptheker, B. (1989). *Tapestries of life: Women's work, women's consciousness, and the meaning of daily experience*. Amherst: University of Massachusetts Press.
Belenky, M. F., Clinchy, B. M., Goldberg, N. R., & Tarule, J. M. (1986). *Women's ways of knowing: The development of self, voice, and mind*. New York: Basic Books.

Collins, P. H. (1986). Learning from the outsider within: The sociological significance of black feminist thought. *Social Problems, 33*(6), 14-32.

Collins, P. H. (1990). *Black feminist thought: Knowledge, consciousness, and the politics of empowerment.* Winchester, MA: Unwin Hyman.

Darrow, K., & Palmquist, B. (1977). *Trans-cultural study guide.* Stanford, CA: Volunteers in Asia Publications.

Frankenberg, R. (1993). *White women, race matters: The social construction of whiteness.* Minneapolis: University of Minnesota Press.

Glaser, B., & Strauss, A. (1967). *The discovery of grounded theory: Strategies for qualitative research.* Mill Valley, CA: Sociology Press.

Mandelbaum, D. (1973). The study of life history: Gandhi. *Current Anthropology, 14*(3), 177-196.

McIntosh, P. (1995). White privilege and male privilege: A personal account to coming to see correspondence through work in women's studies. In M. L. Andersen & P. H. Collins (Eds.), *Race, class, and gender: An anthology* (2nd ed., pp. 70-81). Belmont, CA: Wadsworth.

Reid, I. D. (1940). *In a minor key: Negro youth in story and fact.* Washington, DC: American Council on Education.

Scott, K. (1991). *The habit of surviving: Black women's strategies for life.* New Brunswick, NJ: Rutgers University Press.

Shostak, M. (1981). *Nisa: The life and words of a !Kung woman.* Cambridge, MA: Harvard University Press.

Spradley, J. P. (1979). *The ethnographic interview.* New York: Holt, Rinehart & Winston.

Vaz, K. (1992). A course on research issues on women of color [Special issue]. *Women's Studies Quarterly, 20*(1&2).

Vaz, K. (1995). *The woman with the artistic brush: A life history of Nike Davies.* Armonk, NY: M. E. Sharpe.

Vaz, K., Filippo, M., Thomas, T., & Plant, G. (1993). *Spirit murder: Stopping the violent deaths of black women* [Videotape]. (Available for rental from the Film and Video Distribution Office, Division of Learning Technologies, SVC 1072, University of South Florida, Tampa, FL 33620).

14

EUROPEAN AMERICAN AND AFRICAN AMERICAN MEN AND WOMEN'S VALUATIONS OF FEMINIST AND NATURAL SCIENCE RESEARCH METHODS IN PSYCHOLOGY

LESLIE ANN KINGMAN

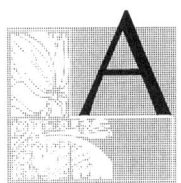A rapid increase of women in psychology in the past 20 years has shifted the gender makeup of recent Ph.D. graduates from predominantly male to over 50% female (Thurgood & Weinman, 1989). Experiences unique to women that have long been ignored in psychology may shift not only the content of what psychology studies but also perhaps even the methods by which we examine human behavior. This study evaluates the claims of some (Ricketts, 1989; Tomm, 1989) that a uniquely feminine or feminist research methodology exists that will be preferred by female psychologists. It also assesses whether "feminist" methods are valued more highly by another oppressed group, African Americans.

Chodorow (1974), Miller (1984), and Gilligan (1982) all have claimed that women have a uniquely feminine sense of self that is defined by less rigid boundaries and that is more relational than the male sense of self. Keller (1989) theorized that our early maternal environment, when coupled with our cultural definition of masculine (that which can never appear feminine), leads to the association of female with merging and of male with separateness. Because of this, the act of separating subject from object—objectivity itself—comes to be associated with masculinity and with a denial of any kind of subjectivity. Keller cautioned, however, against assuming that objectivity is *innately* masculine. Others have suggested that women's more relational sense of self comes out of social hierarchy or power differences (Eagly, 1983; Kaschek, 1988). Mednick (1989) postulated that those in power are more likely to focus their conception of reality on rules and rationality that maintain the power, whereas the disempowered emphasize relatedness and compassion.

Lending support for Mednick's ideas, a number of African American authors have criticized psychology for ignoring context and culture in its research and theorizing (Azibo, 1988b; Kershaw, 1989; Watts, 1987). Azibo (1988b) criticized the "cultural monism" prevalent in American psychology.

FEMINIST ALTERNATIVE METHODS

Many feminists argue that no method is inherently "feminist"; that any research method can be used in a sexist manner or to further the goals of feminism (Peplau & Conrad, 1989). Some feminist psychologists, however, have offered alternative methods. The feminist research methodologies are not universally defined, but rather have included suggestions of a nonhierarchical, participatory research approach in which the context surrounding phenomena is acknowledged and studied and the impact of the researcher's values and emotions on the research process is acknowledged.

Tomm (1989) has called for an "obliteration" of the "we-they" dichotomy in psychological research. She, along with Kleiber and Light (1978) and Walsh (1989), has suggested a nonhierarchical method of research. This methodology includes soliciting orienting questions from the subjects (or participants), involving the participants in the interpretation of results, and providing participants with meaningful, even consciousness-raising, feedback.

Stanley and Wise (1983) believe that to understand a person's context means to start first from the personal and the direct experience of the research participant so as to reach a holistic picture of the phenomenon. They also recommend that the researcher attempt to understand *emotionally* what the experience studied would be like for herself. Others (the *Psychology of Women Quarterly* guidelines as reported in Kimmel, 1990) believe that such extreme measures are not necessary; they believe that research conducted in natural settings with the interests of oppressed groups in mind and with theorizing of appropriate complexity to portray the phenomena studied takes sufficient account of context.

Acknowledgment of the impact of the researcher's values on the research process is important for feminist psychologists. Inherent in this acknowledgment is the recognition of the impossibility of being truly objective in the choice of a research topic, performance of the research, or interpretation of the results (Unger, 1983). Lips (1989) suggested including the researcher's viewpoint as a variable to be studied.

DIFFERENCES AMONG WOMEN

Evidence suggests that women psychologists differ in their epistemological values among themselves. Unger, Draper, and Pendergrass (1986) found that female psychology students who identified themselves as active feminists were more likely than other women students to reject the objectivist view of reality as stable, irreversible, and determined. They tended to favor a view of reality as a matter of cultural and historical definitions. Unger et al. suggested that epistemological values are influenced by social group membership. Because the life experiences of minorities and oppressed groups sensitize those individuals to aspects of reality that are not experienced by the dominant group, they are more likely to question the idea of an objective reality. Feminists who identify women as an oppressed group, therefore, have a stronger tendency to believe that reality is socially constructed and to doubt the objectivity of psychology. Ricketts (1989) found that nonheterosexual women were less likely than heterosexual women to endorse factual approaches to the study of human behavior. These differences in epistemological values among women cast doubt on the notion of a uniquely "feminine" way of knowing.

Although there has been much discussion about masculine and feminine, and objective and subjective, methods of research, Peplau and Conrad (1989) have asserted that "it has not been established that female psychologists and male psychologists actually differ in the research methods they prefer or actually use" (p. 399). This study is an attempt to address the plea by Peplau and Conrad (1989) for evaluation of the claim that female and male psychologists differ in the research methods they prefer. It was expected that the majority of clinical psychologists would value the methods they have been most exposed to (the natural science model) more highly. The question really is, How much do different groups of clinical psychologists *devalue* the feminist methods? It was expected that those psychologists from nondominant, marginalized groups would devalue feminist methods less (women), and more so feminists would value the proposed feminist methods more highly than men and nonfeminists would. Valuing the feminist methods, however, is not just a matter of having a "feminine" identity. African American clinical psychologists (male and female) were also expected to value the feminist methods more highly than European American psychologists do.

METHOD

Subjects

The names of 450 randomly selected full, doctoral-level American Psychological Association (APA) members who are clinical psychologists were obtained from the APA Office of Demographics and Research. Randomly selected were 165 European American, female clinical psychologists; 60 African American, female clinical psychologists; 165 European American, male clinical psychologists; and 60 African American, male clinical psychologists. All those selected received their doctorates after 1970.

Measures

Valuations of Research Methods Scale (VRM)

The Valuations of Research Methods Scale (VRM) was used to measure preference for participatory, socially conscious, and natural science methods. This scale was developed in an earlier stage of this study by Kingman (1992). The VRM is a 31-item scale using a 7-point Likert scale in which respondents indicate how important inclusion of a particular method is when they are assessing the value of psychology research. The 31 items measure participatory, socially conscious, and natural science research methods.

Feminist Identity Development Scale (FIDS)

The Feminist Identity Development Scale (FIDS) was used to measure both degree of feminism and passive acceptance of sexism among women. Bargad and Hyde (1991) developed this scale to measure stages of a woman's feminist identity development. The FIDS is a 39-item scale in which respondents use a 5-point Likert scale to indicate how much they agree or disagree with the various self-descriptive statements. Scores on the Stage V: Active Commitment subscale were used to measure level of feminism, and scores on Stage I: Passive Acceptance were used to measure passive acceptance of sexism. This scale was given only to the women because its utility with men has not been demonstrated.

Mailing Method

The VRM, a demographic data sheet, a cover letter, and a self-addressed, stamped return envelope were sent to all the 450 selected psychologists. The 225 female psychologists also received the FIDS feminism scale.

RESULTS

Of the 450 clinical psychologists, 191 responded to the mailings, for a response rate of 44%: 54% of the respondents were male, and 46% were female; 74% indicated they were European American, and 21% indicated they were African American. All the respondents had earned a doctoral degree in psychology. Because those who had taken the highest number of courses in alternative methods tended to be those who had also taken the highest number of courses in traditional methods, a ratio (alternative courses/traditional courses) was created to measure relative exposure to alternative research methods.

Predictors of Valuations of Research Methods: All Respondents (Men and Women)

Participatory

A stepwise multiple regression was performed on the 191 subjects, with scores on the Participatory scale of the VRM as the dependent vari-

TABLE 14.1 Predictors of Participatory, Socially Conscious, and Natural Science Valuations (all subjects)

Participatory				
Step	*Multiple R*	R^2	*Variable*	*t*
1	.25	.06	Courses	3.147*
2	.33	.11	Ethnicity	2.915*
Socially Conscious				
Step	*Multiple R*	R^2	*Variable*	*t*
1	.38	.14	Ethnicity	5.374*
Natural Science				
		No variables entered/removed		

NOTE: * $p < .01$.

able and gender, ethnicity (European American vs. African American), work role (academician vs. practitioner), and alternative/traditional courses as the predictor variables.

Alternative/traditional courses entered the equation on Step 1 (Multiple $R = .25$, $t = 3.147$, $p < .01$), and ethnicity entered the equation on Step 2 (Multiple $R = .33$, $t = 2.915$, $p < .01$). No other variables entered the predictor equation. Having taken a relatively *higher number of courses in alternative research methods* and *being African American* predicted higher valuations of participatory research methods. See Table 14.1.

Socially Conscious

A stepwise multiple regression was performed on the 191 respondents, with scores on the Socially Conscious scale of the VRM as the dependent variable and the same predictor variables as above. *Being African American* predicted higher valuations of the socially conscious research methods (Multiple $R = .38$, $t = 5.374$, $p < .001$). See Table 14.1.

Natural Science

A stepwise multiple regression was conducted on the 191 respondents, with scores on the Natural Science scale as the dependent variable and the same predictor variables as above. None of the predictor variables predicted scores on the Natural Science scale. See Table 14.1.

TABLE 14.2 Predictors of Participatory, Socially Conscious, and Natural Science Valuations (women only)

Participatory				
Step	Multiple R	R^2	Variable	t
1	.35	.12	Active Feminism	3.073*
Socially Conscious				
Step	Multiple R	R^2	Variable	t
1	.42	.18	Ethnicity	3.978**
Natural Science				
Step	Multiple R	R^2	Variable	t
1	.40	.16	Passive Acceptance of Sexism	2.956*

NOTE: * $p < .01$; ** $p < .001$.

Predictors of Valuations of Research Methods: Women Only

Participatory

A stepwise multiple regression was conducted on the 86 female respondents. Score on the Participatory scale was the dependent variable, with ethnicity, work role, alternative/traditional courses, scores on the Active Commitment to Feminism scale, and scores on the Passive Acceptance of Sexism scale as the predictor variables. Only one predictor variable entered the equation; active commitment to feminism (Multiple $R = .35$, $t = 3.073$, $p < .01$). Those *women who scored highest on the active commitment to feminism* valued the participatory research methods more highly. See Table 14.2.

Socially Conscious

A stepwise multiple regression was conducted on the female respondents, with scores on the Socially Conscious scale as the dependent variable, along with the same predictor variables as above. Only one predictor variable entered the equation: Ethnicity (Multiple $R = .42$, $t = 3.978$, $p < .001$). *African American women* valued the socially conscious research methods more highly than the European American women did. See Table 14.2.

Natural Science

A stepwise multiple regression was conducted on the female respondents. Score on the Natural Science scale was the dependent variable, with the same predictor variables as above. The only variable that predicted scores was the passive acceptance of sexism (Multiple $R = .40$, $t = 2.956$, $p < .01$). Those *women who scored highest in passive acceptance of sexism tended to value the natural science methods* more highly. See Table 14.2.

DISCUSSION

Effects of Gender and Feminism on Valuations of Research Methods

Gender in itself does not appear to predict how clinical psychologists will value different research methods. In this study, no uniquely feminine or masculine approach to research emerged that was based on mere membership in a gender group. Evidence was found, however, that how women psychologists view their own and society's sex roles is related to their valuations of research methods. Women who more passively accept sexism are more likely to rate natural science research methods as more valuable.

It is no surprise that women clinical psychologists who rated themselves as more active feminists were more likely to value a feminist approach: the participatory/nonhierarchical research methods. More surprising was the result that active feminism did not significantly predict valuations of the other feminist approach: socially conscious methods. It may be that socially conscious research methods are more accepted by women in general and that level of feminism does not affect valuations of it (its mean rating, 4.19, is higher than that of the participatory research methods, 3.31).

Effects of African American and European American Group Membership on Valuations of Research Methods

African American clinical psychologists (both men and women) rated both participatory and socially conscious research methods as more valuable than European American clinical psychologists did. That African American clinical psychologists value a more socially conscious approach than their European American counterparts is not surprising. That African American group membership among clinical psychologists (both men and women) predicts higher ratings of participatory/nonhierarchical approaches lends support to Mednick's (1989) supposition that the disempowered emphasize relatedness. These results cast doubt on the theory that a more relational or participatory approach to knowledge is uniquely feminine.

If being a member of an oppressed group leads to questioning of scientific objectivity and the valuing of a more relational approach to research, how do we make sense of the results that gender, in itself, did not predict valuations of participatory and socially conscious research approaches yet ethnicity did? Perhaps oppression is not as salient to most women as it is to African Americans. The women who were most sensitized to women's oppression (active feminists) did value the participatory approaches more highly. Conversely, women who were least sensitized to women's oppression (those high on passive acceptance of sexism) were more likely to value the natural science approaches. It would have been helpful if the African Americans in this study had been given a measure of black or African identity development, which would have been akin to measuring feminism among women (e.g., as in Baldwin & Bell, 1985; or Azibo, 1988a). Then we would have been able to assess whether level of "Africanicity" among African Americans moderates valuations of research methods in a similar way that feminism does among women. It may also be true that if we select doctoral-level psychology as a "world," within that world African Americans are much more of a minority in numbers (3.6%) than women are (55%) (Thurgood & Weinman, 1989). Because of that, African American psychologists see themselves as (and are) less represented and more inaccurately portrayed than European American women. Therefore, they more vigorously question the objectivity of psychological research.

What do these results mean for the future of psychology research? Mere membership in a gender group did not predict valuations of any of the research methods. Both women and men and African and European Americans valued natural science approaches more than the participatory and socially conscious approaches. African American psychologists and feminist women psychologists tended to devalue participatory research methods less than their European American or nonfeminist counterparts, but they valued them much less than natural science approaches. These results may assuage the fears (or dampen the hopes) of some that the feminization of psychology will lead to a fundamental change in the way we conduct research.

REFERENCES

Azibo, D. (1988a). Psychology: Research and methodology relative to blacks. *Western Journal of Black Studies, 12*(4), 220-233.

Azibo, D. (1988b). Understanding the proper and improper usage of the comparative research framework. *Journal of Black Psychology, 15*(1), 81-91.

Baldwin, J. A., & Bell, Y. A. (1985). The African American Self-Consciousness Scale: An Africentric personality questionnaire. *Western Journal of Black Studies, 9*(2), 61-68.

Bargad, A., & Hyde, J. S. (1991). Women's studies: A study of feminist identity development in women. *Psychology of Women Quarterly, 15*, 181-201.

Chodorow, N. (1974). Family structure and feminine personality. In M. Z. Rosaldo & L. Lamphere (Eds.), *Woman, culture, and society*. Stanford, CA: Stanford University Press.

Eagly, A. H. (1983). Gender and social influence: A social psychological analysis. *American Psychologist, 38*, 971-981.

Gilligan, C. (1982). *In a different voice*. Cambridge, MA: Harvard University Press.

Kaschek, E. (1988). Limits and boundaries: Toward a complex psychology of women. *Women and Therapy, 7*(4), 109-123.

Keller, E. F. (1989). Feminism and science. In A. Garry & M. Pearsall (Eds.), *Women, knowledge, and reality*. Winchester, MA: Unwin Hyman.

Kershaw, T. (1989). The emerging paradigm in Black Studies. *Western Journal of Black Studies, 13*(1), 45-51.

Kimmel, E. B. (1990). Gender in academe: Story of a conference. *Psychology of Women Newsletter, 17*(2), 1-5.

Kingman, L. (1992). *European and African American men and women's valuations of feminist and natural science research methods in psychology*. Unpublished doctoral dissertation, California School of Professional Psychology-Fresno.

Kleiber, N., & Light, L. (1978). *Caring for ourselves*. Vancouver: University of British Columbia.

Lips, H. M. (1989). Toward a new science of human beings and behavior. In W. Tomm (Ed.), *The effects of feminist approaches on research methodologies*. Calgary, Canada: Wilfrid Laurier.

Mednick, M. T. (1989). On the politics of psychological constructs: Stop the bandwagon, I want to get off. *American Psychologist, 44*(8), 1118-1123.

Miller, J. B. (1984). The development of women's sense of self. *Work in Progress, 12*, 1-15.

Peplau, L. A., & Conrad, E. (1989). Beyond nonsexist research: The perils of feminist methods in psychology. *Psychology of Women Quarterly, 13*, 379-400.

Ricketts, M. (1989). Epistemological values of feminists in psychology. *Psychology of Women Quarterly, 13*, 401-415.

Stanley, L., & Wise, S. (1983). *Breaking out: Feminist consciousness and feminist research*. Boston: Routledge Kegan Paul.

Thurgood, D. H., & Weinman, J. M. (1989). *Summary report 1988: Doctorate recipients from U.S. universities*. Washington, DC: National Academy Press.

Tomm, W. (1989). *The effects of feminist approaches on research methodologies*. Calgary, Canada: Wilfrid Laurier.

Unger, R. K. (1983). Through the looking glass: No wonderland yet! (The reciprocal relationship between methodology and models of reality). *Psychology of Women Quarterly, 8*(1), 9-32.

Unger, R. K., Draper, R. D., & Pendergrass, M. L. (1986). Personal epistemology and personal experience. *Journal of Social Issues, 42*(2), 67-77.

Walsh, R. T. (1989). Do research reports in mainstream feminist psychology journals reflect feminist values? *Psychology of Women Quarterly, 13*, 433-444.

Watts, R. J. (1987). Development of professional identity in black clinical psychology graduate students, *Professional Psychology: Research and Practice, 18*(1), 28-35.

About the Authors

Georgia W. Brown is Director of the Women's Studies Program at Southern University and Agricultural & Mechanical College in Baton Rouge, Louisiana. She served as a library/informational professional for 35 years before establishing the Women's Studies Program.

Claudia J. Gollop, Ph.D., has spent well over a decade as a library/information professional. She is teaching at the School of Information and Library Science at the University of North Carolina at Chapel Hill and is pursuing research interests in the areas of information resources, health sciences information, and services to special populations.

Martia Graham Goodson is an oral historian and Associate Professor in the Black and Hispanic Studies Department at Baruch College—City University of New York. Her publications include articles in the *Western Journal of Black Studies* ("Slave Narrative Collection: Tool for Reconstructing Afro-American Women's History"; "Considering the Sources: The Significance of 'Race-of-Interviewer' in the Collection and Analysis of Ex-Slave Stories"; and "Medical-Botanical Contributions of African Slave Women to American Medicine") and the edited oral autobiography *Chronicles of Faith: The Autobiography of Frederick D. Patterson* (1991).

Patricia Green-Powell, Ph.D., is Associate Professor of Business Administration and Director of Student Services at South Carolina State University's School of Business in Orangeburg. She has worked in adult education and literacy at the state level for 11 years. She served as coordinator of academic programs for the College of Education at Florida State University, and has been Director of the Florida Adult Literacy Resource Center (FALRC). She has held a variety of management positions and has taught numerous courses on adult literacy education and special education. Her research interests include collecting oral narratives from black women from all walks of life, particularly from the civil rights movement, as well as from black women from rural areas. She pays particular attention to oral history research involving the personal narratives of black women in higher education administration and is interested in conducting qualitative research by means of the case study approach.

Arlene Hambrick, Ed.D., is Senior Manager of the Eisenhower Math and Science Consortia at the Appalachian Educational Laboratory in Charleston, West Virginia. Previously, she was Assistant Professor of Education at Bluefield College in Bluefield, Virginia. Before that, she taught in Chicago and Boston public schools for 25 years. She lectures frequently on the topic of integrating black history, children's literature, and oral history in the form of character reenactment into all aspects of the learning environment. Recent publications include *Implementing Systemic Change in Science Education* (1995). Her current research interests are giving voice to black women's concerns through uncovering and documenting historical biographical data on black women inventors and collecting oral histories through interviewing and analyzing institutional pedagogy for educating black female children.

Leslie Ann Kingman, Ph.D., is a licensed clinical psychologist in private practice in Colorado Springs, Colorado. Her areas of specialization include work with sexual and physical abuse survivors (adults and children), women's issues, and psychological assessment of children.

Joycelyn Moody, Ph.D., is Assistant Professor of English at the University of Washington in Seattle. Published academic works include " 'By Any Other Name': Theoretical Issues in the Teaching of 19th-Century African American Women's Autobiography," and the article "The Holiness of Herself Released: Nineteenth-Century African American Women's Spiritual Narratives and Womanist Research" in *The Womanist: A Newsletter for Afrocentric Feminist Researchers* (1994).

Christine Obbo is a Ugandan social cultural anthropologist whose research has for two decades focused on how change affects relations between men and women. She is also an independent consultant on HIV/AIDS and gender issues in Africa and an Associate of the African Studies Center in the School of African and Oriental Studies at the University of London. Current projects include writing a book about women and HIV/AIDS, and another about her experiences as "other" in gender and global encounters. She is the author of numerous works, including "Bitu: Facilitator of Women's Educational Opportunities" in *Life Histories of African Women* (1987) and *African Women: Their Struggle for Economic Independence* (with Nici Nelson, 1980).

Elizabeth A. Peterson, Ed.D., is Assistant Professor of Community and Occupational Programs in Education at the University of South Carolina, Columbia. Her published studies include *African American Women: A Study of Will and Success* (1992) and "Fanny Coppin, Mary Shadd Cary, and Charlotte Grimke: Three African American Women Who Made a Difference" in *Freedom Road: Adult Education of African Americans* (1996).

Diane D. Turner, Ph.D., is Assistant Professor of Africana Studies at the University of South Florida. She has written a major work on Musicians' Protective Union Local 274 and is documenting jazz in Philadelphia, Pennsylvania. Her areas of specialization are 20th-century African American social and cultural history, Black music history, and the Black Arts Movement. Her forthcoming publications include "Black Music in Tampa," in *Practical Anthropology*, and "Allan Rohan Crite," *Encyclopedia of New England Culture*.

Kim Marie Vaz, Ph.D., is Associate Professor of Women's Studies at the University of South Florida, Tampa. She has been the recipient of a Ford Foundation Postdoctoral Fellowship for Minorities for her book in progress on the place of African mythology in the psychology of black women. She was awarded the 1996 Women of Color Psychologies Award from the Association for Women in Psychology for her paper "Racial Aliteracy: White Appropriations of Black Presences," which was published in *Women and Therapy: A Feminist Journal* (1995, Vol. 16). She is the author of the life history study *The Woman With the Artistic Brush: A Life History of Yoruba Batik Artist, Nike Olaniyi Davies* (1995) and the editor of *Black Women in America* (Sage, 1995).

Jacqueline Walcott-McQuigg is Assistant Professor in the Department of Public Health, Mental Health, and Administrative Nursing at the University of Illinois at Chicago. Her specialty areas are public health, women's health, and occupational health nursing. Research interests are ethnicity and health, psychosociocultural factors influencing weight control behavior (diet control, weight management, exercise), triangulation methodology, and occupational stress. She has been funded to study factors influencing risk-reduction behavior related to obesity, cardiovascular disease, and diabetes in culturally diverse women. She is a co-principal investigator on a NIH-National Institute on Aging study of exercise behavior in minority elderly. She has published in her areas of research interest and has given many presentations on women's health, cultural diversity and health, and African American health issues.

Renée T. White, Ph.D., is Assistant Professor of Sociology at Central Connecticut State University, New Britain. She is coeditor of *Fanon: A Critical Reader* (1996), *Black Texts and Black Textualities*, and *Spoils of War: Women, Cultures, and Revolutions*, and author of *Putting Risk in Perspective: Black Teenage Lives in the Era of AIDS*. Her research is focused on black feminist ideology and practice, race and AIDS research, class inequality, and theories of race and racialism.